FROM
MIDNIGHT
TO DAWN

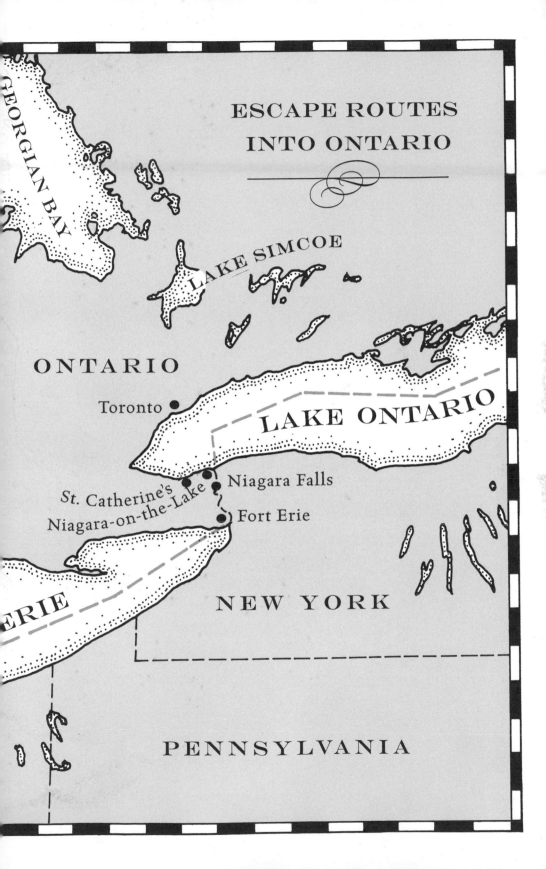

ESCAPE ROUTES
INTO ONTARIO

GEORGIAN BAY

LAKE SIMCOE

ONTARIO

Toronto

LAKE ONTARIO

St. Catherine's
Niagara-on-the-Lake

Niagara Falls

Fort Erie

ERIE

NEW YORK

PENNSYLVANIA

FROM MIDNIGHT TO DAWN

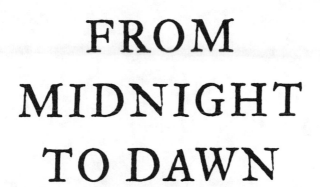

The Last Tracks of the Underground Railroad

JACQUELINE TOBIN

WITH HETTIE JONES

DOUBLEDAY

New York London Toronto Sydney Auckland

PUBLISHED BY DOUBLEDAY

Copyright © 2007 by Jacqueline L. Tobin

All Rights Reserved

Published in the United States by Doubleday,
an imprint of The Doubleday Broadway Publishing Group,
a division of Random House, Inc., New York.
www.doubleday.com

DOUBLEDAY and the portrayal of an anchor with a dolphin
are registered trademarks of Random House, Inc.

Photo credits appear on page 265.

Book design by Kathryn Parise

LIBRARY OF CONGRESS CATALOGING-IN-PUBLICATION DATA

ISBN 978-0-385-51431-6

PRINTED IN THE UNITED STATES OF AMERICA

2 4 6 8 10 9 7 5 3 1

First Edition

This book is dedicated to all those who found freedom in Canada, and to the descendants who are keeping their stories alive.

CONTENTS

Preface:

"One More River to Cross"

At the center of One Hart Plaza in Detroit, Michigan, where United States land ends at the Detroit River, a group of larger-than-life-size bronze figures bear witness to one half of a shared story. Standing with them, following their gaze across the river, a few hundred yards away you can see Windsor, Ontario, in Canada, where the other half of the story took place and where similar figures are part of a companion monument. Even at first glance, both groups reveal the central fact in the story: On the U.S. side, the figures—men, women, and children—face north toward Canada, and from the look of them, you know they're anxious to get there. Yet their anticipation is tinged with uncertainty and a vague weariness.

The monument in Windsor shows another group, this one newly arrived. They're being greeted and they seem thankful, if still hesitant and unsure of what awaits. Only one little girl, holding a doll, is looking back toward something—or, more likely, someone—she has left behind.

For a while during the nineteenth century, the city of Detroit had a code name: Midnight. Fugitive slaves passed through there in secrecy on their way to Canada, sometimes with the help of sympathetic contacts, but more often alone, with little information and without any assistance from others. In either case, they were always in danger. If they were lucky, there was aid on both sides. But what has come to be known as the Underground Railroad was less an organized system than a corridor of subterfuge and chance, and if there were sometimes conductors, safe houses, and tickets to ride, there were also arduous nights in the mountains and days in strange, threatening towns. There was no easy path out of slavery to freedom.

For those who made it to Midnight, the Detroit River became their Jordan, the "one more river to cross" they'd long sung about. On the other side lay their "land of Canaan," and the liberty that still eluded Africans in the United States. For a period of time before the Civil War, even in so-called free states, fugitives could be hunted down and once more enslaved. But that did not stop thousands from running away.

From Windsor, the new arrivals traveled to several black settlements, among them one known as Dawn, where they lived freely under the protection of British law. There, in these places, the story continues. Before the Civil War, more than thirty thousand people crossed into Canada, many of them from Midnight to Dawn, some more than once as they returned to help others. Some of the fugitives who reached Canada stayed on after the Civil War; others returned to the States. But in the passage, all learned, through education and economic self-determination, the ways they might live free. Their story is neither a uniquely American story nor separately a Canadian story, but one that forever unites our two countries and people. It is a story of desperation and resistance, of courage and survival, of men and women who risked their lives in order to claim the life that they, and they alone, owned.

Communication among these settlers was common and considerable, with much travel from one location to another undertaken not only by residents but by interested visitors. The existence of a network of Canadian communities of escaped slaves and refugee free people of color was, of course, known in the United States; newspapers reported about them, abolitionist leaders referred to them. They did not all exist simultaneously during the half century before the Civil War, but— large, small, separate or part of existing towns and cities—they were familiar destinations to all the well-known figures, black and white, whose public positions against slavery inspired many. Harriet Tubman, Frederick Douglass, John Brown, and Harriet Beecher Stowe all knew about, experienced, and wrote about Dawn, Wilberforce, Chatham, and the other places whose stories are told here.

Also, and very importantly, lesser-known—to most Americans— but effective activists contributed to the founding and organization of the "promised lands" in Canada, where black people at last were able to direct their lives. There they practiced agriculture, established and expanded schools, factories, businesses, and places of worship, created civic structures, and published newspapers to keep themselves informed. They argued over whether to become totally self-sufficient or to accept help, but overall they wanted to live as free people and be judged accordingly.

The histories of these Canadian settlements, like the lives of their residents, overlap. But each was unique in origin, organizing principle, and progress, a story in itself. Their individual successes—and failures— have been up to now absent from American histories, and, until recently, from Canadian histories, as well. *From Midnight to Dawn* sets them out here, stories from the nineteenth century shedding light on the twenty-first.

FROM
MIDNIGHT
TO DAWN

Introduction:

Freedom's New Direction

In the eighty-five years between the American Revolution and the Civil War, not only the North and South of the United States but all of North America struggled with the issue of slavery. The Declaration of Independence had set a standard—"all men are created equal"—and the colonies had responded passionately to this promise of a new, egalitarian society. Yet there remained over half a million enslaved Africans toiling on American lands. In addition, living throughout the country were 25,000 free blacks, men and women of African descent who were born free or who had served, earned, purchased, or escaped their way to freedom. The pervasive spirit of liberty and independence was not lost on them. Crispus Attucks, a runaway slave, was the first man to die in the struggle for American independence (though Paul Revere's famous engraving showed him as white).

But the British, in need of manpower, had held out counteroffers: In 1775, Lord Dunmore, the royal governor of Virginia, issued a proclamation stating that slaves who sided with the British would be granted their freedom after the war. Within one month, more than three hundred enslaved black men had responded to Dunmore's call—the first mass emancipation of slaves in American history. These Black Loyalists, as they were called, wore uniforms emblazoned with the slogan "Liberty to Slaves," which became not just a black but also a British rallying cry, though the British based their offer solely on the need for manpower, not on any abolitionist beliefs.

Because Lord Dunmore's call had been such a successful tactic, the British found themselves committed to the concept of freeing slaves owned by the rebellious Americans, who were called patriots, as opposed to Loyalists. This economic tactic, used in conjunction with military tactics, worked. No one knows exactly how many slaves fled to safety behind British military lines after Dunmore's proclamation, but it is likely that more than 100,000 free and enslaved blacks eventually found their way there. Thomas Jefferson is said to have estimated that thirty thousand were "lost" in Virginia alone.

Loss of slave manpower hurt the patriots, who responded with intimidation: Many slave owners threatened severe punishment to runaways. The Virginia Assembly attempted to control the slaves in the colony it governed by threatening them with death if they were caught trying to escape. Southern newspapers printed misinformation about British intentions to sell runaways, after the war, to sugar plantations in the West Indies. Despite the appeal of the British offers, more than five thousand black patriots like Crispus Attucks fought for independence. That number might have increased, but in the South, where enslaved blacks often outnumbered whites and memories of armed insurrections were vivid, the enlistment of blacks was severely opposed. Instead, taking a lesson from the British, patriots began to free slaves from Loyalist farms and plantations. Again, military and economic needs, rather than abolitionist ideas, motivated these acts of emancipation.

In 1780, another North American black man entered the historical record. Enslaved at age sixteen when he was captured in what is now Senegal, Richard Pierpoint later joined the war for independence as a Loyalist. He is listed in military records as a member of the infamous Butler's Rangers, a select group of men skilled in guerrilla warfare as well as in traditional military tactics. Pierpoint felt his loyalties lay with a country that was at least offering the hope of freedom, and he was eventually rewarded: For his services on behalf of the Crown, he received a grant of two hundred acres of land in what eventually became St. Catharines, Ontario, where the legendary Harriet Tubman would later bring her family to freedom.

The American Revolution officially ended with the Treaty of Paris in 1783. Loyalists, both black and white, were forced to leave. Many former slaves chose to move to the West Indies, but others went north. Most considered themselves Americans and did not want to leave the continent. Going to Canada was actually the easiest geographical location to move to without losing ties to family and friends. More than three thousand free blacks had settled in Nova Scotia by the end of 1783.

Reparations and the return of lost property were conditions of the treaty. Since the Americans considered slaves to be property, they demanded compensation for their losses and the return of their slaves. The British balked. British commanders had guaranteed freedom to all slaves who had fought for their side. They held firm in their belief that justice required them to honor their offer, and insisted that Black Loyalists be evacuated along with all others, since they had been free under British rule at the time the treaty was signed. The British did, however, offer to compensate the former slave owners. In order to determine numbers, a "Book of Negroes" was created, which documented all blacks being given free passage to British lands. They were also given "certificates of freedom" to prove their new status.

In the former colonies, now known as the United States of America, weeks of celebration surrounded the election of the victorious general George Washington as the first president of the new nation. But the euphoria didn't last: There were many challenges, foremost among them finding a way to save the Union. Thirteen separate colonies had come together with one purpose; keeping them united required fortitude as

well as fervor. Differences among individual states were already surfacing, the most serious and divisive being the issue of slavery.

In the North, where revolutionary zeal had been strongest, citizens
had begun to question the institution of slavery itself. Many could not
reconcile throwing off their own yokes while still enslaving thousands
of blacks. Gradual emancipation acts were passed in the northern
states. By the first few years of the nineteenth century, Pennsylvania,
New Jersey, New York, Connecticut, Rhode Island, and Vermont had
all abolished slavery altogether.

Meanwhile, the states continued to disagree. In 1787, a Constitutional Convention was called. Delegates felt that individual states held
too much power, but at the same time they were wary of granting too
much power to the federal government. A balance was sought. Since
some states had large populations and others small, representation in
the government became a critical issue: Southerners, in order to bolster
their numbers, wanted slaves counted as whole people; northerners felt
this would give the southern states too much control.

Compromises were reached to placate each area. Northern states
agreed to continue the importation of slaves for another twenty years,
until 1808, when it would then be outlawed. Southern states agreed that
each slave would count as only three-fifths of a person for representation purposes.

The Northwest Ordinance carved up the newly acquired northwestern lands gained from Great Britain, which now include Ohio, Indiana,
Illinois, Michigan, Wisconsin, and parts of Minnesota, forbidding slavery there but adding fugitive slave rules allowing for the pursuit of runaways. On September 17, 1787, the final draft of the United States
Constitution was signed by thirty-nine of the delegates to the convention, including the convention's president, George Washington, who
stated in his letter to Congress the hope of the framers: "that it may promote the lasting welfare of that country so dear to us all, and secure her
freedom and happiness, is our most ardent wish." Hopes for the new
country were high.

———

Britain, too, had been caught up in the fever of egalitarianism that had swept the American colonies toward independence. Emancipation of enslaved blacks during the war was soon followed by legislation in support of it, this time based not on wartime expedience but on rising abolitionism. And there remained a British presence in North America: Canada.

The year 1793 was pivotal: Three events within a few months of one another set in motion subsequent events that pointed to Canada as the land of Canaan, and eventually culminated in the Civil War.

In July, John Graves Simcoe, Upper Canada's first lieutenant governor and an ardent abolitionist, succeeded in passing the first Canadian provincial act against slavery. While the act did not actually free anyone, it stated that no more slaves could be introduced into the province, which later became Ontario. The act also provided that those currently enslaved would remain so until death, and that children born after the act was passed would become free at the age of twenty-five—thus ensuring the eventual eradication of slavery in the province.

Also in 1793, Eli Whitney, an American schoolteacher, invented the cotton gin (a machine for removing seeds from harvested cotton), which gave the South a tremendous economic boost but required increased slave labor. The cotton gin ensured that in the American South slavery would become entrenched. Before then, cotton and slavery were not historically intertwined. Virginia and Kentucky grew tobacco; rice was cultivated in the Low Country areas of South Carolina and Georgia; sugar reigned as king in Louisiana. But the invention of the cotton gin not only revitalized a sagging southern economy; it changed the course of American history. In the ensuing seven years, cotton production would increase more than tenfold. What had been a minor cash crop was to become the road to riches—all you needed was a large plantation and a large number slaves to work it. Solid economic and political divisions were now created between the North and the South.

Although foreign slave trade was to be outlawed as of 1808, the South's rising need for cheap labor simply shifted the trade from foreign to domestic. Cities such as New Orleans would become major venues for the buying and selling of slaves. It is estimated that over 700,000 slaves were eventually moved, in a massive domestic migration, from the North to the South, which now had an enormous economic interest in the institution of slavery and took measures to protect it.

The third event of 1793 was the step taken by Congress to try to hold the South in the young American nation despite rising objections to slavery. Known as the first Fugitive Slave Act, it made aiding escapees a crime.

The problem of runaways was as old as the institution of slavery. Before the Revolution, pacts between the colonies addressed the return of escapees; afterward, southerners succeeded in inserting the following fugitive slave clause into the Constitution: "No person held to service or labor in one State, under the laws thereof, escaping into another, shall, in consequence of any law or regulation therein, be discharged from such servitude or labor, but shall be delivered up, on claim of the party to whom such service or labor may be due."

But no enforcement powers had been granted the federal government until the Fugitive Slave Act of 1793, which empowered slave owners to arrest alleged fugitives and fine anyone harboring fugitives or aiding their escape. There was no provision in this law to protect those unlawfully accused, so kidnapping of free blacks as well as fugitives would soon become common.

After 1793, the North and South struggle escalated: Free states faced off against slave states—the latter augmented by the expansion of U.S. territory with the Louisiana Purchase in 1803 and, eventually, the annexation of Texas in 1845, opening up new lands to the cultivation of cotton and the practice of slavery. To every new pro-slavery law enacted on the federal level by southerners, northern states responded with counteractive state legislation. From 1780 to 1861, northern states passed personal liberty laws that would protect free blacks from possible kidnappings, barred state officials from enforcing fugitive slave laws, and offered fugitives all the protections of due process, including trial by jury.

Up until the War of 1812, when the United States declared war on Britain for its repeated seizures of American ships and sailors, those wishing to escape had no clear direction. Without knowledge of geography and distance, or even political climate, many runaways escaped into the swamps or just outside plantation perimeters, often only to return to their families and familiar ground back on the plantations. After the war, returning soldiers, as well as the slaves who had accompanied them to British lands in Canada, brought back word of places up north where blacks were living freely. Freedom now had a clear direction and a destination.

Wilberforce University, the oldest private African American university in the United States; founded in 1856. Illustration from the 1859 Wilberforce University Catalogue. (Photograph courtesy of the Ohio Historical Society)

Chapter One

Wilberforce

A new black consciousness arose in the decades after the War of 1812. Faced with increased discrimination and violence against them, blacks were no longer waiting for sympathetic whites to protect their interests, but began working actively on their own behalf. Vigilance committees were formed for mutual support and protection; black abolitionist newspapers appeared, representing the thoughts of many free blacks who did not want whites speaking for them. Fraternal organizations, such as the Prince Hall Masons, which had been in existence since the American Revolution, became even more prominent and proactive. When an "Underground Railroad" was laid, on the paths first trod by courageous forebears who had escaped without any white assistance, many of the conductors were free blacks. The term is believed to derive from the story of a young fugitive named Tice Davids, who in 1831 crossed the Ohio River, with his master following in a boat close behind. Supposedly, when Davids reached the Ohio shore, he disappeared and his master could not find him. The master returned to his home in Kentucky, claiming that Davids must have escaped by way of an "underground railroad." (The railroad metaphor continued, as helpers eventually were called "conductors," fugitives became "parcels" and "passengers," and safe houses were referred to as "stations.")

Black emigration, an issue since the early nineteenth century, was now being discussed and redefined by blacks who wanted to decide their own destiny. The movement had begun in 1816 with the American Colonization Society, which included both whites and blacks as members, and was an attempt to effect a compromise between those who owned slaves and those who wanted to free them. The idea was to send free blacks elsewhere rather than emancipate them into the United States population. Established and run for the most part by white men, the society included such notable Americans as Henry Clay, the Speaker of the House; Francis Scott Key, the attorney (and author of "The Star-Spangled Banner"); and Bushrod Washington, a Supreme Court justice and the nephew of George Washington. Liberia, established on the west coast of Africa, was the society's biggest success.

By the 1820s, though, most blacks considered themselves Americans, not Africans, and emigration to Africa was no longer a desirable outcome. "Many of our fathers and some of us have fought and bled for the liberty, independence and peace which you now enjoy," wrote one free black in the North. "Surely it would be ungenerous and unfeeling in you to deny us a humble and quiet grave in that country which gave us birth." Although the American Colonization Society continued until the end of the Civil War, it did so with diminishing support from the black population it was meant to serve.

The very definition of freedom itself had evolved. While it had once meant simply escaping slavery to a state where slavery had been abolished, it now included the concepts of equality under the law, freedom of opportunity, and freedom from discrimination and violence. And the growing numbers of blacks moving to northern states began to force the issue.

Events in southern Ohio in 1829 would serve to emphasize these problems, but they also had far-reaching consequences, including the creation of Wilberforce, the first organized all-black settlement in Upper Canada.

Ohio had abolished slavery in 1802 but in the same decade had also passed so-called Black Laws. Enacted in 1804 and 1807 but rarely enforced, these were harsh attempts to stop the immigration of blacks and to control those already living there. New arrivals were required to register and carry a certificate of freedom, as well as to post a five-hundred-dollar bond within twenty days of entering the state.

Still, blacks were drawn there, especially to the city of Cincinnati, right across the Ohio River from Kentucky, a slave state. Fugitives crossed the river to freedom, free blacks to look for work. The construction of the Miami and Erie Canal, which connected Toledo to Cincinnati, increased the demand for steamships to transport goods throughout the Great Lakes regions and required a large labor pool. Both black and white laborers flocked to Cincinnati. In 1820, blacks made up 2 percent of its population; by the end of the decade, that figure had risen to over 10 percent. In a city already home to hundreds of unemployed citizens, competition for jobs and an eventual downturn in the economy brought about increased tensions. "I thought upon coming to a free state like Ohio that I would find every door thrown open to receive me," wrote John Malvin, a fugitive, "but from the treatment I received by the people generally, I found it little better than Virginia."

New problems beset the black community as well as the white population. Denied access to white institutions, blacks attempted to deal with their increasing difficulties by establishing their own associations, but the increased demand for housing and employment could not be satisfied by existing means; there were just not enough resources to go around. Most blacks congregated in Cincinnati's First and Fourth wards, an area that became known as "Little Africa." Segregation, although not legally sanctioned, became the norm. Early black settlers had lived in good, well-built houses, but when newcomers began pouring in, any structure had to do. Shacks and shanties rose, creating health and fire hazards.

Whites grew increasingly intolerant. Earlier in the decade, they had made attempts through the Colonization Society to remove blacks from the city in the socially acceptable method popular at the time, but nothing came of the discussion. Local newspapers began printing editorials complaining about black people, accusing them of harboring or even kidnapping runaways. Citizens spoke out loudly against the "night walkers, lewd persons, and those who lounge about without any visible means of support." While the nighttime activities of whites were probably not that different from those of the blacks accused, it was the latter who bore the brunt of scrutiny and blame.

By June 1829, Cincinnati was at the boiling point. Town trustees issued a proclamation—posted, ironically, on July 4—stating the city's intent to enforce the Black Laws of 1804 and 1807. As the hot, sticky summer drew to a close, blacks in Cincinnati were made acutely aware of their precarious situation. Threats of violence increased. Free blacks responded by forming their own group to look for other places to live: "If the act is enforced," wrote one, "we, the poor sons of Aethiopia, must take shelter where we can find it. . . . If we cannot find it in America, where we were born and spent all our days, we must beg it elsewhere."

The Cincinnati group chose as their leader James C. Brown, a former slave who had purchased his freedom by hiring himself out as a skilled mason. Having been a member of the American Colonization Society, Brown was well qualified for the task. He had been sent by the society to Texas to explore setting up a black colony there, and though white opposition had canceled the Texas plans, the experience served him well.

Many blacks like Brown, experiencing segregation, prejudice, and lack of legal standing, were at the outset more than willing to explore colonization elsewhere. As intimidation and threats continued to escalate in Cincinnati, the colonization group decided to send two representatives to Upper Canada to look for a location for an all-black settlement.

Even after the Revolution, the Canadian government had continued to extend itself in this respect. Black as well as white veterans of the War of 1812 had been offered land grants in the rolling farmlands northwest of Lake Ontario. Sir Peregrine Maitland, the province's then lieutenant governor, had been trying to protect his territory against an American invasion from Lake Huron and the Georgian Bay; perhaps he saw the area as a potential sanctuary for runaway slaves from the United States. Since Canada was still a colony of Britain, Maitland could have been adopting a similar antislavery stance. It's also possible that he was simply interested in further separating his territory from lands now American. Whatever the motives, many fugitives found the land offered too remote to be easily accessible; many who were granted land never settled on it. However, one group of thirteen did establish Oro, essentially the first "assisted" settlement of blacks in Canada. Because it was so distant, Oro was abandoned eventually, but the precedent for black settlement in Canada had been established.

Bearing a letter from James C. Brown, the Cincinnati group's two representatives, Israel Lewis and Thomas Cresap, met with Gen. John Colborne, then Upper Canada's lieutenant governor, who is reported to have had this response to their request for safe haven: "Tell the Republicans on your side of the line that we Royalists do not know men by their color. Should you come to us you will be entitled to all the privileges of the rest of His Majesty's subjects."

The Canada Company had been incorporated by the British Parliament in 1825 to obtain land in Canada and promote its sale to prospective settlers. Lewis and Cresup returned to Cincinnati not only with Colborne's assurances of legal protection but also an offer by the Canada Company to sell four thousand acres, only eight miles from the shores of Lake Erie, for six thousand dollars.

The Cincinnati group didn't have the money. They asked the Ohio legislature for help but were refused. Finally, Quakers from Ohio and Indiana stepped in and purchased eight hundred acres. Nevertheless, as representatives were completing the land deal, whites in Cincinnati proceeded with their plans to enforce the Black Laws and rid their town of its black population. Threats of mob violence grew. Writing in the *Cincinnati Daily Gazette*, Brown pleaded with the city for a three-month extension: "Withhold your mighty arms until our representatives return, we beg your sympathy until we find shelter."

As designated leader of the black population, and aware that it would take time to move over two thousand people to a new community, Brown did everything in his power to placate the whites until the blacks could leave. He wrote articles for the *Gazette* to keep the public informed about the black community's plans for emigration to Canada and their efforts thus far. But even this did not satisfy the whites. On August 15, 1829, a mob of three hundred attacked the black community, beating the inhabitants and demolishing their homes and businesses. The violence went on for three days. Over fifteen hundred African Americans fled for their lives.

Those who left the city fell roughly into two groups, each pushed into immediate action by the violence, but each having different motives. As historian Nikki Taylor has noted, some were refugees, escaping the mob violence of Cincinnati, going anywhere for safety; those led by Brown were emigrants, having already organized and made plans to leave the city to create a new life elsewhere.

Some of the refugees moved to cities just outside of Cincinnati, seeking safety close to home. Many even returned later the same year, when the Cincinnati city fathers realized that they were losing much of their cheap labor pool and the mayor promised he would try to repeal the Black Laws. Of those who continued on to Canada, most settled right across the border from Detroit, near the town of Amherstburg. Their goal was to move only far enough away to get outside the reach of American prejudice and violence toward them.

But at least five families moved on to the lands purchased from the Canada Company and became the nucleus of the settlement that came to be known as Wilberforce. During its nearly ten-year existence, settlers established two churches, a temperance society, a gristmill, a sawmill, and schools. One visitor noted that twenty to thirty children were at school; others made mention that even some white children from the neighboring areas were in attendance. The desire for a quality education superseded any belief in segregation.

When James C. Brown left Wilberforce soon after the first settlers arrived (his wife having grown disillusioned with living in Canada), Israel

Lewis recruited Austin Steward, a successful grocer from Rochester, New York. Steward was supportive of the new settlement. He believed that rural areas, not cities, were the best places for blacks to find opportunity for independence and self-sufficiency. In his memoir, *Twenty-Two Years a Slave, and Forty Years a Freeman*, he wrote, "Our people mostly flock to cities where they allow themselves to be made hewers of wood and drawers of water; barbers and waiters—when, if they would but retire to the country and purchase a piece of land, cultivate and improve it, they would be far richer and happier than they can in a crowded city."

It was Steward who had first given the community the name Wilberforce, in honor of William Wilberforce. Known as "the Liberator" for his eighteen-year effort to end slavery in the British Empire, Wilberforce deserved the honor. Religious influences had moved him to his abolitionist beliefs, among them John Newton, his rector in London, a reformed slave trader who had been inspired to write the song "Amazing Grace" in testament to his conversion. Just three days before Wilberforce died, the House of Commons finally passed the British Emancipation Act. He lived to know that the first organized all-black settlement in Upper Canada had been named for him and that his abolitionist efforts had succeeded.

Austin Steward assumed leadership of Wilberforce, as he had been asked to do, but it became clear that he had taken on the role, at least in some part, to propel himself to a seat in Parliament. Israel Lewis, however, wanted the recognition of leading the community himself. Internal struggles ensued, personally as well as financially; Lewis was eventually accused of absconding with moneys he had solicited for the settlement. These problems were aired publicly, affecting what until then had been favorable American press about the community, especially on the part of Benjamin Lundy, a Quaker abolitionist who published the *Genius of Universal Emancipation*, an antislavery newspaper.

Before 1830, Lundy had been the foremost figure in the antislavery movement in the States. His lifelong efforts influenced many of the early abolitionists of the time, including William Lloyd Garrison, who credited Lundy with "awakening" him to "the holy cause of emancipation." Garrison, writing in his own newspaper, the *Liberator,* also supported Wilberforce: "As it increases in population, intelligence and power, it will render the prolongation of that accursed and bloody system more and more insecure, and increase more and more the necessity of abolishing it altogether and without delay."

Benjamin Lundy had attended the 1823 meeting of the American Convention for Promoting the Abolition of Slavery, where he became acquainted with antislavery pamphlets from Britain circulating at the time. He began reprinting them in his paper as he received them, keeping Americans abreast of the rising tide of British antislavery efforts. In addition to his work as a publisher, Lundy was an agent of the American Colonization Society, and in his newspaper actively promoted its positions. He began looking toward British North American lands for possible locations for colonization efforts, though he made it very clear that his motivation was in freeing the slaves, not getting rid of them.

In 1832, Lundy decided to see for himself what conditions for blacks were like in Upper Canada. He included Wilberforce in his travels. While at a meeting there, he witnessed firsthand the community's internal conflicts. Despite this experience, he printed a hearty endorsement of the settlement when he returned home, writing glowingly about the fertile land surrounding it, the legal protections offered by the British government, and the mild climate of the area. He even sold a map drawn by one Hezekiah Grice, which showed routes that could be used to travel there.

In his diary, Lundy prophesied that of the black settlements in Canada, Wilberforce would be "by far the most important, as there are men of known intelligence and public spirit there who will give it a consequence that probably will not, at least very soon, be attached to the others. It will indeed be viewed by the colored people as a nucleus for an extensive emigration from the northern and middle parts of the union, especially from Virginia and several contiguous states."

But Lundy's prophecy was never realized. Despite his attempts, as well as those of other abolitionists, to promote the community, records reveal that Wilberforce was never home to more than two hundred people. Blacks did not flock there as expected, and the reduction of the original land sale hadn't set a good precedent for relations between the settlers and the Canada Company. There had also been pressure from newly arriving Irish immigrants, who petitioned the company to not sell any more land to blacks. The company's subsequent refusal to extend the original acreage effectively curtailed the settlement's continued growth. Members of Wilberforce's original community scattered, some back to the United States. By 1878, only four of the original settlers remained in the area.

Nevertheless, before its demise less than ten years from its inception, and despite its failure to live up to expectations, Wilberforce became a symbol and inspiration for antislavery and abolitionist causes. Hezekiah Grice, who had created the map of the route to the settlement, wrote a letter to national black leaders in the States asking whether it was now time to consider emigration "en masse" to Canada.

His question prompted black leaders to come together in Philadelphia, on September 15, 1830, for the first National Negro Convention (beginning an institution, the National Negro Convention Movement, that was to last for the next thirty years). This first gathering lasted ten days and hosted over forty prominent blacks from all over the country. Presiding over the convention was Richard Allen, a former slave who had become a respected leader of Philadelphia's black community. In 1787, Allen and his friend Absalom Jones had broken away from St. George's Methodist Episcopal Church in Philadelphia when refused seating on its main floor. Some blacks followed Jones and formed the African Protestant Episcopal Church of St. Thomas; others followed Allen to found the African Methodist Episcopal Church, of which he would be elected bishop.

Delegates to the first convention outlined their objectives in the creation of a more permanent organization, the American Society of Free Persons of Color, for the purpose of "improving their condition in the United States; for purchasing lands; and for the establishment of settlement in the Province of Canada." This position made clear that colonization outside North America was no longer seen as acceptable but that emigration to North American British-held lands would be encouraged. Although supporting emigration to Canada, delegates also declared their intention to work for better conditions in the United States. At the convention's close, Richard Allen wrote an address on behalf of the delegates to "Free Persons of Colour of these United States," in which he referred to "life, liberty and the pursuit of happiness" as "incontrovertible facts," and concluded that "our forlorn and deplorable situation earnestly and loudly demand of us to devise and pursue all legal means for the speedy elevation of ourselves and brethren to the scale and standing of men."

Allen's address credited the African Colonization Society but emphasized that the convention's position differed: ". . . we beg leave to say, that it does not meet with our approbation." Delegates instead made a clear distinction between colonization imposed on them by others and emigration on their own terms, recommending only "the formation of a settlement in the British province of Upper Canada," which would be "a great advantage of the people of colour." Accordingly, the delegates pledged "to aid each other by all honourable means, to plant and support one in that country." The address was, as Allen stated, an "appeal to our coloured brethren, and to all philanthropists here and elsewhere, to assist in this benevolent and important work."

Today, what remains of Wilberforce is a plaque and a subdivision called Wilberforce Heights in the town now named Lucan, in honor of the Irish who continued to settle the area. The plaque credits "fugitive slaves" for the founding. No mention is made of James C. Brown and the group of Cincinnati blacks who had first envisioned this free all-black settlement and took the necessary steps to create it.

Nevertheless, the legacy of Wilberforce is not that it failed, but that it happened at all. Not only was it the first organized black settlement in Canada, it also indirectly inspired the national scale of the Negro Convention Movement. The shackles of slavery were being shed mentally as well as physically. It took another ten years, but what had begun in Wilberforce impelled others and opened new doors.

And though there were to be more ambitious and successful black settlements in Upper Canada, Wilberforce holds a special position. As historian Fred Landon has written, none of the others "attracted more attention or had fixed upon them higher hopes. Even across the sea, there were people watching this experiment in Negro colonization. Its failure was probably inevitable; all the Negro colonies in Upper Canada disappeared as such in time, but while they lasted, they were one of the indirect influences undermining the system of slavery in the United States."

Illustration of Josiah Henson making a presentation to Queen Victoria at Windsor Castle. (Photograph by Jacqueline Tobin, courtesy of Uncle Tom's Cabin Historic Site and Museum)

Chapter Two

Dawn and "Uncle Tom"

By 1834, colonization versus abolition was a hot topic throughout the United States, debated most passionately on college campuses. Students at Lane Theological Seminary in Cincinnati were no exception. Lane was a Presbyterian-affiliated school, its purpose the education of young men for Christian ministry, its president the well-respected Reverend Lyman Beecher (father of Harriet Beecher Stowe, who would later write *Uncle Tom's Cabin*).

Students at Lane had already founded extracurricular clubs for discussing pertinent subjects such as missions and colonization. Now they petitioned the board of the college to create an antislavery society. Dr. Beecher approved but the trustees didn't, fearing loss of funding and an impact on recruitment of new students. Professors, while privately supporting the idea, advised the students against any action that might create divisions within the student body.

While Dr. Beecher was traveling on seminary business, the Lane trustees ordered the students to discontinue both antislavery and colonization societies. Beecher's position when he returned was that he didn't want to suppress the students' right to free discussion on any topic of their choice. Nevertheless, faced with the determination of the trustees, he asked the students to bide their time until the new rule could be overturned.

But the students refused to back down and asked for the right to transfer without penalty to other seminaries of their choice. A "Statement of Reasons," signed by fifty-one of them, laid out their beliefs. Many of the "Lane Rebels," as they were called, relocated across Ohio to the more liberal Oberlin Theological Seminary after receiving assurances of their right to free speech there.

The students' bold action caused much public reaction. Newspaper articles condemned them and accused them of trying to infuse politics into a Christian seminary. Theodore D. Weld, one of the Lane Rebels, responded, "But in solemn earnest, I ask, why should not theological students investigate and discuss the sin of slavery? . . . Is it not the business of theological seminaries to educate the heart, as well as the head? To mellow the sympathies, and deepen the emotions, as well as to provide the means of knowledge? If *not,* then give Lucifer a professorship."

Hiram Wilson, another one of the Lane Rebels who had transferred, graduated from Oberlin in 1836 and immediately began his mission work. Oberlin's president, Charles Finney, was interested in the status of blacks who had made their way to Canada. He gave Wilson twenty-five dollars to travel to Upper Canada to investigate and report back on their status. Wilson traveled throughout the province from the fall through the following spring, when he returned to the United States to attend a meeting of the American Anti-Slavery Society as a delegate from Upper Canada. Wilson had a firm personal belief in the importance of education for everyone, especially former fugitives. During his travels, he observed firsthand the discrimination they were facing. Specific educational opportunities for them had to be created, he reported. Wilson solicited financial help from this group, and with five other Oberlin students, he returned to Canada to create schools primarily for but not restricted to black students, under the auspices of his new organization, the Canada Mission.

Wilson's efforts drew the attention of James Fuller, a Quaker philanthropist in New York State. Fuller, although interested in aiding in the rehabilitation of former fugitives, was reluctant to interfere in the internal affairs of a foreign country. Wilson's Canada Mission gave him the opportunity he was looking for. He began raising money for the schools.

At about the same time Hiram Wilson was attending Lane Seminary in Cincinnati, arguing the right to have campus discussions about slavery, Josiah Henson, a fugitive slave from Kentucky, was making his escape through the same city and finding his way across Lake Erie to Canada. Henson had been born in 1789 to slave parents on a farm near Port Tobacco, Maryland. His first memory was of seeing his father walking toward him, bleeding profusely from a beating—he'd struck back at an overseer who had assaulted Henson's mother. As a result, his father was "sold south." Henson, his mother, and six siblings continued to live on the same farm until their master drowned while stumbling home drunk. To settle the estate, the Henson family was sold off, separately.

In his autobiography, written in 1849, Henson wrote: "I remember being torn from a dear and affectionate mother; I saw her tears and heard her groans. . . . From a little boy up I have remembered my mother . . . I have heard her pray for me; for she was a good Christian woman before I was born. . . ."

At eighteen, allowed to hear a sermon, Henson had a conversion experience that drew him toward a life of preaching. When he was twenty-two, he married a woman from a neighboring plantation; they had twelve children, seven of whom reached adulthood. At one point during his forty-one years of enslavement, Henson suffered a crippling injury from a beating; both shoulder blades were broken as a result, but no physician was ever called. "From that day to this," he wrote, "I have been unable to raise my hands as high as my head." Despite this disability, he tried to purchase freedom for himself and his family, but after he had saved the necessary funds, his master asked a higher price and set out with Henson to sell him south. During their journey, when his master fell ill, Henson nursed him back to health, despite having had the opportunity to kill him and flee. Henson, whose faith guided him all his life, felt that a Christian would not commit murder, even though he traveled back to the plantation knowing that at the first opportunity an effort would be made to sell him again.

Once at home with his family, Henson made up his mind. On a Saturday night in mid-September 1830, he, his wife, and four of their children escaped. Henson carried the two youngest in a knapsack on his back. They made their way on foot to Cincinnati and on to Sandusky, Ohio, mostly alone but with some help from Indians and white people they encountered on the way. In Sandusky, Henson met a sympathetic ship captain who took the family across Lake Erie to Buffalo, where they found a man who ferried them to Canada. Describing his elation and relief, Henson wrote, "It was the 28th of October, 1830, in the morning, when my feet first touched the Canada shore. I threw myself on the ground, rolled in the sand, seized handfuls of it and kissed them, and danced around, till, in the eyes of several who were present, I passed for a madman."

Newly escaped fugitives often settled near the first place they reached, hiring themselves out to white farmers in the area. Initially, the Hensons settled close to Fort Erie. Henson built a small home, worked on local farms, and began preaching to his fellow fugitives who had also settled there. But he soon realized that no progress would be made if they did not become independent through owning their own land. Already seen as a leader as well as a powerful orator, Henson convened a meeting to discuss the issue. They needed "energy, enterprise, and self-reliance," he said, and his neighbors agreed. Henson was sent to scout out a suitable location.

An area near the Sydenham River, where there was already a small settlement called Dawn, seemed ideal. But first Henson's group would have to earn money for the purchase of the land, and so they settled temporarily near Colchester, a small community on the southwestern tip of Ontario, near Lake Erie, where land was already cleared and they could grow crops to sell.

Henson often preached about the important obligations the group was bound to honor, not only to God for their deliverance but to their fellowmen. Always a man who acted on his beliefs, during these years he made numerous trips back to the States to bring other fugitives to Canada. As he would write, "I have been instrumental in delivering one hundred and eighteen human beings out of the cruel and merciless grasp of the slaveholder."

It was while living in Colchester that Henson met Hiram Wilson and was eventually introduced to James Fuller. In June 1838, Wilson and Henson called a convention of Canadian blacks to discuss the establishment of a school. "Our children could gain those elements of knowledge which are usually taught in a grammar-school," Henson urged. In addition, boys should be taught the practice of a mechanical art, like millwork, carpentry, and blacksmithing, and girls be instructed in the domestic arts, "the proper occupation and ornament of their sex." He argued that a school would train those who could then instruct others, which would gradually enable them all "to become independent of the white man for our intellectual progress, as we could be for our physical prosperity."

In a report to the Canada Mission Board, Hiram Wilson explained their reasoning: "This institute is not to rival Oberlin or Oneida, but it is necessary because neither of these is safe for the fugitive. Our arms are thrown open . . . to receive and instruct them, where no tyrant can molest or make them afraid." (Oneida Institute, a Presbyterian-supported school near Utica, New York, where students earned their tuition by doing manual labor, had been founded in 1827 to prepare students for mission work in the West. In 1833, Beriah Green, a staunch abolitionist, became its president, with the promise that he could direct the school toward the cause of black freedom, "transform the Institute into an interracial abolitionist training ground.")

Given the go-ahead by the Canada Mission Board to find a site that would be safe for fugitives, Henson and Wilson decided on Dawn, where Henson had first wanted to settle. Perhaps he had been drawn to the area because religious camp meetings were held in the "flats" (the lowlands) near the Sydenham River. Possibly he'd met Weldon Harris and Levi Willoughby, two blacks already living there. In any case, the land was heavily forested, with wetlands and grasslands providing plenty of game to support the community. For the school, which had been named the British American Institute, Henson and Wilson purchased two hundred acres on the river; Henson bought two hundred adjacent acres for himself. The school eventually built at Dawn must be credited to Hiram Wilson and James Fuller as well as to Josiah Henson, though it was Henson whose name would be forever linked to it.

In 1842 work began. First the school was built, then a sawmill to generate income from the vast surrounding forests, and a gristmill for grinding wheat and other grains. Soon Dawn had become synonymous with the British American Institute and many blacks were drawn there because of the promise of education and jobs. By 1844, American abolitionists began publicizing the area. Levi Coffin, a Quaker abolitionist from Cincinnati who was known as the "president" of the Underground Railroad, made his first trip there that year. Others like Coffin arrived to see for themselves the status of fugitives they were aiding to escape to Canada. By 1845, the school had seventy students under the tutelage of one of the Institute's first teachers, Hiram Wilson's wife, Hannah.

It was a new Fugitive Slave Act, passed in 1850, that served as both cause and effect in antislavery opinion. The 1793 law had stated that a slave maintained his status, even in states and territories that did not have slavery. But many states did not enforce this rule. Southern states pushed through new legislation, making the federal government rather than the states responsible for enforcement. Historian Eric Foner notes the irony: The same southerners who had used the argument of states' rights to defend slavery were now demanding federal intervention to help protect those rights. The 1850 law specifically required the involvement of marshals to assist in the apprehension of fugitives and commanded citizens to aid in their capture. It forbade interference with any persons attempting to apprehend fugitives. And it denied fugitives the right to trial by jury or even to have their testimony considered in court.

The harshness of this law, while placating southern slave owners, resulted in increased abolitionist sentiment and action among blacks and whites. The *Liberator,* an antislavery newspaper, noted that nearly all the waiters in the hotels in Pittsburgh fled en masse two weeks after the signing of the bill by President Fillmore. Hiram Wilson estimated that in the first three months after the law's passage, at least three thousand people crossed the border into Canada.

Free blacks did not wait passively for sympathetic whites to protect them. Many formed vigilance committees for mutual protection. Abolitionist newspapers appeared; the Underground Railroad was expanded; fraternal organizations such as the Prince Hall Masons became even more proactive. Colonization organizations were formed to explore emigration to Africa. And when people were directly threatened, individual acts of violent resistance occurred. One incident in particular, in 1851, in the small town of Christiana, Pennsylvania, focused the country's attention on the new Fugitive Slave Act and the federal government's ability to enforce it.

The incident made national headlines. It was called the "Christiana Riot" by the white press; Frederick Douglass called it "the battle for liberty," and a local Pennsylvania newspaper ran the headline CIVIL WAR, FIRST BLOW STRUCK. Southerners were stunned at the audacity of blacks fighting for their own freedom and angered by what they saw as lack of white support for enforcement of the Fugitive Slave Act. North-

erners felt pressure to enforce a law they did not support. The line in
the sand had been clearly drawn. Emigration by both slaves and free
blacks increased, and Dawn saw an influx of newcomers.

By the 1850s, blacks made up most of Dawn's population. Their development of shops, schools, churches, and mills provided the infrastructure for what eventually became the town of Dresden, which was
incorporated in 1871. Today, Dresden is a small town of about 2,500,
its economy based on recreation and tourism.

East Coast builders, as well as Europeans seeking a new source of
lumber, especially valued the black walnut in the forests surrounding
Dawn. It was suggested to Josiah Henson that he take some of it to the
1851 World's Fair in London, for exhibit in the Crystal Palace located in
Hyde Park. Built almost entirely of iron and glass, the Crystal Palace
contained such marvels as a fountain constructed from four tons of crystal glass, a massive sideboard carved from a single oak tree, a giant thirty-
one-ton steam locomotive, and a statue of a naked Greek slave girl. The
building was basically a giant greenhouse designed much like a conser-
vatory. Among its more than 100,000 exhibits were included yellow
graphite pencils, Bowie knives, Swiss watches, Colt pistols, and life-size
models of dinosaurs, the first ever created. The theme of the fair was
modern industrial technology and design. Henson crossed the Atlantic
aboard an American ship with four black walnut boards—each seven
feet long by four feet wide—which had been finished by former slaves
who worked at the Dawn sawmill. When he arrived at the fair, the
American Department insisted he exhibit in the American section, but
Henson objected, demanding to be allowed a space in the Canadian Department, and insisting that he was a Canadian citizen displaying Canadian goods.

Though the American Department eventually prevailed, it was
Henson who had the last word. He set up his boards in the American
section with a sign that read THIS IS THE PRODUCT OF THE INDUSTRY OF
A FUGITIVE SLAVE FROM THE UNITED STATES, WHOSE RESIDENCE IS

DAWN, CANADA. English visitors to the fair loved the public insult to America.

As the only black man to display a product at the fair, and self-identified as a former slave, Henson drew the attention of many of the over six million visitors. Queen Victoria, who with her children visited every exhibit in the building, is said to have inquired as to whether he was, indeed, a fugitive.

Henson had never learned to read, but he had a marvelous memory that masked this shortcoming. When his son Tom became aware of it, he began to teach him. "I did really learn to read a little," Henson later wrote. "It was, and has been ever since, a great comfort to me to have made this acquisition; though it has made me comprehend better the terrible abyss of ignorance in which I had been plunged all my previous life. It made me also feel more deeply and bitterly the oppression under which I had toiled and groaned. At the same time it made me more anxious than before to do something for the rescue and the elevation of those who were suffering the same evils I had endured."

While in England, Henson was in demand as a speaker. At one venue, he met the archbishop of Canterbury, who asked him, "Which university did you attend?" To which Henson replied, "The university of adversity."

Until the early 1850s, most of Henson's public lectures were conducted on behalf of the British American Institute. But in 1852, Harriet Beecher Stowe published *Uncle Tom's Cabin,* and soon after, the public began connecting him with her character, Uncle Tom. From then on, Henson himself became the focus of attention, rather than the British American Institute he was promoting.

Stowe had been inspired to write her book after witnessing slavery during her early years in Cincinnati and after passage of the 1850 Fugitive Slave Act. The first year alone, over 300,000 copies were sold in the United States, and the book had a dramatic international impact as well (a British edition was published within two months of the first American edition). While slave narratives such as Frederick Douglass's *Narrative of the Life of Frederick Douglass* had been popular, and abolitionist newspapers such as William Lloyd Garrison's *Liberator* and Douglass's *North Star* were quite successful in spreading the antislavery message, it was *Uncle Tom's Cabin*, notably written by a white woman, that had the biggest public impact on the mostly white reading public. Southerners were outraged, insisting that the characters were based on lies and an exaggeration of the conditions of slavery. A bookseller in Alabama was run out of town for selling copies; the southern press called the book "a caricature of slavery."

But the North, and Europe as well as Canada, embraced the book. Newspapers praised it: "We welcome the work as amongst the most powerful agents that human genius has yet produced for the removal of the one fearful curse that rests upon our country" *(Christian Register, Boston).*

Response in the English press was similar: "We have here the most singular and absorbing specimen of American Literature, which ever came to our shores. It will be read, and must be read, by everybody, everywhere" *(Tait's Edinburgh Magazine).* "The work . . . has inflicted a wound upon the infernal system of slavery, from which it will never recover" *(Brighton Herald).*

While the black press mostly lauded the work, some took issue with Stowe's story line, which concluded by sending George Harris, one of the two main black characters, to Liberia as part of the colonization movement. An editorial in *The Provincial Freeman,* a black-owned newspaper in Canada, called the book "a piece of needless and hurtful encouragement of the vile spirit of Yankee Colonizationism."

Stowe was under such intense public pressure to explain her characters that she felt compelled to write *A Key to Uncle Tom's Cabin,* a 259-page document, in 1853, only one year after she had published the original book. Southerners especially were not used to having slaves characterized as having the same attributes as themselves. Stowe defended her characterization of Uncle Tom as a gentle, intelligent, religious and courageous black man, and went on to relate several stories of real slaves to prove the accuracy of her characterization, ultimately connecting Uncle Tom to Josiah Henson:

> A last parallel with that of Uncle Tom is to be found in the published memoirs of the venerable Josiah Henson. . . . With a degree of prudence, courage and address, which can scarcely find a parallel in any history, he managed, with his wife and two children, to escape into Canada. Here he learned to read, and, by his superior talent and capacity for management, laid the foundation for the fugitive settlement of Dawn, which is understood to be one of the most flourishing in Canada.

There has been considerable debate over whether Josiah Henson was indeed the prototype for Stowe's "Uncle Tom." Henson had published his autobiography in 1849. His descendants believe (a position shared by those at the Harriet Beecher Stowe Center) that while conducting her extensive research, Stowe most probably came across Henson's autobiography and incorporated into her character some of his life and personal attributes.

Perhaps more important than the argument is each of their legacies. As Dawn Adiletta, curator of the Stowe Center, puts it: "Stowe wrote a novel that rocked the world, whether one liked it or not, and became an icon of social justice. Henson did his best to behave honorably while trapped in a dishonorable situation (slavery); risked his life for his own freedom and the freedom of his family; risked it again as he returned to the United States to help others . . . and enabled others to become self-supporting. His legacy is remarkable."

Nevertheless, Henson's true story, as dramatic and as daring as it was, became overshadowed by the fictional. Regrettably, his legacy was distorted by readers who judged him through the prism of later racial sensitivities, and who ascribed to him the subservience that was in fact created largely by the black minstrel shows popular at the time, which depicted blacks in stereotypical fashion. When the public began to identify Henson as Uncle Tom, neither he nor Stowe ever denied the link; Stowe even wrote an introduction for a later edition of his auto-biography, thereby giving tacit approval to the connection. But though Henson was continually introduced on the lecture circuit as Uncle Tom, he did not use the name himself. He is quoted as saying, in at least one lecture after the Civil War, "It has been spread abroad that 'Uncle Tom' is coming, and that is what has brought you here. Now allow me to say that my name is not Tom, and never was Tom, and that I do not want to have any other name inserted in the newspapers for me than my own. My name is Josiah Henson, always was, and always will be. I never change my colours."

For her part, Stowe responded with a somewhat evasive answer when questioned about Henson and Uncle Tom, writing that she was pleased to endorse a "noble man" and admitted that his autobiography had been the source of many of her ideas and scenes for her book. She mentioned in particular the scene in which Uncle Tom refuses to kill his master in order to free himself. She also wrote that Henson had once visited her, confirming the "high esteem" she had for him.

The impact of Stowe's book cannot be overestimated. It challenged many ideas and influenced some people in direct ways. Alexander Ross, a Canadian doctor and ornithologist, and eventually a famous Underground Railroad conductor, covered his clandestine activities in the South with the subterfuge of bird-watching. Of *Uncle Tom's Cabin*, he said, "It excited the sympathies of every humane person who read it. . . . To me it was a command. . . ."

After two years of study with northern abolitionists, Ross began his work in the South, seeking to educate enslaved blacks about methods of safe escape and travel to Canada and using his bird-watching cover to gain access to the homes of southern plantation owners. A mid-nineteenth-century back-to-nature movement was then sweeping the Western world, and included such individuals as Charles Darwin, who was developing his theory of natural selection and evolution, and the American naturalist John James Audubon, who was painting the various birds he encountered in his travels. Southerners, aware of these trends, accepted Ross's credentials; Ross himself employed his cover to great advantage. While out in the fields, purportedly watching birds, he would gather the slaves, find those ready to risk escape, instruct them about methods and destinations, and give them a compass, a knife, and some food.

Ross's activities were undertaken at great risk to himself, as well as to the fugitives. On several occasions, he was arrested after suspicious plantation owners made the connection between his arrival and the escape of their slaves. At least two times, Ross, himself a member of a Masonic lodge, was able to get himself out of the situation by flashing the Masonic distress signal. In this case, the fraternal connection superseded any political allegiances. In his memoirs, he credited Stowe for inspiring his actions: "A settled conviction took possession of my mind that it was my duty to help the oppressed to freedom."

Stowe's controversial novel inspired aboveground as well as underground action. In the United States, the Massachusetts antislavery senator Charles Sumner began to push for repeal of the 1850 Fugitive Slave Act. He called Stowe "another Joan of Arc," who "with marvelous powers sweeps the chords of the popular heart. Now melting to tears, and now inspiring to rage, her work everywhere touches the conscience, and makes the slave-hunter more hateful."

And Abraham Lincoln, as legend has it, said upon meeting Stowe, "So you are the little woman who wrote the book that started this great war."

Uncle Tom's Cabin inspired many theatrical productions, songs, and poetry in the United States as well as in Canada. Stowe's depiction of black people challenged prevailing myths about them. But her honesty was met by a resistant culture. Minstrel shows, with white actors in black face portraying blacks, had already become popular, especially in the North. Soon "Tom shows" were written, with actors interpreting some of the more dramatic scenes from the book. Stephen Foster, considered a "minstrel composer," wrote songs such as "My Old Kentucky Home" and "Old Folks at Home" that were often performed in the context of the Tom shows.

Thus the character of Uncle Tom, written by Stowe to represent a noble black man, a Christ-like figure, was diluted to reflect the racist views of the times. Uncle Tom onstage became a shuffling, grinning black man who would do anything to ingratiate himself with whites. The term *Uncle Tom* was coined: a slur used to define blacks who would demean themselves and their culture for the approval of whites. Lost was the fact that there really was a man, Josiah Henson, whose life displayed all the virtues with which Stowe had imbued her character: courage, intelligence, compassion, and leadership of his people.

Henson himself made three journeys to London, the last when he was eighty-eight years old. It was on this final trip that he and his wife were personally received by Queen Victoria at Windsor Castle. Henson thanked Her Majesty for himself as well as "on behalf of all the other coloured brethren in Canada . . . for her august protection when they were poor fugitive slaves." The next year, after an introduction by Frederick Douglass, he went to the White House to meet President Rutherford B. Hayes. Josiah Henson died in 1883, at the age of ninety-four, in the house now known as "Uncle Tom's Cabin." His funeral was one of the largest ever seen in the area. Thousands of people lined the route to the British Methodist Episcopal Church in Dresden, Ontario, the town that had grown from Dawn.

While the British American Institute enjoyed initial success and good publicity, it quickly came under attack. At least some of the controversy arose, according to historians Marie and Jeffrey Carter, because of opposing views in the abolitionist movement itself. The British American Institute represented to many the viewpoint of colonization, providing a safe haven for former fugitives, a place where they could live and learn away from the pressures of the rest of society. But many abolitionists believed that fugitives should be fully integrated into society, become entirely self-sufficient, and, above all, should not beg for money or other support. These two views were clearly defined in the pages of the two black newspapers of the time in Upper Canada. The *Voice of the Fugitive* supported Henson and the concept of black communities in general. The *Provincial Freeman* attacked and criticized the British American Institute and Henson specifically because of his reliance on solicitation for support. The argument was fiercely debated in the black community and to this day continues to define how the history of the British American Institute and Henson are, to a large degree, depicted.

Additionally, the Institute suffered from lack of good management. Neither Hiram Wilson nor Josiah Henson was a competent manager. Both were careless, at best, with the finances of the organization, and thus came under intense scrutiny by other blacks as well as by whites. The financial records of the school were challenged on many occasions by various individuals and groups, with the blame early on being laid at the feet of Wilson and Henson (the latter at least had a legitimate excuse in that he had never learned to read and write). But even the concept of the Institute as a "segregated" school came under attack, as segregation versus integration was already an issue. Dawn's debts, which included the cost of employing teachers, building mills and other facilities, and just the overall business of trying to keep the Institute afloat, continued to rise. New trustees were brought in but they too were accused of stealing school funds. By 1872, with the Institute in financial ruin, the board sold its land and assets.

Today, the history of Dawn and Henson is kept alive at the Uncle Tom's Cabin Historic Site and its museum in Dresden, on land once owned by Henson near the British American Institute. The site, which is managed by his descendants, consists of Henson's home and grave, a nineteenth-century schoolhouse, and a museum that also commemorates Dawn and the Underground Railroad. Henson's artifacts, including an autographed picture from Queen Victoria, are on display.

Because of his fame and the leadership roles he played in the history of Canadian blacks, Henson became, according to historian Robin Winks, "the best known of all Negro Canadians, his narratives the

most frequently used sources, his life the archetypical fugitive experience." In Canadian history, he is remembered along with "the North
Star, the Underground Railroad, and the fugitives' haven 'under the
lion's paw.' "

In 1983, Josiah Henson was honored with a commemorative stamp,
the first black man to receive such an honor in Canada.

Chapter Three

Chatham

Although Chatham wasn't solely a black town, it was a town that attracted blacks, free and fugitive, and a place where they prospered. They may have been drawn there because of Chatham's location at the fork of the Thames River, which provided not only navigational access to Detroit but also the safety of distance from the American border (by 1837, there were two steamships daily between Detroit and Chatham). There were also economic opportunities here not found elsewhere, especially beginning in the early 1850s, when the Great Western Railway was constructed. Some years later, a visiting American minister was moved to write of Chatham that it was "not a mecca only. In a broader and truer sense, it was the colored man's Paris. Even now, after the experience and growth of 20 years of liberty we scarcely know a city of the land blessed with a society more varied and refined, more opulent and gay, than was this little Canadian city during the decade that opened up the second half of our century."

The *North Star* offered this description of Chatham in 1855:

John Brown, famed abolitionist and organizer of the raid on Harpers Ferry. (Photograph courtesy of the Ohio Historical Society)

In this town, forty-five miles from Detroit, is a principal settlement of fugitive slaves. It contains between five and six thousand
inhabitants, mostly black, who have gained their liberty, a boon
more dear than life. They have their own schools and churches,
and their houses present as fair and comfortable an appearance as
any on the route from Detroit. Many of them own land . . . and
whenever a fugitive arrives, he meets a joyous welcome, and at
once finds employment and good support. The land is good, and
the temperature is moderated both summer and winter by the
vicinity of the Great Lakes. It is a "blessed city of refuge" for the
downtrodden. . . .

Though many people arrived in Chatham unskilled and uneducated,
many others brought skilled trades. A *New York Herald* article about the
town listed four cabinetmakers, one gunsmith, six master carpenters,
plasterers, three printers, two watchmakers, two ship's carpenters, two
millers, four blacksmiths, one saddler, six master shoemakers, six gro-
cers, and a cigar maker. Black-owned businesses included shoemaker
James Charity's Charity Block, a building with shops on the ground
floor and apartments above. The Villa Mansion Hotel, owned by black
businessman Sherwood Butler, often served as a meeting center for the
community.

Another visitor to Chatham in 1855, Benjamin Drew, a former public school teacher and part-time journalist, wrote:

Here indeed, more fully than anywhere else, the traveler realizes
the extent of the American exodus. At every turn, he meets members of the African race, single or in groups: he sees them building
and painting houses, working in mills, engaged in every handicraft
employment; here he notices a street occupied by colored shop-
keepers and clerks; if he steps into the environs, he finds the blacks
in every quarter, busy upon their gardens and farms. The white
population of Chatham is reckoned at four thousand; the number
of colored persons in the town may be safely estimated at eight

hundred. If to this estimate is added the number residing in the neighborhood, the total amount cannot be less than two thousand.*

Drew had been asked by antislavery forces to report on the status of blacks in Canada. His tour of southern Ontario included fourteen communities, where he interviewed over a hundred refugees, using letters of introduction from people such as Hiram Wilson to make his connections. In his 1855 book, *A North-Side View of Slavery,* Drew presented his findings and interviews, offering fugitives the opportunity to speak for themselves. Like the slave narratives of the time, these interviews stand today as witness to slavery, to flight, to a new, free life.

Drew's book was intended to counter the recently published *A South-Side View of Slavery,* by Reverend Nehemiah Adams, who, in an attempt to challenge *Uncle Tom's Cabin,* portrayed slave owners as "guardians, educators and saviors of the African race." Both Drew's and Adams's books contributed to the increasingly heated debate over slavery that had begun with the 1850 Fugitive Slave Act. After the 1852 publication of *Uncle Tom's Cabin* came the 1854 Kansas-Nebraska Act, which divided the land west of Missouri into two territories, Kansas and Nebraska, with the population living in each to determine themselves whether slavery would be legal.

By 1856, the debate in "the colored man's Paris" was less over slavery itself than how to fight it. Chatham had not only industry but infrastructure: three black Baptist churches, an African Methodist Episcopal church, whose members had separated from its American conference and formed the British Methodist Episcopal Church, black private schools, and many organizations and societies, among them a lodge of the Prince Hall Freemasons, a benevolent society, a debating society, a literary society, and the Walter Hawkins singing group. The True Band Society, which supported and encouraged self-reliance in the commu-

*While population figures varied most records indicate that the black population usually numbered one-third of the total population.

nity, counted over three hundred members in its first year of existence. Chatham was also the home of Ontario's second black newspaper, the *Provincial Freeman*, run by Mary Ann Shadd and Isaac Shadd, her brother. William Wells Brown, a black abolitionist, remarked that in Chatham "every other person whom I met was colored. The population here is made up entirely from the slave states, with but few exceptions. Every shade of the southern sons and daughters of oppression, from the polite house servant down to the coarsest field-hand, is seen upon the unpaved and dusty streets. . . ."

Along with its prosperity and community, though, Chatham had its share of racial discrimination. Edwin Larwill, a town councillor, school board commissioner, and editor of the white newspaper, the *Chatham Journal*, attempted to bar black students from attending public schools, to block blacks from voting, and to levy a poll tax on blacks living in the city. His racism rivaled the U.S. black codes: "Imagine our Legislative Halls studded and our principal departments managed by these Ebony Men," he wrote. "It would be impossible to keep them out of the smaller elective offices. . . . The genius of our institutions would be destroyed."

That Larwill did not succeed is testament to the strong network that had been created among the people of Chatham and the nearby communities of Wilberforce, Dawn, and the Elgin settlement in Buxton, all within fifty miles of Chatham. If anything, Larwill brought people together, often in conjunction with white sympathizers, in a refusal to let discrimination stand in the way of creating success for themselves and their children in matters of education, business, or religion.

In 1856, Dr. Martin Delany, a free black man who had already made a name for himself in the States as a writer and physician, moved to Chatham to pursue his interests under the security of the British flag. Born in Virginia of a free mother and an enslaved father who later purchased his freedom, Delany proudly traced his roots to an African chieftain. In Pittsburgh, he had founded and edited *The Mystery*, his own newspaper, which he then sold to the AME church. Then he became a coeditor and reporter for the *North Star*. As traveling correspondent, he undertook a "western tour" of the United States, and reported his observations of free black life in nine essays and twenty-three letters. The importance of Delany's travel narratives is often overlooked. His writings documenting the free black experience, studied beside the slave narratives, reveal a more complete picture, the full range of mid-nineteenth-century black life in America.

Delany's western tour on behalf of the *North Star* ended in April 1849. Three months later, he and Frederick Douglass ended their collaboration. There is speculation that the two split over ideological differences. Douglass, the son of an enslaved black woman and a white slave master, lived his early life enslaved. After escaping he created a successful life in the midst of white society and became, at least for many whites, the quintessential example of how a black man, once in bondage, might succeed in America through his own endeavors. Douglass's success moved him to believe in the concept of black assimilation into white society; his suggestion was to "avail yourself of white institutions, not because they are white, because they afford a more convenient means of improvement."

Delany, on the other hand, had been born free, the son of a "free seamstress and a plantation slave," and constantly touted his "pure" black blood, in contrast to Douglass's mixed heritage. Delany had quite different life experiences, which led him to see himself as an outsider in white society. One of the first black men to study medicine at Harvard, he did not graduate. White students, though they claimed to have "no objection to the education and elevation of blacks," nevertheless objected to their admission to the medical lectures as "highly detrimental to the interests and welfare of the institution of which we are members" and protested "their presence in college with us." Delany was expelled.

After the passage of the 1850 Fugitive Slave Act, he felt that the time for talking had ended and the time for action was at hand. To a crowd in Pittsburgh, he shouted, "Sir, my house is my castle . . . If any man approaches that house in search of a slave . . . if he crosses the threshold of my door, and I do not lay him a lifeless corpse at my feet, I hope the grave may refuse my body a resting place, and righteous Heaven my spirit a home. O, no! He cannot enter that house and we both live."

In 1852, the same year *Uncle Tom's Cabin* appeared, Delany published *The Condition, Elevation, Emigration, and Destiny of the Colored People of the United States, Politically Considered,* a book that set forth his views on the necessity for black emigration and nation building outside the borders of the United States, specifically in Central and South America. His views angered most abolitionists, including Frederick Douglass, who were still wedded to the idea of blacks staying in America and fighting for their rights and freedom. In what was a clear insult, Douglass did not review Delany's book, though he wrote several glowing reviews of *Uncle Tom's Cabin.*

Delany was outraged that Douglass would embrace Stowe's work yet not even mention his, and wrote several letters to Douglass expressing his views. "I beg leave to say that she knows nothing about us, the Free Colored people of the United States," he wrote about Stowe, "neither does any other white person—and, consequently, can contrive no successful scheme for our elevation; it must be done for ourselves."

To his credit, Douglass published Delany's letters, creating a written dialogue that represented, in essence, their philosophical differences. "To scornfully reject all aid from our white friends," Douglass responded, "and to denounce them as unworthy of our confidence, looks high and mighty enough on paper; but unless the back ground is filled up with facts demonstrating our independence and self-sustaining power, of what use is such display of self-consequence?" Believing that Stowe's book was having a dramatic impact on the minds and hearts of Americans, he defended her: "The assertion that Mrs. Stowe 'knows nothing about us' shows that Bro. Delany knows nothing about Mrs. Stowe."

Delany objected to Stowe's sending one of her main characters, George, to Liberia, which he considered a statement of support for the patronizing policies of the American Colonization Society. Delany himself was an emigrationist, not a colonizationist. He believed that blacks should choose to emigrate rather than allow themselves to be colonized—in effect sent away—by others. Douglass's public support of Stowe and lack of similar consideration for Delany was not just a public insult; it was a way of creating a public dialogue about the differences in the black community at that time.

In 1853, Douglass attended a convention of black leaders in Rochester, New York, to discuss the Fugitive Slave Act and other issues, including colonization, especially in light of the arguments surrounding Stowe and *Uncle Tom's Cabin*. The convention passed many resolutions, including, "Resolved, That we recognize in 'Uncle Tom's Cabin' a work plainly marked by the finger of God, lifting the wall of separation which has too long divided the sympathies of one class of the American people from another . . ."

Delany boycotted the convention, angered by the participants' seeming equation of colonization with emigration as both being bad for blacks; he called another convention, to be held in Cleveland in 1854, to discuss the importance of self-reliance especially as it pertained to emigration. With his keynote address, "Political Destiny of the Colored Race on the American Continent," Delany earned his title as the "Father of Black Nationalism." He argued that "blacks can call themselves free only when they constitute an essential part of the ruling element of the country in which they live," and stated that blacks had "inherent traits, attributes, so to speak, and native characteristics, peculiar to our race." Delany's message of black pride, black power, and black separatism had heretofore not been heard. The Cleveland convention, which included voting women for the first time, approved a resolution that "as men and equals, we demand every political right, privilege and position to which the whites are eligible in the United States, and we will either attain to these, or accept nothing." With emigration as its focus, the attendees voted to publish a journal, the "African American Repository," to document the successes of the black man through history. Committees were set up for exploring emigration to Africa, Haiti, and Central America. Delany was chosen to lead the African exploration.

It was at this point that he found himself increasingly estranged from the abolitionist movement in the United States, feeling as he did that in relationships with antislavery friends as well as pro-slavery elements, "we find ourselves occupying the very same position . . . a mere secondary, underling position." In 1856, Delany moved to Chatham.

His move did not go unnoticed by the *Provincial Freeman*. Its issue of February 23 made this clear: "We are pleased to state to our readers, the arrival of our esteemed and talented friend, Dr. M. R. Delany, of Pittsburgh, Pa, in this town, yesterday morning, who intends making this his home." Dr. Delany's reputation was noted: "as a physician, having been long in practice and thoroughly known by all the professional men of the States and inhabitants generally; and, as a writer, and orator, is distinguished among the numbers that now occupy the field, in the distribution of knowledge for the elevation and improvement of mankind, which is certainly commendatory to all friends of progress here and elsewhere. The Doctor proposes to resume the practice of medicine immediately, when he will doubtless be at the service of all who may call at his office, on William Street, east of King." An advertisement for his services appeared in the same issue. "Doctor Delany, Physician & Surgeon, Will, Until Further notice, Have his Office in the front Private Parlor of Mr. T. Bell's Hotel. Entrance on William Street, East of King. "References: J. P. Gazzam, Esq., M.D. George M. Cook, Esq., M.D., Late Prof. Of Surgery in the Washington Medical College, Baltimore, Md.—Pittsburgh. Pa." The advertisement noted that Delany "practices in Chronic Diseases, and the Diseases of Women and Children, in particular."

Delany also continued his writings while living in Canada. When Douglass wrote an editorial in his own newspaper, *Frederick Douglass' Paper,* praising the black communities in Canada, Chatham specifically, Delany responded by writing an editorial for the *Provincial Freeman* of July 12, 1856, taking Douglass to task for his apparent sudden turnaround regarding black emigration and his new awareness of black success in Canada. During the next several years, while living in Chatham, Delany also finished his book, *Blake; or, The Huts of America,* a novel of black revolution. Chapters 1–23 and 29–31 were first published serially by a New York monthly, *The Anglo-African Magazine,* in 1859. The following excerpt (from chapter 31) is often quoted but never attributed to him:

> I'm on my way to Canada,
> That cold and dreary land;
> The dire effects of slavery
> I can no longer stand.
> My soul is vexed within me so,
> To think that I'm a slave,
> I've now resolved to strike the blow,
> For Freedom or the grave.

Delany may have been responding to the 1856 publication of Harriet Beecher Stowe's follow-up novel, *Dred: A Tale of the Great Dismal Swamp.* Feeling the backlash of black abolitionist anger over her Uncle Tom character and her seeming support for colonization, Stowe had left Uncle Tom behind and had written from a new perspective; her novel touted the life of a black revolutionary. Through *Dred,* Stowe suggested that there might be a need for radical action to abolish slavery. Though they may have been widely divergent philosophically in their early writing careers, the fact was that Stowe and Delany, through *Blake* and *Dred,* both now embraced, at least in their novels, radical action by blacks on their own behalf.

Another name enters Chatham's story around this time: John Brown, the fiery abolitionist whose actions are often said to have precipitated the Civil War. Born in 1800, Brown was the first son of an intensely religious father, Owen, who immersed his family in strict religious dogma that also encompassed abolitionism. Owen was a tanner and shoemaker who, in Ohio, became a successful landowner. He remembered receiving an antislavery pamphlet that changed his life when he was nineteen years old. Supported in his beliefs by his wife, Ruth, Owen raised his children the same way.

The Kansas-Nebraska Act of 1854 set off a firestorm of activity between pro- and antislavery forces in the new western territories. Antislavery supporters were especially outraged by the act because it negated a previous agreement, called the Missouri Compromise, which had outlawed slavery in both territories. But now both pro- and antislavery settlers rushed to Kansas, each side hoping to determine the results of the first election. The *North Star* urged blacks to relocate there to prevent southern sympathizers from adding another slave state to the Union. But while many northern whites who moved to the area were against slavery, they were also not interested in having free blacks in their midst. They were antislavery but also antiblack.

In 1855, John Brown's half sister, Florilla, and her husband, Samuel Adair, both graduates of Oberlin, moved to Osawatomie, a fairly new settlement about fifty miles southwest of Kansas City. Staunch abolitionists, the Adairs wrote to Owen Brown that Missouri pro-slavery elements were invading the territory. Though Osawatomie was a "free state" community, the Adairs were keenly aware that they were surrounded. More of the Brown family arrived later that year. When one son wrote his father that the free staters needed ammunition, John Brown himself, traveling with another son, Oliver, carried a load of weapons to the area.

In 1856, pro-slavery forces attacked Lawrence, Kansas. Free staters in general were being personally threatened throughout the territory. Brown decided to take action to protect his family, his community, and his beliefs. Along with four sons and a son-in-law, he seized five pro-slavery men, and in the ensuing skirmish, the pro-slavery men were killed. Word of the killings spread. Despite the fact that he was not the actual killer, Brown certainly had been in charge. Historians still debate the morality of his actions, which earned him the name "Osawatomie Brown," and led people to refer to "bleeding Kansas."

Brown soon left Kansas to begin soliciting funds and support for more antislavery activities. His experiences had convinced him that slavery would not be overturned at the ballot box, but on the battle-field, and he had a larger plan in mind than just Kansas. In January 1857, he invited himself to be a guest at the home of Frederick Douglass in Rochester, New York.

For three weeks, at the Douglass home, Brown devoted his time to drafting a constitution to present to a select group of "friends of freedom" in Chatham, Ontario. He had decided, by this time, that the geographical focus of his abolitionist actions was going to be Virginia, not Kansas, but that to recruit men for his activities, he needed to hold a convention in Canada, away from American scrutiny.

Also in March 1857, the United States Supreme Court, led by Chief Justice Roger B. Taney, handed down the Dred Scott decision, which decreed that slaves were not citizens of the United States and thus did not have the rights of citizens. Those in the antislavery movement grew increasingly alarmed. Any rights blacks had thus far gained seemed to be rolling back. Many were now convinced that radical action was necessary. Douglass and Delany both voiced their belief in the right to resist slavery by violent means. Against this backdrop, in April 1858, John Brown made his way to Chatham, Ontario, to meet with Dr. Martin Delany.

American history hardly recalls this important event or the reasons Brown went to Canada. Entering the country at St. Catharines, across the border from Niagara Falls, he met first with Harriet Tubman, who had moved there with her family for safety in 1851. He tried to solicit her support. After their meeting, which Brown thought successful, he described Tubman to his son, using a male pronoun as a form of honor: "He [Harriet] is the most of a man, naturally, that I ever met with."

Then Brown moved on to Chatham. Delany wasn't at home when he arrived; without giving his name, Brown told Delany's wife he'd return in two weeks. Describing him later, she reported a "long, white beard, very gray hair and a sad but placid countenance . . . like one of the prophets." Out walking shortly after the two weeks had passed, Delany spotted the man his wife had described. When he approached and introductions had been made, Delany exclaimed, "Not Captain John Brown of Osawatomie!" Brown's reputation had preceded him.

There on the street, he stated his purpose: "I have come to Chatham expressly to see you . . . I must see you at once, sir . . . in private, as I have much to do, and but little time before me. If I am to do nothing here, I want to know it at once."

At the Villa Mansion Hotel, after securing a private back room, Brown explained further: "Sir, the people of the Northern States are cowards; slavery has made cowards of them all. The whites are afraid of each other, and the blacks are afraid of the whites. You can effect nothing among such people. . . . it is men I want, and not money; money I can get plentiful enough, but no men. Money can come without being seen, but men are afraid of identification with me, though they favor my measures."

Delany agreed to host the convention Brown wanted to call. In May 1858, Brown would present the constitution he had drafted. Invitations were sent to the select few he considered trustworthy.

> *Chatham, Canada, May 5, 1858*
>
> *My dear friend:*
>
> *I have called a quiet convention in this place of true friends of freedom. Your attendance is earnestly requested. . . .*
>
> *Your friend,*
> *John Brown*

According to historian Benjamin Quarles, while most of the invitations went out to blacks, at least one went to a white sympathizer, Dr. Alexander Milton Ross, the Canadian physician who used the cover of bird-watching for his abolitionist activities.

Several years prior to this time, while in Cleveland awaiting further trips, Ross had received a telegram from John Brown, stating that he wished to meet him. Ross, in his memoir, described his night with Brown:

During our long . . . interview, which lasted from 8 p.m. to 3 a.m. in the morning, he related many incidents of his life bearing upon the subject of slavery. He said he had for many years been studying the guerilla [sic] system of warfare adopted in the mountainous portions of Italy and Switzerland; that he could, with a small body of picked men, inaugurate and maintain a Negro insurrection in the mountains of Virginia, which would produce so much annoy-ance to the United States government, and create such a feeling of dread and insecurity in the minds of slave-holders, that slavery would ultimately be abolished.

On the appointed date, May 8, 1858, approximately seventy dele-gates gathered in Chatham to discuss Brown's plans and the constitu-tion he had drafted. Besides John Brown and about a dozen of his supporters, and Martin Delany, who chaired the meeting, other notable attendees included James Madison Bell, a plasterer and poet; Isaac Shadd of the *Provincial Freeman;* James Monroe Jones, a gunsmith and engraver; Alfred Whipper, a schoolteacher; and William Lambert, a tailor and the head of the Detroit Vigilance Committee. (Vigilance committees had been established throughout the North by sympathetic white and black citizens to aid escaping fugitives by providing food, shelter, possible employment, and safe passage to the next leg of their journey.) Another Michigan man, William Charles Monroe, the rector at St. Matthew's Protestant Episcopal Mission and a staunch emigra-tionist, became the presiding officer of the convention.

Knowing that the townspeople would be curious about the gather-ing, the delegates met furtively, and a rumor was deliberately spread that their intention was to form a racially mixed Masonic lodge, a good cover as many of the participants were known Masons, including the chair, Dr. Martin Delany, himself a past Grand Master in Pittsburgh. Brown had clearly pinpointed his base of support and sought help from those most involved in black progress. With the delegates sworn to se-crecy, he presented his plans, read aloud by John Henry Kagi, the cho-sen secretary of the convention.

William Wilberforce, British reformer who first introduced legislation to stop the importation of slaves into British colonies.
(Photograph courtesy of the Ohio Historical Society)

Reverend Josiah Henson in 1875, age 86. *(Photograph by Jacqueline Tobin, courtesy of Uncle Tom's Cabin Historic Site and Museum)*

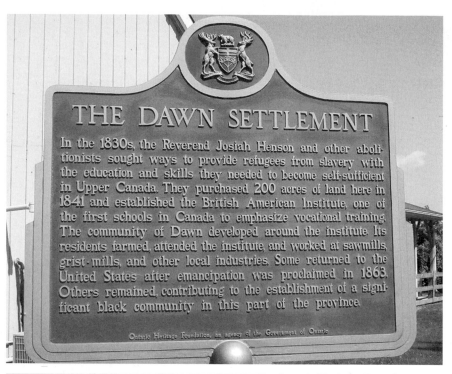

Ontario Heritage Foundation plaque at Uncle Tom's Cabin celebrating the Dawn settlement. *(Photograph by Jacqueline Tobin)*

Rocking chair hand-carved by former slaves for Reverend Josiah Henson. Note Masonic symbols and detailing. *(Photograph by Jacqueline Tobin)*

Reverend Josiah Henson and his wife, Nancy Gambril. *(Photograph by Jacqueline Tobin, courtesy of Uncle Tom's Cabin Historic Site and Museum)*

Harriet Beecher Stowe. *(Photograph courtesy of Harriet Beecher Stowe Center, Hartford, Connecticut)*

Alexander Ross, Canadian physician, ornithologist, and Underground Railroad conductor. *(Photograph courtesy of Library and Archives Canada)*

Maryland home of Reverend Josiah Henson. The house was a part of a 3,700-acre tobacco plantation where Henson was enslaved. *(Photograph courtesy of Montgomery County Department of Park and Planning in Maryland)*

Reverend Josiah Henson's log cabin home in Dresden, Ontario. *(Photograph by Jacqueline Tobin)*

ABOVE: Hand-carved pulpit and organ used by Reverend Josiah Henson. *(Photograph by Jacqueline Tobin)*
RIGHT: Barbara Carter, great-great-granddaughter of Reverend Josiah Henson. *(Photograph by Jacqueline Tobin)*

Josiah Henson 1789-1883

Canada 32
postage/postes

Reverend Josiah Henson was honored by the Canadian government with the issuing of the country's first stamp to commemorate a black citizen.

Benjamin Drew, a Boston abolitionist who toured Canada interviewing former slaves. His book *Refugees from Slavery* was an important part of the pre–Civil War dialogue about the impact of slavery. *(Photograph courtesy of Ohio Historical Society)*

Dr. Martin Delany, a free black man who moved to Chatham and later enlisted in the United States Army. He was commissioned a major in the 104th U.S. Colored Troops.
(Photograph courtesy of Ohio Historical Society)

First Baptist Church, Chatham, Ontario. Site of the last meeting held by John Brown in Canada to recruit blacks for his liberation army. *(Photograph by Jacqueline Tobin)*

Chair and table used by John Brown during his Chatham Convention meeting at the First Baptist Church, Chatham, Ontario. *(Photograph by Jacqueline Tobin)*

Burnside marine carbine rifle circa 1850 on display at the Heritage Room in Chatham-Kent, Ontario; believed to have been owned by abolitionist John Brown. *(Photograph by Jacqueline Tobin)*

Osborne Perry Anderson, the only black combatant to survive the raid on Harpers Ferry. *(Photograph courtesy of Western Archives, University of Western Ontario)*

Left to right: Gwen Robinson, historian at Chatham-Kent Black Historical Museum; Walton (Kip) Stowell, former mayor of Harpers Ferry; and James A. Addy, current Harpers Ferry mayor, celebrating their town's historical connections. *(Photograph courtesy of Gwen Robinson)*

Original small printing press
used by Mary Ann Shadd;
housed at Buxton Museum.
(Photograph by Jacqueline Tobin)

Laura Haviland, Canadian-
born Quaker, known as
"the Superintendent of the
Underground Railroad."
*(Photograph courtesy of the
Ohio Historical Society)*

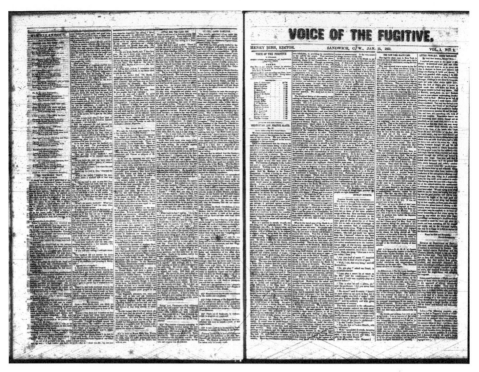

Voice of the Fugitive publication. *(Photograph courtesy of Library and Archives Canada)*

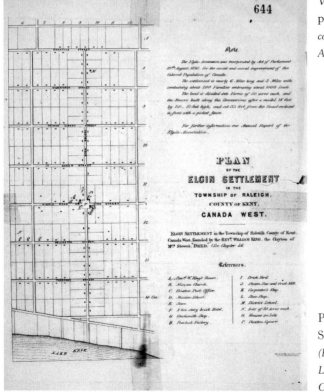

Plan of the Elgin Settlement, 1860. *(Photograph courtesy of Library and Archives Canada)*

London, 13 Feby 1860.

This is to Certify that Mr. *John Millar* has Subscribed *One* Share in the Stock raised for the purpose of developing the material resources of the *Elgin Settlement* in Canada West; that he has paid *Twelve pounds 10/—* thereon, and is to receive Six per Cent Interest, semi-annually, upon each instalment from the date of its payment, until the principal is repaid, four years from this date, according to the terms of the Prospectus.

Archd McKellar

Agent of Elgin Association.

Share certificate indicating fund-raising for Canadian black settlements such as Buxton. *(Photograph courtesy of Library and Archives Canada)*

863

FUGITIVE SLAVES
IN
CANADA.
BUXTON MISSION.
A PUBLIC MEETING
WILL BE HELD IN THE
FREE CHURCH
GEORGE STREET, DUMFRIES,
On MONDAY Evening, September 3d,
At Eight o'Clock, when the
REV. WILLIAM KING
Formerly a Slave-owner in Louisiana, United States,
Will Address the Meeting on the subject of
Slavery in the United States, and the Social and Moral Improvement of the Fugitive Slaves in Canada.

At the close of the address a Collection will be taken up in aid of the Mission and Schools at Buxton, Canada West.

Dumfries, August 29, 1860.

Dumfries—Printed at the Standard Office, by Walter Easton.

Fugitive Slaves in Canada poster advertising meetings on behalf of Buxton Mission. *(Photograph courtesy of Library and Archives Canada)*

Engraving of the Liberty Bell given to Buxton citizens by black towns-people of Pittsburgh. *(Photograph by Jacqueline Tobin)*

1860s Buxton school-house, newly restored. *(Photograph by Jacqueline Tobin)*

Interior of newly restored Buxton school-house. *(Photograph by Jacqueline Tobin)*

St. Andrews Church, South Buxton, built by Reverend William King and community in 1859. *(Photograph by Jacqueline Tobin)*

The Christiana, Pennsylvania, home of William and Eliza Parker; scene of the Christiana Resistance. *(Photograph courtesy of Toni Parker and Lancaster Historical Society)*

Toni Parker, great-great-granddaughter of William and Eliza Parker, at the site of the Christiana "riot." *(Photograph courtesy of Toni Parker)*

The "Crossing Stone" near Fort Erie, Ontario, looking across the Niagara River toward Buffalo in the United States. Site where many fugitives crossed over from the U.S. to Canada. *(Photograph by Jacqueline Tobin)*

Poster warning of slave-catchers in the Niagara region. *(Photograph taken by Jacqueline Tobin in Bertie Hall, Underground Railroad safe house on the Niagara Shores)*

Harriet Tubman. *(Photograph courtesy of Library and Archives Canada)*

Bertie Hall, Underground Railroad safe house. *(Photograph by Jacqueline Tobin)*

Sandwich First Baptist Church, dedicated on August 1, 1851. The congregation was formed in 1840 by eleven freedom seekers from the United States. *(Photograph by Jacqueline Tobin)*

Nazrey African Methodist Episcopal Church, built by hand in 1848 to serve Amherstburg's black population. *(Photograph by Jacqueline Tobin)*

Monument by Ed Dwight commemorating Canada's part in the Underground Railroad. The tower represents the Eternal Flame of Freedom, and fugitives are being welcomed by Canadian Underground Railroad conductors. *(Photograph by Jacqueline Tobin)*

The first meeting was held at the Methodist Episcopal church. After-ward, though, alarmed by the revolutionary cast of the enterprise, some attendees, including the Methodist Episcopal minister, withdrew their support for it, and further use of the church was denied. Alfred Whip-per arranged to have the next meeting at the schoolhouse on Princess Street, where Brown's constitution was adopted and signed.

The convention was concluded the next day with a final session held at yet another location, the First Baptist Church at 135 King Street East in Chatham, now landmarked as the "John Brown Meeting House."

According to historian Jean Libby, it was Brown's intent to create a constitutional framework for a "moving population" of freed slaves, much as the Mayflower Compact had provided a body politic for the Pilgrims. The means Brown proposed would guarantee both unity and security. Libby explains that Brown wanted to establish a "separate country for liberated slaves . . . with the Underground Railroad being the route chosen for movement. He did not intend to kill slaveholders unless they resisted."

As Martin Delany later reported, Brown told those assembled in Chatham that his plan was to reroute the Underground Railroad so that it terminated not in Canada but in Kansas, in order to "test, on the soil of the United States territory, whether or not the right to freedom would be maintained." The constitution he presented included a total of forty-eight articles outlining specifics. There were to be three branches of the provisional government, the legislative, the executive, and the judicial, and a commander in chief as well as officers, including a secretary of war. The constitution encouraged the sanctity of marriage and the death penalty for "forcible violation of any female prisoner."

Article XLVI prompted considerable debate: "The foregoing Arti-cles shall not be construed so as in any way to encourage the overthrow of any State Government, or of the General Government of the United States; and look to no dissolution of the Union, but simply to Amend-ment and Repeal. And our Flag shall be the same that our Fathers fought under in the Revolution."

As might be expected, those fugitives who had made their escape to

Canada and gained freedom only under the British flag were reluctant to approve the use of the American flag. Too many of them thought, as James Monroe Jones wrote, that they carried this "emblem on their backs." But Brown prevailed and convention members ratified the constitution as written. According to participants, Martin Delany, who was first and foremost a black nationalist, was very involved in the convention discussions and was a strong proponent of Brown's plans.

It was Brown's intent to conduct a raid within weeks of the close of the Chatham convention, but money trouble and a betrayal by Hugh Forbes, one of the convention members, made postponement a necessity. Brown's northeastern financial backers, known as the "Secret Six," convinced him to return to Kansas to refute Forbes's public pronouncements that a raid in the East was imminent. In his autobiography, Martin Delany claimed that the idea of an imminent raid was never mentioned at the convention. Others present, including Isaac Shadd and John Kagi, stated otherwise. Perhaps Delany, at the time he wrote, did not yet feel safe enough to report the truth. It is also likely, as has been suggested, that Brown never revealed all his plans to any one person.

The Secret Six were mainly financial backers of Brown, but they also gave advice. They devised a blind arrangement with him: They would provide him with money, but Brown would not disclose any specific plans to them, lest his raid fail and they all be implicated. Brown followed their advice and left for Kansas. Not content to lie low, he aided in the rescue of eleven slaves, leading them over a thousand miles to freedom in Canada. And then, seventeen months after the Chatham convention, he struck a blow for emancipation at Harpers Ferry, in what is now West Virginia but was then a small Virginia town of about 2,500 people, with an equal number of free blacks as whites, and about ninety slaves. Harpers Ferry was a prosperous town, then twice as large in population as today. It was the site of a federal arsenal with stores of weapons and ammunition and a rifle-works factory.

It was Brown's intent to capture the arsenal and then distribute guns and ammunition to slaves in the area. This mountain-based army of

African Americans would then make sporadic raids into the South to free others. But after Brown and his men captured the arsenal, they were trapped inside by local townspeople, and remained there until U.S. Marines stormed the building early the next morning.

Twenty-one men fought with Brown at Harpers Ferry. Of that group, ten were killed, and seven captured and executed. The only black Canadian, Osborne Perry Anderson, a printer at the *Provincial Freeman,* survived the raid and made his way back to Canada with the aid of Underground Railroad conductor William Still.

The *Shepherdstown Register,* a local newspaper, printed this account:

> FREDERICK, OCT. 17—Information has been received here this morning of a formidable Negro insurrection in Harper's Ferry and the United States Arsenal. The express train was fired into twice, and one of the hands, a Negro, was killed whilst trying to get the train through the town. . . . The engineer states that amongst them there were several strapping Negroes who occasionally shouted that they longed for liberty, as they had been in bondage long enough. . . .

Much was written about the raid nationally, mostly from a white perspective. The most underreported fact of the Harpers Ferry raid is that of the seventeen men who died there, *several were black.* According to Brown historian Jean Libby: "Two of the five black men who were in John Brown's original army of twenty-two young men died in the battle in Harpers Ferry. One black man (Osborne Anderson) escaped and wrote an eyewitness-participant account stating that fifty slaves and local free blacks joined in the fighting. Three of those fifty died in the fighting, and one more died in jail with John Brown during the following week.

When he was arrested at Harpers Ferry on October 18, 1859—ironically, by Col. Robert E. Lee—Brown's original handwritten constitution was found on his person. Its preamble states:

Whereas, slavery throughout its entire existence in the United States, is none other than a most barbarous, unprovoked, and un-justifiable war of one portion of its citizens upon another portion, the only conditions of which are perpetual imprisonment and hopeless servitude or absolute extermination; in utter disregard and violation of those eternal and self-evident truths set forth in our Declaration of Independence: Therefore,

We, citizens of the United States, and the Oppressed People, who, by a recent decision of the Supreme Court are declared to have no rights which the White Man is bound to respect; together with all other people degraded by the laws thereof, Do, for the time being ordain and establish ourselves, the following Provisional Constitution and Ordinances, the better to protect our Persons, Property, Lives, and Liberties, and to govern our actions.

Other documents, found in Brown's hideout, included letters from the Secret Six. When these men discovered that the raid had failed, they organized to send high-powered attorneys to represent Brown, but they also fretted over whether to run themselves. Gerrit Smith, a wealthy man who had already given Brown land to live on in the Adirondacks, is said to have had a nervous breakdown; Thomas Wentworth Higginson, a minister and former boxer, felt remorseful that he had not stopped Brown "from himself." Franklin Sanborn, a Concord, Massachusetts, schoolmaster and friend of Ralph Waldo Emerson and Henry David Thoreau, fearing arrest, went to Canada twice to hide until he felt safe enough to return to the United States. Dr. Samuel Gridley Howe, an educational reformer and husband of poet Julia Ward Howe (author of the "Battle Hymn of the Republic"), and George Luther Stearns, who financed antislavery homesteading in Kansas territory, both left for Canada until after Brown's execution.

Indeed, by the time of the Harpers Ferry raid, many of Brown's supporters had moved in different directions. Dr. Martin Delany was already on his way to Africa to explore the Niger Valley; Reverend William C. Monroe and his family were on the same ship to Africa as

Delany, preparing for mission work. James Monroe Jones was on the American Pacific coast. Harriet Tubman could not be reached; it is said that she was too ill to respond.

Frederick Douglass, who was not a direct participant and who had tried to convince Brown that his actions were futile, barely escaped arrest after Harpers Ferry. Southerners such as Virginia's governor Wise felt that the leading black man of the day was somehow involved. Wise told groups that he "wanted Douglass badly." And he said, "If you manage to get holt of that Boy, and send him to me, I will make my Negro Jim take him out and whip him until he says thank you Sir, or Please Master." Luckily, Douglass had been tipped off and left for Great Britain just days before a warrant could be executed.

Brown was convicted of treason, conspiracy with slaves to rebel, and first-degree murder. That blacks were not supportive of the raid, as some have speculated, cannot be supported by facts. According to local newspapers, there was a noted change among the slaves in the Harpers Ferry area immediately afterward. Insolence was reported, as well as work stoppages, stock poisonings, secret gatherings (conjuring memories of Nat Turner), and many fires in the county. A Richmond newspaper reported that "the heavens are illuminated by the lurid glare of burning property." John Brown, in jail while awaiting execution, voiced concern that he and his men would somehow be accused of setting the fires.

Martin Delany, while not at Harpers Ferry, shared one last connection to John Brown. After his arrest, Brown was imprisoned in Delany's birthplace, Charles Town, Virginia. His jailer, John Avis, who befriended Brown, was a childhood playmate of Delany and remained in touch with him after Brown's death. It is said that Brown willed one of his guns to Avis before he was hanged.

Delany himself was pursuing his dream of African emigration. In Abbeokuta, Nigeria, he signed a treaty with eight chiefs, who agreed that Delany's settlers could move onto any land of theirs not yet occupied in return for the North American settlers providing, "intelligence, education, a knowledge of the Arts and Sciences, Agriculture, and other Mechanical and Industrial Occupations."

Brown was hanged in Charles Town, Virginia, on December 2, 1859. In his last written statement, he said he was "quite certain that the crimes of this guilty land will never be purged away, but with Blood. I had as I now think, vainly flattered myself that without very much bloodshed, it might be done." His words were prophetic. Less than two years later, Abraham Lincoln would be elected president, the South would secede from the Union, and the Civil War would begin. Upon hearing of Brown's execution, the sixth of the Secret Six, Reverend Theodore Parker, a Unitarian minister then dying of tuberculosis in Rome, said, "The road to heaven is as short from the gallows as from the throne."

Canadian blacks as well as blacks in the United States along with white sympathizers responded with great emotion to John Brown's death. Memorial services were held throughout Ontario. In Chatham, Benjamin Quarles wrote that "every moment seemed to be devoted to the sad event." Prayer vigils were held at black churches. According to historian Bryan Prince, the diary entry of the Reverend John Renne, an Ontario Presbyterian minister in Buxton, a black settlement about twenty miles from Chatham, had this to say: "Dec. 29, 1859—Last night col'd people here held a meeting to express sympathy with the family of John Brown who was executed at Charleston lately. Immense crowd. All col'd orators except another persona and myself. Great extravagance at some of their speeches. One declared, 'No slaveholder should ever be in heaven,' another hoped streets of America would be filled with the blood of slaveholders next year."

In America, on the day of Brown's execution, the poet Henry Wadsworth Longfellow made this diary entry: "This will be a great day in our history, the date of a new Revolution—quite as much needed as the old one." Henry David Thoreau stated, "This morning, Captain Brown was hung. He is not Old Brown any longer; he is an angel of light."

John Brown was also memorialized in song, but not exactly as history has mythologized. While "John Brown's Body" was indeed a song sung during the Civil War, the words were not originally about abolitionist John Brown, but about a young Scotsman in the Massachusetts Volunteer Militia who also happened to bear that name. His fellow soldiers supposedly sang it in order to tease him:

> John Brown's body lies a-mouldering in the grave,
> John Brown's body lies a-mouldering in the grave,
> John Brown's body lies a-mouldering in the grave,
> But his soul goes marching on.
> Glory, glory, hallelujah!"

Most soldiers, though, had heard about the legendary John Brown, so as the song passed from one military unit to another, the lyrics were changed to refer to him directly. And Julia Ward Howe, after viewing a military parade and hearing the soldiers sing "John Brown's Body," wrote her own words to the same melody. Her song was later published in *The Atlantic Monthly* as the "Battle Hymn of the Republic."

Before Martin Delany's treaty with the Nigerian chiefs could be implemented, the American Civil War began. Delany abandoned his emigration plans and returned to America to fight. No explanation for his change of mind was ever stated specifically, but his actions indicate he now felt it his duty to fight in his own country and not abandon the cause there. He moved his family to Wilberforce, Ohio, and began recruiting black men for the Union army. In 1865, at a meeting with President Abraham Lincoln, he proposed "an army of blacks, commanded entirely by black officers . . . to penetrate through the heart of the South, and make conquests, with the banner of Emancipation unfurled . . . sustaining and protecting it by arming the emancipated, taking them as fresh troops . . . keeping this banner unfurled until every slave is free, according to the letter of your proclamation."

Lincoln responded by asking Delany to take command of such a regiment. He handed Delany a card of introduction to be given to Secretary of War E. M. Stanton: "Do not fail to have an interview with this most extraordinary and intelligent black man." During the course of the Civil War, Delany succeeded in enlisting thousands. Eventually he was commissioned a major, making him the highest-ranking field-grade officer in the United States Colored Troops. Following the war, he worked with the Freedman's Bureau in the South, becoming noted for his oratory on behalf of blacks owning land. He continued to pursue his dreams of African emigration through his public support for the Liberian Exodus Joint Stock Exchange Company, the intent of which was to transport emigrants to Liberia. As part of the expedition, the company purchased a boat called the *Azor*.

In 1879, in response to Charles Darwin's *The Origin of Species*, Delany published a treatise titled *The Origin of Races and Color*, using various methodologies, including biblical and scientific, to refute Darwin. He never made the journey to Liberia. Noting the economic problems facing his family, Delany returned to Ohio to practice medicine and support them. He died of consumption in 1885.

The Canadian connection to Harpers Ferry was not lost on Americans. The American South had no use for meddling Canadians any more than they'd had for the British before the American Revolution. Governor Henry A. Wise of Virginia claimed that the "compact of fanaticism and intolerance" had sprung from British soil, and the 'predatory war' of the abolitionists was being carried on from Canada itself."

Brown's visit would forever connect the city and people of Chatham to the small town of Harpers Ferry. Today Canadians recognize and respect this connection. In a ceremony on October 19, 2003, the Municipality of Chatham-Kent was officially "twinned" with Harpers Ferry, West Virginia. These words appear on the Ontario Heritage Foundation plaque erected in front of the First Baptist Church in Chatham:

On May 10, 1858, American abolitionist John Brown held the last in a series of clandestine meetings here at First Baptist Church. Brown planned to establish an independent republic within the United States and wage guerilla [sic] war to liberate the South from slavery. He came to Upper Canada to recruit blacks who had fled here in the wake of the Fugitive Slave Law (1850). On October 16, 1859, Brown and twenty-one supporters seized the government arsenal at Harpers Ferry, Virginia, and held it against a counter-attack for two days. Brown, executed as a traitor, became for many a martyr and a hero. His actions escalated the tensions between North and South that led to civil war in 1861.

Mary Ann Camberton Shadd (Cary), the first known black woman to edit a North American newspaper. (Photograph courtesy of Library and Archives Canada)

Chapter Four

Mary Ann Shadd and the Provincial Freeman

T hat Chatham was "the colored man's Paris" was due in no small part to a woman.

Mary Ann Shadd's contributions—not only to the black communities of Canada but to the United States as well—have largely gone unnoticed. Yet Frederick Douglass once remarked of her that "we do not know her equal among the colored ladies of the United States."

It could be that Shadd's relative obscurity is based on the fact that, like Martin Delany, she was never enslaved. Perhaps her gender also lessened the attention paid to her. In any case, Shadd's accomplishments as an abolitionist, a journalist, and an educated black woman set her apart from the racial and gender stereotypes of her time, and earn her a place in history among the more familiar names.

Born to free black parents in Wilmington, Delaware, in 1823, Mary Ann was introduced to abolitionism early. Her father, Abraham Shadd, a successful shoemaker, businessman, and property owner, became involved during the 1830s in the anticolonization movement. The Shadd family story, while not altogether typical, in many ways represents a population of free blacks whose freedom was always equivocal as long as slavery was legal.

The Shadds traced their history back to 1755, when Hans Schad, a Hessian mercenary, came to America to fight for the British in the French and Indian Wars (known as the Seven Years War in Europe, it was fought for control of North America). Wounded at Fort Duquesne (now Pittsburgh), Schad was nursed back to health by a Mrs. Jackson, a widowed free black woman, and her daughter. He eventually married the daughter, Elizabeth, choosing, as did thousands of other soldiers, to stay in America after the war. Hans and Elizabeth moved from Pennsylvania to Wilmington, Delaware, where he earned his living as a butcher, and later as a shoemaker, and Elizabeth opened a tea shop, "celebrated for its nice refreshments, where everything was the best of its kind," and died "in old age, much respected, leaving valuable property," as mentioned in a memoir written by a local Wilmington woman, Elizabeth Montgomery. Their second son, Jeremiah, Mary Ann's grandfather, continued his father's butcher business through the American Revolution. Amelia, Mary Ann's grandmother, who emigrated from Santo Domingo, was known in Wilmington as "old Mother Shadd" and described as "nearly white and very Frenchy and polite." Amelia did her own butchering and sold sausages, along with cakes and coffee, in a market stand. Of the twelve children born of this marriage, one was Abraham Doras Schad, Mary Ann's father, born in 1801. Jeremiah died in 1819 at the age of sixty-one, a very successful free person of color. An inventory of his large estate included silverware, wineglasses, china, carpeting, furniture, and tools. Around this time the spelling of the family name was changed to Shadd, and all were recorded as mulatto or colored (according to the racial categories in place at the time).

Abraham Shadd was eighteen when Jeremiah died. He continued his father's career as a shoemaker and married Harriet Parnell. Little is known of Harriet except that she, too, was a mulatto. Harriet and Abraham's first child, Mary Ann Camberton Shadd, was born October 9, 1823, and benefited from her family's social position and relative wealth. According to Jane Rhodes, her biographer, despite many family members' ability to pass as white, "there was a conscious decision to claim an identity as persons of color and to cast their lot with the darker members of the race."

This decision placed them directly in the midst of a growing antiblack fever in the United States at the time, affecting both free and enslaved. Delaware was in a unique geographical position. Although a slave state, it was in the upper reaches of the South. Free people of color like the Shadd family had to contend with all the repressive constrictions found in most slave states. Black codes were becoming increasingly harsh as word of slave uprisings in the Deep South filtered northward, creating fear not just among slaveholders but also among persons who lived around free blacks like the Shadds.

Abraham Shadd became involved in abolitionist activities in Delaware after being provoked by the rising tide of the American Colonization Society, which was active there. He saw through their paternalistic rhetoric and was able to discern their real sentiments. "We will not permit them to associate with us," one colonizationist stated. "We will not tolerate any notion of equality with them." Shadd became a delegate to the 1830 National Negro Convention in Philadelphia, the meeting prompted by antiblack violence in Cincinnati that led to the founding of Wilberforce. Those attending the convention denounced the colonization movement and its push for Liberian emigration, but did discuss Canada as a possible alternative. Mary Ann Shadd, seven years old then, grew up in the midst of intense discussion about abolitionism and Canadian emigration.

Free blacks in Delaware did not have access to good education; perhaps this is the reason Abraham moved the family to Pennsylvania, a free state, where Quakers were advancing the cause of education among blacks. When Mary Ann was ten, the family moved to West Chester, Pennsylvania, a scant fifteen miles north, to get away from increasing pressure in the southern state of Delaware and also to be closer to abolitionist activities in Philadelphia, less than twenty miles north. Abraham remained an active participant in subsequent black conventions, where the emphasis shifted to educational opportunities; he also became a vocal opponent of colonization, an increasingly active abolitionist, and a subscription agent for the *Liberator*. When the American Anti-Slavery Society was created in 1833, Abraham was named one of six black persons on its board.

William Still, an Underground Railroad conductor who documented his experiences in a memoir, *The Underground Railroad*, called West Chester the site of "more Underground Railroad routes than anywhere else in the North," since it was on a direct line north from Wilmington, in the slave state of Delaware, to Philadelphia, in the free state of Pennsylvania, and other points north. Based on Abraham's abolitionist activities and the geographic location of their farm, it is believed that the Shadd home was indeed an Underground Railroad safe house, and many accounts indicated that Abraham was a prominent conductor.

Mary Ann Shadd thus spent her adolescence surrounded by the activities of the Negro Convention Movement, the American Anti-Slavery Society, and the Underground Railroad. She was also influenced by another organization: In 1835, Abraham Shadd, having grown tired of the Negro Convention Movement's "going nowhere," gravitated to the American Moral Reform Society, which argued that the "universality of mankind" superseded racial identities. This society's belief in "the ability of women to have an equal role in reform and abolition organizations" certainly must have attracted Mary Ann's attention.

It was in Philadelphia that she first met William Still, who became a lifelong friend and supporter of her work. It is presumed, but cannot be proven, that she had a Quaker education, the best that blacks could have received then. Thus, her education would have been classical in nature and she would have been exposed to the beliefs of the Quaker community and their antislavery actions. One Quaker belief, based on the biblical teachings of Paul, asserted that "male and female are one in Jesus Christ." During the early nineteenth century, in many parts of the country, a significant number of women were acknowledged ministers in the Society of Friends (Quakers). Thomas Clarkson, an English abolitionist, after observing Quaker women's status within the Society of Friends, stated that it "gives them, in fact, a new cast of character. It produces in them a considerable knowledge of human nature. It produces in them thought, and foresight, and judgement. . . . elevates in them a sense of their own dignity and importance." Indeed, when the first Woman's Rights Convention was held in 1848, at least four of the organizers were members of the Society of Friends.

Mary Ann felt strongly enough about education to return to Wilmington after her own education to start a school for black children. She began her teaching career while still a teenager. Interestingly, despite her education and all the exposure to discussion of "equal rights" that her life circumstance provided, when her father gave the keynote address in Wilmington at a "First of August" celebration (an annual event to celebrate the British 1833 abolition of slavery in British-held territory), Mary Ann, because of her gender, was not permitted to attend. Nevertheless, it didn't take her long to begin formulating her own ideas on the importance of education and self-reliance for blacks. While still in her twenties, she expressed her concerns in a letter to Frederick Douglass about the lack of action by free blacks. Coming to the same conclusion as her father, Mary Ann stated, "We have been holding conventions for years—have been assembling together and whining over our difficulties and afflictions, passing resolutions on resolutions to any extent; but it does really seem that we have made but little progress, considering our resolves. We should do more, and talk less."

Douglass printed her letter in the *North Star*, thus giving Shadd her first public forum. It gave her a taste of the power of the printed word that she never relinquished. At a time when women in general and blacks in particular had little opportunity to be heard, Mary Ann was breaking new ground. At the same time her letter appeared in Douglass's paper, she was writing *Hints to the Colored People of the North*, a twelve-page pamphlet further articulating her ideas about black self-reliance. Shadd argued her case for the importance of education, economic self-sufficiency, and moral refinement if blacks were to achieve the equality with whites that they sought.

By becoming a public voice for her people, Shadd attracted both admiration and animosity for overstepping what were believed to be the bounds of the "cult of true womanhood," a phrase referring to the nineteenth-century ideal that women should be pure, pious, submissive, and domestic, sexual stereotyping that impacted both white and black women at that time. Mary Ann Shadd was clearly a feminist, and she expressed her beliefs not only on the subject of equality for blacks but also on the subject of equality for women. Even Martin Delany, who became her friend, and held the view that Shadd was "a very intelligent young lady," described her as "peculiarly eccentric." The interpretation of her behavior as "eccentric," which had also been voiced by Frederick Douglass, followed her the rest of her life. A black activist in New York City related this story about Shadd hailing a taxi: "Coming down Broadway at a time when colored women scarcely dared to think of riding in the stages, Miss Shadd threw up her head, gave one look, and a wave of her hand. There was such an air of impressive command in it that the huge, coarse, ruffianly driver, who had been known to refuse colored ladies as though suddenly seized with paralysis, reined up to the curb, and she entered, and, without hindrance, rode to the end of her journey."

The 1850 Fugitive Slave Act had a definite effect on Shadd as it did on other northern blacks. Emigration was once again becoming a topic of discussion among blacks, but it was emigration by choice, not coercion, that some, including Shadd, would come to embrace.

When a call came for an antislavery convention to be held in Toronto in 1851, Shadd decided to go and listen to what Canadian black leaders had to say about emigration in general and emigration to Canada specifically. There she met black leaders who would play a large role in the rest of her life—men such as Henry Bibb, who had just begun Canada's first black newspaper, the *Voice of the Fugitive*; Martin Delany; and Thomas Cary, a barber from Toronto who would become her husband. Speaker after speaker extolled the virtues of black settlements in Canada West. (After 1841, the area previously known as Upper Canada was referred to as Canada West.) Shadd must have been swayed, because less than a week later, at the age of twenty-eight, she moved to the settlement of Windsor, in Canada West. To her younger brother Isaac, who would later become a partner in many of her projects, she wrote, "I have been here more than a week, and like Canada. Do not feel prejudice and repeat if you were to come here or go west of this where shoemaking pays well and work at it and buy lands as fast as you made any money, you would do well." Shadd was to make Canada West her home until the Civil War.

Her interest in Canada—as well as, no doubt, increasing pressures because of the Fugitive Slave Act—prompted the entire Shadd family to emigrate. The following year, according to the *Voice of the Fugitive* for June 17, 1852, Abraham Shadd, described as "the father of the accomplished and talented Miss Mary A. Shadd," arrived in Windsor "on a tour of observation through this section of Canada, to obtain some necessary information preparatory to the removal of his family, and a large number of others from Pennsylvania, to settle on the Queen's Free Soil."

Contributing to Mary Ann Shadd's decision to move to Canada had been Henry Bibb's call for teachers in the first issue of the *Voice of the Fugitive*. Bibb, a former runaway, had moved with his wife, Mary, to Sandwich, Ontario, across from Detroit, in order to support a black settlement program undertaken by the Refugee Home Society. There, Mary Bibb started a school for fugitives and Henry began publishing his newspaper. The paper's agenda, as stated, was "While we intend this to be a mouth piece for the refugees in Canada especially, yet we mean to speak out our sentiments as a FREEMAN upon all subjects that come within our sphere."

Initially, the Bibbs were enthusiastic about Shadd's arrival, and they wholeheartedly supported her efforts to begin a school in the nearby settlement of Windsor. They often extolled her virtues, calling her "a lady of high literary attainments." Shadd returned the compliment, describing their paper as "one of the most important publications now in circulation, for the elevation of our people in North America, but especially in Canada." It was not long, however, before the relationship between the Bibbs and Shadd began to deteriorate. Shadd had become quite vocal about her beliefs, and had already expressed her conviction that schools should not be solely for blacks or whites, but opened to children of all ethnicities. Unfortunately, this strongly held belief in black assimilation would pit her against many of her own race on issues of education and religion. She included, in her attacks on segregated institutions, Bibb's project, the Refugee Home Society, which was open only to fugitives, not free blacks like herself.

But she did not stop with just verbal attacks. In June 1852, Shadd once again employed the power of the press to make her points and claim her status as a voice for the black community. She published *A Plea for Emigration; or, Notes of Canada West,* a forty-four-page essay, to "set forth the advantage of a residence in a country, in which chattel slavery is not tolerated, and prejudice of color has no existence whatever. . . ." Shadd's biographer describes *Notes of Canada West* as "an unabashed propaganda tract that exaggerated the benefits of the Canadian haven while ignoring many endemic problems."

Nevertheless, the pamphlet served Shadd's goal of promoting emigration to Canada. It also helped to establish her as an authoritative voice for the black fugitives there. Particularly, it served as a platform from which to attack Henry Bibb and the act of "begging" on behalf of fugitives, especially as Shadd viewed it in relationship to the Refugee Home Society. She asked if it was "really a benevolent act to send old almanacs, old novels, and all manner of obsolete books to the fugitives." In a more telling statement, she made her views very clear about the policy of the Refugee Home Society to sell land only to former slaves, not free blacks. "The Fugitive Bill makes insecure every northern colored man—those free are alike at the risk of being sent south. They arrive in Canada destitute . . . but may not settle on the land of the Refugees' Home, for the accident of nominal freedom."

Notes of Canada West appeared the same year Martin Delany published *The Condition, Elevation, Emigration, and Destiny of the Colored People of the United States, Politically Considered,* which advocated emigration to Central and South America. Shadd and Delany were both promoting emigration but did not yet agree on the best destination. Leading somewhat parallel lives and holding similar beliefs about self-reliance and emigration, they also agreed on the need for racial unity. In Shadd's case, she put forth the premise that free blacks and those enslaved shared common grounds and should not be divided. Both she and Delany eventually found themselves living in the same town, Chatham, when Delany moved there in 1856.

Meanwhile, Shadd continued her vicious attacks on the Bibbs, eventually alienating them and finally losing access to the public forum provided by the *Voice of the Fugitive*. Her choice to have her pamphlet printed in Detroit by white printers was a deliberate affront to Bibb, who ran his own printing press and could have used the business. Without a platform, Mary Ann had to find another, or create one.

In 1853, she closed the financially strapped school she had been running, and, with support from her family and friends, began publishing the *Provincial Freeman*. She chose Samuel Ringgold Ward, a prominent figure in antislavery circles, to be on the editorial board. Ward not only shared Shadd's beliefs about segregated institutions and begging but was already a newspaper publisher in the States. A former slave who had written his autobiography, Ward was also a Congregational minister whose skills prompted Frederick Douglass to write, "As an orator and thinker he was vastly superior to any of us."

While Ward was listed as an editor, the paper was clearly Shadd's. In a testimonial, her friend William Still gave the credit to her: "As she stands connected with the press, she is justly entitled, doubtless, to the credit of being the first colored woman on the American continent to establish and edit a weekly newspaper."

The philosophical differences between the Bibbs and Shadd are clear from the titles each chose for their papers. As her biographer notes, "Shadd and Ward sought to represent Canada's black population as independent and autonomous 'freemen' rather than dependent and oppressed 'fugitives,' as portrayed by the opposition." Shadd was adamant that blacks coming to Canada embrace their new country as British citizens, not as American fugitives.

The *Voice of the Fugitive* ceased publication upon Henry Bibb's death in August 1854. By 1855, Shadd had moved the offices of the

Provincial Freeman from Windsor to the Charity Building in Chatham, right in the midst of Chatham's swirling abolitionist activities.

Mary Ann Shadd always acted outside the bounds of what was, for her time, acceptable female behavior. As a feminist and an educated, out-spoken black female journalist with her own newspaper, she publicly used her tongue and pen to vent her anger as well as her views. She did not marry until she was thirty-two, and had an unusual marriage arrangement in that much of the time her husband, Thomas Cary, continued to live in Toronto while she lived in Chatham. They had two children of their own, and Shadd was stepmother to Cary's other three children. Little is mentioned about the children in any of the accounts of Shadd's life, other than that they were often at her sister's home while Shadd herself continued to travel around the United States and Canada, lecturing in support of the *Provincial Freeman.*

Nevertheless, despite her ability to stretch the boundaries of her race and gender, Shadd could not gain entrée into one of the most im-portant abolitionist gatherings of her time, John Brown's Chatham convention, held in her own hometown. Records indicate that no women were invited, but there can be little doubt that had Shadd been a man, she would have been there. And certainly, though barred due to her sex, she was privy to the convention's discussion since among the attendees were her husband, her brother and coeditor, and friends such as Martin Delany and Osborne Perry Anderson, a friend of the Shadds from Pennsylvania who had been brought by her uncle to Canada to manage his farm and who was now a printer at the *Provincial Freeman.* In addition to the direct involvement of Shadd's inner circle, it is said that she and her brother lent their press and offices to John Brown.

It was through Anderson that Shadd eventually found another way to remain a part of the action and serve her cause. As the only black Canadian to join John Brown at Harpers Ferry and the only black man to survive the event, Anderson had a story to tell, and Shadd under-stood the importance of getting it into the historical record. Thanks to

her, the story of Harpers Ferry was not entrusted solely to white historians; she edited and published Anderson's eyewitness account in *A
Voice from Harper's Ferry.*

Like most events involving blacks during this time period, what occurred would be documented differently depending on the sympathies
of the writer and newspaper. Seen from the perspective of white southerners, as in the Mason Committee report to Congress about the event,
Harpers Ferry would be remembered for the "entire disinclination of
the slaves to insurrection, or to receive aid for that purpose." But it is
important to know that James Mason, the author of the above report,
was the man who had drafted the 1850 Fugitive Slave Act and had interviewed John Brown for over three hours after his arrest. He was totally vested in the institution of slavery. On the Senate floor, Mason
articulated his view that "Brown's failure was due to the loyalty of the
slaves, to the affection, the kindness, the love which they bear to their
masters and to their master's homes." Anderson's account was intended to debunk those myths.

> The truth of the Harper's Ferry "raid," as it has been called, in re-
> gard to the part taken by the slaves, and the aid given by colored
> men generally, demonstrates clearly: First, that the conduct of the
> slaves is a strong guarantee of the weakness of the institution,
> should a favorable opportunity occur; and, secondly, that the col-
> ored people, as a body, were well represented by numbers, both in
> the fight, and in the number who suffered martyrdom afterward.

One particular anecdote about Brown's activities preceding the "raid,"
as cited in Anderson's book, offers great insight into Brown's thinking regarding the overall symbolic importance of this event. Anderson writes
that Brown gave his men eleven orders before proceeding to Harpers
Ferry. The eleventh stated that "Colonel A. D. Stevens . . . proceed to the
country with his men, and after taking certain parties prisoner bring
them to the Ferry. In the case of Colonel Lewis Washington [great-
grandnephew of George Washington] who had arms in his hands, he

must, before being secured as a prisoner, deliver them into the hands of Osborne P. Anderson. Anderson being a colored man, and colored men being only things in the South, it is proper that the South be taught a lesson upon this point." Brown had found out that Lewis Washington owned a sword given to the first president by Frederick the Great, king of Prussia, a contemporary of George Washington and widely respected as a military man.

When Lewis Washington was indeed captured by some of Brown's men, including Anderson, he was told to "hand over the sword of Frederick the Great" to Anderson. Taking a relic from a descendant of the "Father of the Country" and giving it to a black man was an act of immense symbolism. This story might never have been told had not Anderson and Shadd partnered to publish his memoir. Shadd was committed to preserving and shaping abolitionist history, an act Frederick Douglass was to admonish a black crowd to do in an 1871 Memorial Day speech:

> We are sometimes asked, in the name of patriotism, to forget the merits of this fearful struggle, and to remember with equal admiration those who struck at the nation's life and those who struck to save it, those who fought for slavery and those who fought for liberty and justice.
>
> I am no minister of malice. . . . I would not repel the repentant; but may . . . my tongue cleave to the roof of my mouth, if I forget the difference between the parties to that terrible, protracted, and bloody conflict.
>
> . . . if this war is to be forgotten, I ask in the name of all things sacred, what shall men remember?

During the Civil War, Anderson maintained his commitment to end slavery by recruiting slaves for the United States Colored Troops in Indiana and Arkansas. When he died in Washington, D.C., at the age of forty-two, after a lengthy period of bad health, his pallbearers included Lewis H. Douglass, son of Frederick Douglass and soldier in the Fifty-fourth Massachusetts Infantry. Anderson was eulogized at his funeral as "the last survivor of the only army of freedom ever recruited in the United States."

Constant financial struggle, especially during the severe depression that hit Canada in 1857, resulted by the end of the decade in the final demise of the *Provincial Freeman*. The 1860s brought dramatic changes to Shadd's personal world as well as to North America in general. On November 29, 1860, her husband died at the young age of thirty-five. At the time, Shadd was carrying their second child. Ironically, Thomas Cary was buried on land held by the British American Institute in Dawn; Josiah Henson, a man Shadd had rebuked incessantly, gave the eulogy. One month after Cary's death, South Carolina seceded from the Union, precipitating the Civil War, which began four months later.

Martin Delany and Frederick Douglass had been selected by the new president, Abraham Lincoln, to recruit black troops for the Union army. In 1863, Delany turned to Shadd to aid him. She chose to recruit throughout the Northern United States, tapping into the relationships she had made in her travels for the *Provincial Freeman*. And she was not the only Canadian black to respond to the Civil War: Her brother Abraham, as well as a Shadd cousin, along with Martin Delany's son, Toussaint L'Ouverture, all moved south to join the Union army, while Josiah Henson and Osborne Perry Anderson recruited men across Canada to join the ranks.

Mary Ann Shadd continued her recruiting efforts until 1864, then returned to Chatham after the Civil War ended. But it had become a much different town from the one she had left. The war had given new hope to those blacks who had escaped to Canada. With the Emancipation Proclamation, many returned to friends and family left behind in the States. As Shadd's biographer explains, "She was an abolitionist in a world that no longer needed abolitionists; an emigrationist for a people who no longer sought a new homeland. But her abilities as an organizer, educator and journalist made her valuable to African Americans in the midst of Reconstruction, and the changes in the States held out promise for her own advancement." Responding to this new challenge, she left the country she had embraced as home for over a decade to re-create herself in the country of her birth.

Along with her extended family, Shadd found her way to Washington, D.C. There she watched as other abolitionists, her friend William Still among them, raced to write the history of their movement. In his book on the Underground Railroad, Still did not include her as one of the heroines of the cause, though he did ask her to contribute to a chapter on the Christiana Riot, which had occurred in her home state of Pennsylvania. Still believed that Shadd must have interviewed William Parker, one of the men most directly involved in that 1851 act of resistance. Parker, along with his wife and friends, had resisted the efforts of slave owner Edwin Gorsuch to capture his escaping slaves. Perhaps Still thought Shadd knew Parker and his family had gone to Canada West to live after their escape. Shadd apparently did not respond to Still's request. She did, however, become an agent for his work. At the same time, he encouraged Shadd to write her own book. But though she had already considered it, and was thinking of writing a book on John Brown, her book ideas never came to fruition.

Instead, Shadd became one of the first students in the School of Law at Howard University. For reasons unknown, she did not complete her degree until 1883, when she was sixty years old. In the interim, she found another cause to work for, that of women's suffrage. Once again, she found herself in the middle of conflict. The antislavery movement had, in essence, postponed any focus on women's rights. The passage of the Thirteenth Amendment abolished slavery, the Fourteenth Amendment granted citizenship to all blacks, and the Fifteenth Amendment granted voting rights to people regardless of race, color, or previous condition of servitude. But that did not include women.

Mary Ann Shadd did not live to see her latest cause succeed. At the age of seventy, she died of stomach cancer. There is no record of any obituary or article about her in the Chatham daily paper. Her obituary in the Washington *Bee* did not do justice to the lifetime she had spent in pursuit of black freedom and achievement. It simply stated: "Mrs. M.S. Carey [sic], one of the best-known women in this country, died at her residence on last Monday morning at 4:50 a.m. Mrs. Carey was a woman of excellent traits of character and loved by all who knew her. While she may have been eccentric at times, she was a woman of kind disposition."

Despite having been all but disregarded at the time of her death, Shadd has since been commemorated in Chatham with a plaque which reads:

Mary Ann Shadd (Cary) (1823–1893)

Born in Wilmington, Delaware, Mary Ann Shadd became a prominent activist in the Underground Railroad refugee communities in Upper Canada during the 1850s. Arriving in 1851, she taught refugee children and urged skilled Blacks to seek haven in Canada from the increasingly dangerous conditions in the United States. In 1853, Shadd established the *Provincial Freeman,* an influential newspaper that encouraged self-reliance and argued for the rights of Blacks and women. The paper waged war on slavery and bigotry, becoming the leading voice of the refugees in Canada.

In a long overdue tribute by the country of her birth, in 1998 Mary Ann Shadd was inducted into the National Women's Hall of Fame in Seneca Falls, New York.

Henry Bibb. (Photograph courtesy of University of North
Carolina, DocSouth; Joyner Library, East Carolina University;
and University of Wisconsin Press)

Chapter Five

Henry Bibb

In 1842, Henry Bibb, a fugitive from Kentucky, settled in Detroit. He rose quickly in stature, and was one of the most famous black abolitionists in the United States and Canada West until his untimely death in 1854. That so little is known about Bibb in both countries is unfortunate, for his life, like the lives of Frederick Douglass, Mary Ann Shadd, and Harriet Tubman, stands as witness to the antebellum history of both countries.

A biographical survey of Bibb's life reads like a review of Canadian and American black abolitionist history; historian Afua Cooper has called him a "trans-border" figure, because, like others, he was entwined with both countries. Bibb was involved in the Negro Convention Movement, emigrationism, the antislavery movement, and the Underground Railroad. Both orator and writer, he was not content to be just a participant, and despite his short life, he rose to become a leader in almost every endeavor with which he involved himself.

Much of what is known about Bibb's time as a slave comes from his autobiography, the *Narrative of the Life and Adventures of Henry Bibb, An American Slave, Written by Himself,* published in 1849. His later years can be viewed through his letters to various abolitionist newspapers, as well as editorials in his own newspaper, the *Voice of the Fugitive*. Other abolitionists wrote much about Bibb as well. While he left no personal diary, all these writings, read in the context of his involvement in abolitionist activities, give us a good picture of his life.

Born in Shelby County, Kentucky, in 1815, of a slave mother and a white man, Bibb was the oldest of seven sons born to Milldred Jackson (his spelling of her first name), who told him that his father was James Bibb. In his autobiography, he discussed this: "It is almost impossible for slaves to give a correct account of their male parentage. All that I know about it is that my mother informed me that my fathers name was James Bibb. He was doubtless one of the present Bibb family of Kentucky; but I have no personal knowledge of him at all, for he died before my recollection."

Of his early childhood, Bibb wrote that he was "brought up . . . Or, more correctly speaking, . . . I may safely say, I was *flogged up;* for where I should have received moral, mental, and religious instruction, I received stripes without number, the object of which was to degrade and keep me in subordination."

Often he was hired out to work for various other plantation owners; it was those experiences that first revealed to him the horrors of slavery: "Reader, believe me when I say that no tongue, nor pen ever has or can express the horrors of American Slavery." While not allowed to learn to read and write, Bibb explains that "all that I heard about liberty and freedom to the slaves, I never forgot." Religiously oriented, he was committed to seeking freedom from a very young age: "Among other good trades I learned the art of running away to perfection. I made a regular business of it, and never gave it up, until I had broken the bands of slavery, and landed myself safely in Canada, where I was regarded as a man, and not as a thing." He detailed several attempts he made to escape, all with no success, and wrote that he would have continued his efforts were it not for the fact that he was drawn to a young mulatto woman named Malinda, who was enslaved on a farm four miles from him.

When he approached Malinda and her mother to discuss marriage, he presented them with his philosophy of life, using it as a sort of litmus test for the relationship. "I informed her [Malinda] of the difficulties which I conceived to be in the way of our marriage; and that I could never engage myself to marry any girl only on certain conditions; near as I can recollect the substance of our conversation upon the subject, it was, that I was religiously inclined; that I intended to try to comply with the requisitions of the gospel, both theoretically and practically through life. Also, that I was decided on becoming a free man before I died; and that I expected to get free by running away, and going to Canada, under the British Government. Agreement on those two cardinal questions I made my test for marriage."

Despite objections from his mother and Malinda's mother, the wedding took place with the support of Malinda's master, and Bibb wrote later that he often looked back on that time period with Malinda as being the happiest of his life. Eventually he was sold to Malinda's master, but despite the seeming benefit of this proximity to his wife, there was a negative side; he often had to watch when Malinda was abused by their master. In time, Malinda gave birth to their daughter, Mary Francis. While the birth of a child should bring joy to most parents, Bibb described returning from his work at night to find his young daughter "bruised black with the whole print" of the mistress's hand. "I am the father of a slave," he wrote, "a word too obnoxious to be spoken by a fugitive slave. . . . I have the satisfaction of knowing that I am only the father of one slave. . . . She was the first and shall be the last slave that ever I will father, for chains and slavery on this earth."

Bibb made good on his commitment to gain freedom; he escaped in the winter of 1837 and made it all the way to Canada West, but then moved back to Cincinnati, where he worked to save money to return for his wife and child. But he was betrayed by blacks and was returned to his master.

On at least one occasion, Bibb attempted to take his family with him. In his narrative, he described the scene in which he and his wife and child were surrounded in the swamps by a pack of wolves. They were captured and returned. Bibb's owner was determined to make an example of him; he was bound and his clothing ripped off, and he was forced to lie facedown on the ground, where they staked his arms and legs. A horn was sounded to call the rest of the slaves to view his punishment. The overseer gave him fifty lashes with the whip and then the owner took a paddle and gave him eight or ten blows on top of those wounds to give Bibb, in his words, "something to remember me by." Bibb recalled what occurred subsequently:

> My wounds were then washed with salt brine, after which I was let up. . . . I was so badly punished that I was not able to work for several days. After being flogged as described, they took me off several miles to a ship and had a heavy iron collar riveted on my neck with prongs extending above my head, on the end of which there was a small bell. I was not able to reach the bell with my hand. This heavy load of iron I was compelled to wear for six weeks. I never was allowed to lie in the same house with my family again while I was the slave of Whitfield. I either had to sleep with my feet in the stocks, or be chained with a large log chain to a log over night, with no bed or bedding to rest my wearied limbs on, after toiling all day in the cotton field.

One might question the wisdom of Bibb's returning after reaching safety, but he was concerned about achieving the same freedom for his wife and daughter. Throughout his narrative, he refers constantly to his family as the central motivating factor in his life during this time period. After another escape attempt, he and Malinda were to be sold apart. The parting scene described by Bibb has become, according to Cooper, "a classic piece of literature in African American autobiography." In later lectures, Bibb related this story, often bringing his audience to tears.

> When the dear woman saw there was no hope for us, and that we should soon be separated forever, . . . to meet no more as husband and wife, parent and child—the last and loudest appeal was made

on our knees. We appealed to the God of justice and to the sacred ties of humanity; but this was all in vain. The louder we prayed the harder he whipped, amid the most heart-rending shrieks from the poor slave mother and child, as little Frances stood by, sobbing at the abuse inflicted on her mother.

After a total of six escape attempts, he finally succeeded in reaching freedom again in 1842, when he arrived in Detroit, joining other "professional fugitives," including Frederick Douglass and William Wells Brown, in telling stories of slavery and escape. Bibb, Douglass, and Brown were among an elite group of former slaves who began to earn their living from their stories, being hired by antislavery groups and sent on lecture tours around the country on behalf of the abolitionist cause. Good speakers and writers were considered major weapons in the abolitionist arsenal, and Henry Bibb was deemed one of the best of both.

In Detroit, Bibb began the next phase of his life. The city already had an active community of free blacks, with a literary society, a debating club, a temperance society, and a library. Bibb entered into the community activities wholeheartedly, joining the Reverend William Monroe and other black leaders in the antislavery cause. He started school at Second Baptist Church under Monroe but could afford to attend for only three weeks. His concern for his family left enslaved caused him to wander from job to job. "I was not settled in mind about the condition of my bereaved family for several years, and could not settle myself down at any permanent business," he wrote.

He attended his first black convention, the State Convention of Colored Citizens, in Detroit in 1843. William Lambert and William Monroe had called the convention to discuss abolitionism and the improvement of living conditions for blacks in the state, but most of their attention was focused on achieving voting rights, an issue being raised on the national as well as the local level.

Black leaders had already realized the futility of working through the Whigs and the Democrats, the two existing political parties. White antislavery activists were equally as disgusted with the lack of support for their cause. In 1839, the Anti-Slavery Society, under the leadership of William Lloyd Garrison, had split, and a rival organization, the American and Foreign Anti-Slavery Society, was established. The divide had occurred over dissatisfaction with Garrison's reliance on "moral suasion" to move the abolitionist cause; dissidents were not willing to wait until people could be convinced to end slavery and legalize suffrage for blacks (males only). They wanted an immediate emancipation and were willing to use political action to get results. Frederick Douglass was among the blacks remaining aligned with Garrison, while Henry Highland Garnet and Samuel Ringgold Ward, along with Bibb, joined the new organization. By 1840, the new group had formed the Liberty party, the first political party in the United States organized to oppose slavery.

Lambert and Monroe were already active in Liberty party politics when Bibb arrived in Michigan. Historian David M. Katzman states that "Michigan's Negroes exerted their greatest militancy in the political sphere. The central issue for them in Michigan was the denial of suffrage to the black man, and they fought this restriction in every way possible—by petition, convention, referendum, and court test. Occasionally Negroes balloted by fraudulently swearing that they were eligible electors." Bibb was one of those who tried to cast his ballot, but was stopped at the polls. The *Signal of Liberty,* the Michigan abolitionist newspaper tied to the Liberty party, actively supported the black suffrage movement by printing petitions that subscribers could rip out and circulate for signatures.

In 1848, the abolitionist Liberty party joined with like-minded members of the Whig party to form the Free Soil party—a compromise measure—which adopted the slogan "free soil, free speech, free labour, and free men." Its platform did not go so far as to demand an end to all slavery, but simply opposed its extension into any new states or territories. Bibb took a public stand and lectured on behalf of the Free Soil party, despite his concern that the platform did not go far enough. In the 1848 election, during which Martin Van Buren was selected as its presidential contender, the Free Soil party did well, despite losing the presidential election to Whig candidate Zachary Taylor. Five Free Soil party members were elected to office, giving the antislavery issue a place at the political table.

Despite being a relative newcomer to the city, Bibb was an active participant during the 1843 Detroit convention. He placed one of the resolutions on the floor for consideration: "Resolved, that we, the colored citizens of Michigan, be united in sentiment and action and never to consent to emigrate or be colonized from this, our native soil, while there exists one drop of African blood in bondage in these United States." The resolution is telling in that it is a strong statement against emigration. Bibb was probably responding to the efforts of the American Colonization Society to move blacks out of the country. He soon became one of the most popular antislavery lecturers in the country. "The first time that I ever spoke before a public audience," he wrote later, "was to give a narration of my own sufferings and adventures, connected with slavery. I commenced in the village of Adrian, State of Michigan, May, 1844." It is possible that he was invited there by Laura Haviland, a resident of Adrian, who had by this time helped establish the first antislavery institute in Michigan. Several years later, after having changed his mind about emigration, Bibb returned the invitation by asking Haviland to come to Canada to teach school.

In the winter of 1845, Bibb made one last attempt to free his family. He arrived in Indiana, only to be told that his wife was now the concubine of the white man to whom she had been sold. Their daughter, Mary Frances, was living with her. "From that time I gave her up into the hands of an all wise Providence," he wrote. "As she was then living with another man, I could no longer regard her as my wife. After all the sacrifices, sufferings, and risks which I had run, striving to rescue her from the grasp of slavery; every prospect and hope was cut off. She has ever since been regarded as theoretically and practically dead to me as wife . . . I resolved, in 1846, to spend my days in traveling, to advance the anti-slavery cause."

In identifying Bibb as a "trans-border" figure, Cooper has noted that Bibb would cross the Canadian/U.S. border whenever the occasion called for it, and even publicized his forays by sending letters to abolitionist newspapers. From Canada West, he wrote to the *Emancipator* in May 1847, "It gives me great pleasure to take by the hand so many of my fellow countrymen from the Southern prison house. Almost everyday we have an arrival. How strange it is that men, women and children are willing to suffer from exposure and hunger, and run the risk of being seized by bloodhounds, or of death by torture, for the sake of liberty!"

In August of that same year, Bibb was part of a group of celebrants who crossed from Detroit to Windsor in order to welcome new fugitives to freedom. Most likely, the group was celebrating Emancipation Day, August 1, 1834, the date Sir Thomas Buxton's Emancipation Act had gone into effect; August 1 celebrations were held throughout the British colonies in its honor. Bibb's speech to the group was printed in the *Emancipator*:

> Dear Brethern, we are happy to meet you here on Freedom's soil, we congratulate you, we rejoice with you, and some of us can sympathise with you from experience. I can imagine that I see you traveling by night through the dark swamps, some with their little children on their backs, and their wives and others by their side, guided by the North star; and in the distance I seem to hear the slaveholder and his bloodhounds. But you are now in Canada, free from American slavery; yes the very moment you stept upon these shores you were changed from articles of property to human beings.

This speech indicates that at least some blacks, Bibb included, felt free to cross and recross the border at will, thus confirming Afua Cooper's concept of a "fluid frontier" and border at the Detroit River.

While his courage to speak and act publicly cannot be underestimated, Bibb was certainly freer to cross the border without some of the concerns other fugitives had. While he was still a fugitive from slavery, Bibb's last owner had already died, so that he could move about without fear that his master was actively hunting him.

Bibb's personal life took a turn: "In the month of May, 1847, I attended the anti-slavery anniversary in the city of New York, where I had the good fortune to be introduced to the favor of a Miss Mary E. Miles, of Boston; a lady whom I had frequently heard very highly spoken of, for her activity and devotion to the anti-slavery cause, as well as her talents and learning, and benevolence in the cause of reforms, generally." Bibb established a relationship with Miles through visits and letters. In June 1848, the two were married. "Not in slave-holding style, which is a mere farce, without the sanction of law or gospel; but in accordance with the laws of God and our country. My beloved wife is a bosom friend, a help-meet, a loving companion in all the social, moral, and religious relations of life," he wrote. In what seems to be a reference to his first wife, Malinda, Bibb revealed some of his sadness and anger when speaking of his new wife, Mary. "She is to me what a poor slave's wife can never be to her husband while in the condition of a slave; for she can not be true to her husband contrary to the will of her master. She can neither be pure nor virtuous, contrary to the will of her master. She dare not refuse to be reduced to a state of adultery at the will of her master. . . ."

Bibb concluded his autobiography with this commitment: "I trust that this little volume will bear some humble part in lighting up the path of freedom and revolutionizing public opinion upon this great subject. And I here pledge myself, God being my helper, ever to contend for the natural equality of the human family, without regard to color, which is but fading *matter,* while *mind* makes the man." Below this text, the city and date were recorded: "New York City, May 1, 1849."

Bibb's autobiography went through three editions within the next two years. It was reviewed favorably by much of the abolitionist press. "It is certainly one of the most interesting and thrilling narratives of slavery ever laid before the American people," Frederick Douglass wrote. "The exposure which the author makes of the horrors of slavery—the separations, the whippings, and the accumulated outrages inflicted on the slave, must stir the blood of every reader who has the pulsations of a man. . . . We deem the work a most valuable acquisition to the anti-slavery cause; and we hope that it may be widely circulated throughout the country."

Henry and Mary Bibb settled in Detroit, where they both threw themselves full-time into the abolitionist cause. Much of what is known about their activities comes from letters Henry Bibb wrote to abolitionist presses, including the *North Star*. These letters and editorials trace the evolution in thought of many blacks in the three decades before the Civil War, in essence creating a documented dialogue among blacks in Canada and the United States. Issues such as separatism versus assimilation, "begging" versus self-reliance, emigrationism versus colonialism, and moral suasion versus political action were all a part of the dialogue. Bibb was an active participant in all these discussions.

According to Cooper, the first letter found written by Bibb had been sent to Silas Gatewood, his former owner. The letter contained the pamphlet of the proceedings from the 1843 State Convention of Colored Citizens. Bibb was obviously flaunting his new stature as a freeman and his importance in the political sphere. Gatewood's reaction at receiving this pamphlet is not known, though he actually responded and wrote Bibb news about his mother, who was still enslaved. He even asked Bibb to say hello to two of his former slaves.

Bibb wrote back, this time expressing his anger at all Gatewood had done to his family:

> To be compelled to stand by and see you whip and slash my wife without mercy, when I could afford her no protection, not even by offering myself to suffer the lash in her place, was more than I felt it to be the duty of a slave husband to endure, while the way was open to Canada. My infant child was also frequently flogged by Mrs. Gatewood, for crying, until its skin was bruised literally purple. This kind of treatment was what drove me from home and family, to seek a better home for them. . . . I subscribe myself a friend of the oppressed, and Liberty forever.

What a powerful affront these letters must have been to Gatewood. In many states, slaves were not allowed by law to read or write. Here was one of his own former slaves who had emancipated himself, now reading, writing, and acting politically on behalf of those still enslaved by men like Gatewood. Cooper calls this letter writing by former fugitives to their former masters "the journey of engaging in a process of mental and psychological emancipation."

In 1848, Bibb wrote a letter to the *North Star* stating his views against separate black institutions. In it, he congratulated Douglass on his stance against separate black churches: "We should contend for the natural equality of the human family, without regard to color or sect. I see no more use in having a colored church exclusively, than having a colored heaven and a colored God. I regard prejudice to be just as wicked in a colored person as in a white one." Despite this public testimony, years later Mary Ann Shadd accused Bibb of being a separatist.

After the Cleveland convention of 1848, participants were asked to return to their own communities and hold similar meetings. In Detroit, Bibb helped convene an assembly, a record of which was also sent to the *North Star*. By request of the delegates, he opened the meeting by singing a song (Bibb often sang "plantation songs" or "liberty songs" either before or after his lectures, emotional lamentations much like spirituals, or more celebratory songs of freedom). Audiences were often moved to give him a standing ovation, both for his oration and his singing. Bibb was appointed to a committee to draft the assembly's objectives. Several resolutions were passed:

Resolved, That we hold our liberty dearer than we do our lives, and we will organize and prepare ourselves with the determination, live or die, sink or swim, we will never be taken back into slavery.

Resolved, That we will never voluntarily separate ourselves from the slave population in the country, for they are our fathers and mothers, and sisters and our brothers, their interest is our interest, their wrongs and their sufferings are ours, the injuries inflicted on them are alike inflicted on us; therefore it is our duty to aid and assist them in their attempts to regain their liberty.

Other resolutions were passed stating that the delegates would always abide by the U.S. Constitution and laws of any states that did not allow slavery. They agreed to draft a resolution to Congress praying for the repeal of the 1793 Fugitive Slave Act. Recording secretary George DeBaptiste noted that Bibb closed the meeting "by calling on the colored people of this city and state to prepare themselves with the means of self defense, for said he, ye are property in the eye of the laws of this free nation, equalized with the horse and the ox, and being held in this light by the mansstealers of the south and liable to be seized as such at any moment by himself or his agents, all protection that is left you is that which nature has bestowed; therefore, as you have no other means, you must protect yourselves by whatever means you possess."

One prime example of Bibb's religious zeal was his involvement in 1849 in a movement by the American Missionary Association to provide Bibles for slaves. He was a firm believer that the Bible was an antislavery document and that it could be a potent resource against slavery if enough slaves were given it. But he was publicly chastised for his views by Frederick Douglass in a *North Star* editorial:

It seems to us that no scheme of giving Bibles to the slave, while he is a slave, can succeed without the co-operation of the slave holders themselves; and this co-operation Mr. Bibb, in the speech in question virtually told the audience could never be obtained. . . . thus involving himself in a contradiction. He said, on that occasion, "As well might they expect the fox to guard the geese, or the wolf to protect the lamb, as to think that slaveholders would circulate the Word of God among their slaves." On this assertion, though it is diametrically opposed to Mr. Bibb's scheme, we most fully unite, and conclude from it, that the first to be done, is to break the power of the slaveholder, as the first means of giving the Bible to the slave. Mr. Bibb, contrary to our experience, and the experience of many others whom we have consulted [claimed that on most plantations there were at least some slaves able to read].

This disagreement between Douglass and Bibb became personal. When Bibb's autobiography was published later that same year, Douglass prefaced his positive review of the narrative with an aside attacking Bibb: "After waiting several weeks, we have received a copy of this little work. Why it did not come to hand sooner, we do not know, unless its author felt it proper to serve a black editor last."

In the hundred years prior to the Civil War, over one hundred slave narratives were written. Bibb's autobiography is seen as unique among them for several reasons: He was one of the few to have labored in the Deep South, so he was able to depict vividly the horrors of slavery in the cotton fields, and why slaves feared being "sold south." He also wrote about slave religion, and made specific reference to the use of conjuring to achieve some desired action, such as protection against beatings and help in attracting members of the opposite sex. He even mentioned his use of such techniques himself, although they proved to be of no avail. But what stands out most in Bibb's narrative is his emphasis on the importance of his family. The prevailing view among whites at that time was that blacks did not believe in family ties as they did. Of course, they refused to acknowledge that they themselves had ripped the family structure of blacks to shreds. Bibb expressed over and over again his frustration and sadness regarding his futile attempts to free his family and reestablish his marriage to Malinda. Cooper has labeled Bibb's narrative, "a love story" because of his focus throughout it on his relationship with Malinda.

Bibb was a prolific letter writer. His letters have been found published in many antislavery newspapers, not only the well-known *North Star*, the *Emancipator*, and *Frederick Douglass' Paper*, but lesser-known, short-lived abolitionist papers: the *Signal of Liberty*, the *Palladium of Liberty*, and the *Anti-Slavery Bugle*, published in Ohio. The *Anti-Slavery Bugle* was started by abolitionist and women's rights advocate Abby Kelley Foster, who began it after realizing while on a lecture tour of the West that eastern abolitionist newspapers took too long to reach the western territories.

Although newly emancipated slaves were able to claim their voices through public lectures and written narratives, they had to preface their autobiographies with testimonials written by white people in order to prove the authenticity of their narratives. Bibb's editor, Lucius C. Matlack, addressed those concerns:

> To many, the elevated style, purity of diction, and easy flow of language, frequently exhibited, will appear unaccountable and contradictory, in view of his want of early mental culture. But to the thousands who have listened with delight to his speeches on anniversary and other occasions, these same traits will be noted as unequivocal evidence of originality. . . . Moreover, the writer of this introduction is well acquainted with his handwriting and style. The entire manuscript I have examined and prepared for the press. Many of the closing pages of it were written by Mr. Bibb in my office.

In addition to testimonials by Matlack and others verifying the truthfulness of Bibb's narrative, an investigative report conducted by the Detroit Liberty Association also prefaced his book. "Slave owners, slave dealers, fugitives from slavery, political friends and political foes contributed to a mass of testimony, every part of which pointed to a common conclusion—the undoubted truth of Mr. Bibb's statements. . . . The Committee have no hesitation in declaring their conviction that Mr. Bibb is amply sustained, and is entitled to public confidence and high esteem."

Other corroborating letters, from Hiram Wilson and ironically even his old master, Silas Gatewood, also prefaced Bibb's narrative, and a supporting letter from a committee of "respectable" Detroit men concluded them. While these testimonials may seem excessive and unnecessary, editors and publishers of fugitive narratives knew that southern and northern racial bigotry required as much. That even Harriet

Beecher Stowe was hounded into providing *A Key to Uncle Tom's Cabin* to prove the veracity of facts in her story indicates the lengths to which any abolitionist author, white or black, had to go in order to overcome prevailing racial stereotypes.

Bibb published a pamphlet in 1849 on two slave rebellions: It was entitled *Slave Insurrection in 1831 in Southampton County, Va., Headed by Nat Turner. Also a Conspiracy of Slaves in Charleston, South Carolina, in 1822.* In 1852, probably at the request of audiences who had heard him sing, he published a collection of songs, *The Anti-Slavery Harp,* which was reissued in 1852, after he moved to Canada.

In 1850, the Bibbs moved to Sandwich, Canada West. While many fugitives and free blacks were crossing the border to escape possible reenslavement, Cooper suggests that the Bibbs chose to go in order to better serve the hundreds of fugitives who were moving into Canada. Mary Bibb immediately started a school in their home. Within one month, she had moved her school to another location and was teaching forty-six students. The school was described as "ill ventilated, with uncomfortable seats and a shortage of desks and apparatus"; still, the quality of education offered must have been publicly respected, as six white students also attended classes.

One of Henry Bibb's first acts upon arriving in Canada was to organize the Sandwich Convention, held in November of 1850, its purpose to discuss solutions to the problems, including housing, that faced new arrivals. Delegates formed the Fugitive Union Society, to "enable every fugitive from slavery, if possible, to become an owner and tiller of the soil, and so promote the cause of temperance and education among our people; and that any person who does not sell or use intoxicating drinks as a beverage, and who bears a good moral character, may become a member of this Society." Bibb was chosen as recording secretary; Josiah Henson was elected president. While housing and land ownership were the main objectives of the convention, a newspaper was also proposed. Those now living in Canada West had access to American abolitionist newspapers, but the group understood the importance of establishing their own press in their new country. Bibb took the mandates of the convention seriously. He not only attempted to alleviate the problems of settling the new fugitives; he also began publication of his own abolitionist newspaper, the *Voice of the Fugitive*, in January 1851.

That same year he organized the North American Convention of Colored People, held in Toronto. There were fifty-three delegates to this important convention, including Martin Delany, Josiah Henson, Abraham Shadd, William Lambert, and Hiram Wilson. (Jane Rhodes suggests that Mary Ann Shadd was present as well.) Bibb had many good reasons to choose Toronto for the convention. It was home to over five hundred blacks now living in this city of thirty thousand. The Anti-Slavery Society of Canada had originated in Toronto, and transportation to the city by rail and water had already been developed, making it accessible from many North American locations. The *Globe*, the Toronto antislavery newspaper edited by abolitionist George Brown, publicized the event: "A great North American Convention of colored people is appointed to meet in this city on the 11th, 12th, and 13th. Numerous and efficient delegates are expected to be present from the West and also from the Northern states. One important subject of deliberation will be the question of colonization which has been touched on in our columns lately in several letters."

Just one year before, the issue of emigration had been denounced because it sounded too much like colonization schemes; now elective emigration to Canada was given particular emphasis. Among the important resolutions passed at this convention was one advocating such emigration: "Resolved, that the convention recommend to the colored people of the U.S. of America, to emigrate to the Canadas instead of going to Africa or the West India Islands, that they, by so doing, may be better able to assist their brethren who are daily flying from American slavery."

Other resolutions were passed offering thanks to the British government for protection and for encouraging those still enslaved in the United States to "come out from under the jurisdiction of those wicked laws." Convention delegates encouraged those already in Canada to purchase land in order to ensure their independence. One other resolution passed stated that "in the opinion of this convention, the establishment of exclusive churches and schools for colored people, contributes greatly towards the promotion of prejudice, heretofore unknown in the Canadas, and we do hereby recommend that all such organizations be abandoned as speedily as may be practicable."

Bibb can be credited for much of this convention's success. He called for it, organized it, and was one of the most active participants in guiding the discussion topics. He was also chosen, along with two other delegates, to author and publicize its proceedings, which were eventually published as an "Address to the Colored Inhabitants of North America."

Beginning with reference to the Declaration of Independence, Bibb and his coauthors wrote:

This political or practical falsehood looks well on paper, and strikes harmoniously on the American ear, especially on the 4th day of July; but it sounds like base hypocrisy to every colored American who knows that under the same government three millions and a half of his race are tyrannically robbed of their manhood. . . . With the map and the history of human bondage before us, we are led to believe that the abolition of American slavery is now in the hands of the people of color in North America. Not that we would have the true-hearted abolitionists, who have stood by us in the darkest hours of adversity, to cease their efforts until the work is done; but we should be found standing in the front ranks of the battle, until our kinsmen, according to the flesh are disenthralled.

After laying out the problems facing blacks in North America, they suggested some remedies, including self-emancipation, emigration to Canada or the West Indies, the establishment of a network to aid fugitives, and the importance of education: "Let there be put into the hands of the refugee, as soon as he crosses Mason and Dixon's Line, the

Spelling Book. Teach him to read and write intelligibly, and the slave-holder won't have him on his plantation among his slaves."

The proceedings concluded with an admonition to free people of color that "the eye of the civilized world is looking down upon us to see whether we can take care of ourselves or not. If our conduct is moral and upright, in spite of all the bad training we have had, it will reflect credit on ourselves, and encourage our friends in what they are doing for our elevation."

The Fugitive Union Society mandated by the Sandwich convention later joined forces with a Michigan Anti-Slavery Society endeavor, the Refugee Home Society. When the two projects came together, Bibb voiced both his support and his concerns: "God speed the Society in its noble undertaking. May it become auxiliary to societies which have been organized for the same object and work with them in union until the object is obtained." He was making it clear that Canadian fugitives had no desire to be controlled by American whites, no matter how philanthropic their projects.

By November 1851, the joint Canadian/Michigan venture (also called the Refugee Home Society) purchased their first parcel of two hundred acres of land. Bibb exalted: "The Refugee Home Society has just purchased a beautiful tract of unimproved Canada land, for the benefit of the homeless refugees in this section of the Province. The land is to be divided into 25-acre lots for actual settlers. It is known to be well stocked with good marketable timber, and that wood will command a liberal [profit] on the land if chopped and corded."

The purpose of the society was outlined in its constitution:

Whereas it is supposed that there are, at the present time, between thirty-five and forty thousand refugee slaves in Canada, whose number has been constantly increasing since the passage of the Fugitive Slave Bill. And, whereas, on their arrival, they find themselves in a strange land, uneducated, poverty-stricken, without homes, or any permanent means of self-support; however willing they may be to work, they have neither means to work with, nor land to work upon. . . . This Society would therefore represent to the refugees from Southern slavery, who are now in Canada destitute of homes, or who may hereafter come, being desirous of building themselves up in Canada, on an agricultural basis, and who do not buy, sell or use intoxicating drinks as a beverage, shall, by making proper application to this society, and complying with its Constitution and By Laws, be put into possession of 25 acres of farming land, and their children shall enjoy the blessings of education perpetually.

In an editorial, Bibb wrote about the importance of owning land, "because it is the best way to encourage industry among this class, to put a stop to so much begging, and to provide means of self-support. While we must admit that there are many among us who are poor and needy object of charity, which is caused by slavery, we must strive to have as little of it as possible." Bibb was already articulating the importance of self-reliance and independence and his stance against begging, a topic that was on the minds of many in the community. In later lectures, given to garner support for the Refugee Home Society, Bibb addressed the matter of begging outright: "If our people must beg, we hope they may beg for something that is permanent."

When fund-raising efforts and stock sales were not producing the revenue needed for the project, Reverend Charles C. Foote was authorized to act as an agent to travel and solicit funds. Other agents were added later. All were required to give a written accounting of the moneys received and spent.

The Refugee Home Society seemed similar in many ways to other black settlements, but there were some important differences, one of the most contentious being that land could be sold only to settlers who were "refugees from Southern slavery and who are the owners of no

land." Free blacks were barred from purchasing land under its auspices. Another difference was that land would be purchased wherever
possible and would not be limited to one contiguous area.

The Refugee Home Society managers were aware of the monetary
squabbles that had plagued the Dawn settlement. They attempted to
circumvent any similar issues by requiring that any society checks issued be signed by three members of the executive board; this number
would later be increased to six signatures. Another unique form of
checks and balances included the designation of a special auditor to
monitor all transactions.

As with other settlements, temperance was also listed as a requirement for any settlers purchasing society land. Houses were required to
have two rooms and deeds to the properties had to include the names of
wives and children in order to protect any widows surviving their husbands from losing their land. Five acres were to be given outright, free
of charge, out of the twenty-five-acre parcels to be purchased. Land
had to be cleared within two years and payment for it could take up to
ten years. Half of the moneys collected were to go to the education of
those who had settled. The society was to exist until slavery ended in
the United States.

To fulfill the society's educational requirements, Bibb called on
Laura Haviland, an old friend. She opened her school in 1852, on
Refugee Home Society land in the Puce River district.

In her autobiography, Haviland recalled:

While visiting friends in Detroit and Canada previous to reopen-
ing Raisin Institute, as I designed, I was earnestly solicited by
Henry Bibb, Horace Hallack and Rev. Chas. C. Foote, the committee authorized to employ a teacher, to open a school in a new
settlement of fugitives, eight miles back of Windsor, where the
Refugee Association had purchased government land, on long and
easy terms, for fugitive slaves. They had erected a frame house for
school and meeting purposes. The settlers had built for themselves
small log-houses, and cleared from one to five acres each on their

heavily timbered land, and raised corn, potatoes, and other garden vegetables. A few had put in two and three acres of wheat, and were doing well for their first year. After prayerful consideration, I reached the conclusion to defer for another year my home work, and enter this new field.

As Haviland recalled, the settlers "made great effort to improve their homes by taking trees from their woods to the saw-mills to be cut up into boards for better floors than split logs, and for partitions to make their little houses more comfortable." She also noted her success: "In six weeks of steady attendance fifteen young men and women could read the second reader, and write a legible hand, and draft a negotiable note." Remarking the settlers' mixed religious backgrounds and their desire for religious services, Haviland formed a Christian Union Church, explaining that she "was not there to present particular religious tenets, but to present the crucified, risen, and glorified Savior."

She related one incident involving two brothers who had successfully escaped to Canada. When their former master from Kentucky came trying to trick them back into slavery, the brothers ambushed him, stripped him, and gave him forty lashes. "They applied the lash until the forty stripes their mother had received at his hands had been given," and then they let him go. The lash they used, Haviland noted, was a "plantation slave whip kept by Henry Bibb as a reminder of his slave life."

Benjamin Drew visited Refugee Home Society land in 1854 and noted the details of land acquisition:

At about nine miles from Windsor, in the townships of Sandwich and Madison, the Refugees' Home Society have made a purchase of nearly two thousand acres of land, on which reside some twenty families, each on a farm of twenty-five acres. Forty 25 acre lots have been taken up. A school is maintained there three fourths of the year. . . .

By the constitution adopted in 1852, it appears that each family of actual settlers receives twenty-five acres of land, five of which they receive free of cost, provided they shall, within three years from the time of occupancy, clear and cultivate the same. . . .

The Refugee Home Society, its officers and agents, possess the entire confidence of the American public: at least of that portion which sympathizes with the wandering outcasts from the United States.

Drew interviewed several settlers in the area. While he had drawn his own conclusions about the society's project, it was his intention to let the fugitives speak for themselves. Some he interviewed had negative opinions. Thomas Jones, a fugitive from Kentucky living in Windsor, expressed his view:

The colored people are doing very well. They are poor, some of them, but are all able to have enough to eat and wear, and they have comfortable homes, with few exceptions. . . . In the Refugee's Home they are not doing very well. Land was to be sold to the refugees at cost, giving them five acres, and they to buy twenty. Some dissatisfaction exists because there have been an advance made of four shillings an acre for surveying, although the land had been surveyed once. The refugees refused to pay it.

Jones explained what was perhaps his main complaint:

I came here without anything. I had no money or aid of any kind. I went right into the bush chopping wood. I brought my lady with me, and we were married. . . . With what I earned by hard licks, I bought land and have built me a frame-house.

If a man have aid furnished him, he does not have so much satisfaction in what he has,—he feels dependent and beholden, and does not make out so well. I have seen this, ever since I have been here,—the bad effects of this giving. I have seen men waiting, doing nothing, expecting something to come over to them. . . . My opinion is, that the fugitive on the road, should be assisted, but not after he gets here. If people have money to give, they had better give it to those who suffer in trying to help them here.

Other settlers thought differently. The descendants of John Freeman Walls, a fugitive from North Carolina who moved to Canada with his master's widow, credit the Refugee Home Society with much of their family's success. John Walls settled on land purchased from the forerunner of the Refugee Home Society near the Puce River and became a successful farmer as well as an accomplished carpenter, ensuring his self-sufficiency. He cleared his land by hand and constructed a two-story log home, designed "shotgun" style after a form of plantation architecture. Church services for neighboring settlers were held in the Walls home for several years until a church building could be erected. His descendants still live on the same land settled by their ancestor.

The Refugee Home Society and especially Henry and Mary Bibb were not immune from attacks that had plagued other black settlements, but they drew their largest opposition from their former friend and colleague Mary Ann Shadd. The first public indication of Shadd's opposition to the society came in *A Plea for Emigration; or, Notes of Canada West,* the pamphlet she published just nine months after her arrival in Canada. In this treatise, Shadd expressed her anger that free blacks were barred from purchasing land from the society, saying that this "would cause friction and factionalism between persons of freeborn origin and those of slave origin." She accused Bibb and the society of "begging" on behalf of the fugitives and even accused Bibb of stealing funds that had been collected. She also complained that the society was being run by white men from Detroit who wanted to control the project. In addition to personally attacking Bibb, she cast aspersions on the character of the settlers themselves. To the American Missionary Association, from which she had sought support for the school she had opened, she wrote:

It is no slander to say that Henry Bibb has hundreds of dollars belonging to fugitives, probably thousands, would be nearer the truth. Henry Bibb is a dishonest man, and as such must be known to the world. To expose him is a duty which though painful, involving as it does loss of confidence in coloured men, who assume to be leaders of their people, must be performed. . . . Within the present year and during the time he has been asking for "donations" etc. to help him out of difficulty, he has built a house, bought a vessel, bought a house and lot, on which he lives, leased another, and Mrs. Bibb has purchased a farm, and there are other business operations I can mention beside the paper, the *Voice of the Fugitive.*

Many of Shadd's arguments do not hold up to scrutiny and could have been applied to other settlements, as well. Although a big proponent of assimilation versus separate institutions for blacks, she did not attack the Buxton settlement for creating a separate black community, nor did she acknowledge that, by policy, the Refugee Home Society assimilated its settlers into already existing communities by its decision not to purchase one large contiguous land block. In regard to the begging issue, Shadd did not acknowledge that all the black settlements had to seek support, at least initially, from outside sources, mostly white. It seems there must have been other reasons for her attacks.

The historian Robin Winks suggests that Shadd "resented any evidence of dependency upon whites, denounced begging in all its forms as 'materially compromising our manhood, by representing us as objects of charity,' and attacked the Refugee Home Society in particular since its trustees were white, its financial base lay in Michigan, its local Negro spokesman, Bibb, was a mulatto, and a white man, Reverend Charles C. Foote, was its principal almoner and agent."

Cooper probably comes closest with her argument that the main issue driving Shadd's attacks was the lack of resources available to the black community as a whole, noting that each new project had to compete for moneys from the same pool of usually white benefactors who held the purse strings, thus creating rivalries within the black community for white funding.

In September 1854, a True Band Society was set up in Amherstburg, in part to attack the "begging system." Just two years later, there were fourteen True Band Societies throughout Canada West. Their purpose extended beyond the begging issue and included development of emergency funds for refugees, creation of a board of arbitration to deal with internal community issues before they could be reported in the national press, support for integration and assimilation into society at large, and encouragement of school attendance. But even these efforts did not stop the arguments regarding begging.

While there seems to be no one identifiable reason for all of Shadd's ire, at least one incident may be pinpointed for causing some of her personal animosity toward Bibb. He had published a report indicating that Shadd was getting funds from the American Missionary Association to run her school, in essence accusing her of "begging," just as she was accusing others of doing. He wrote:

> At this we understand that there was an offence taken by Miss Shadd, where there was none intended by us. We heard her say that she was receiving "three york shillings, from each of her pupils per month," which sum was not enough to support her from about 20 children and after we learned that the above society [AMA] had granted her the sum of $125, we thought that they did well, and we ventured to give publicity to the fact, for the encouragement of our people in Windsor as they were entirely ignorant of it up to that time, so this was good news to them, and as our business is to give the news, and not knowing that she wished this information kept from the parents of the children, we gave publicity to it and for which Miss Shadd has said and written many things which we think will add nothing to her credit as a lady, for there should be no insult taken where there is none intended.

The result of all this publicity was that the AMA withdrew its support for Shadd's school.

When the attacks got more vicious and personal, Bibb was forced to defend himself publicly. He used the best venue at his disposal, the new Canadian black newspaper, the *Voice of the Fugitive*.

The first edition of this pioneering paper appeared on January 1, 1851, in Sandwich, a direct result of the mandate put forth by the Sandwich convention in 1850:

> Whereas, We as a people, have a great work to accomplish and we have no instrument that we can use with more effect than the public press—as we struggle against opinions, our warfare lies in the field of thought, embodying ourselves to field, we need a printing press—for the press is the vehicle of thought—the ruler of opinions. We need a press, that we may be independent of those who have always oppressed us—we need a press that we may hang our banners on the outer wall, that all who pass by may read why we struggle, and what we struggle for.
>
> Resolved, That we make immediate effort to have a newspaper established in our midst, which shall be the advocate of the colored people of Canada West.

As the first black newspaper in Canada, the *Voice of the Fugitive* was an important step in creating a distinct voice, one that was separate from the abolitionist press in the United States and served the interests of the fugitives in Canada. Bibb drew on his own journalistic experience in letter writing and publishing as well as his personal experience as both fugitive and freeman when setting its tone and structure. He realized that the paper needed to be international as well as local in focus. Again, drawing on contacts he had made in abolitionist circles, he commissioned agents throughout Canada as well as in the United States and Great Britain. Martin Delany, then publisher of his own paper, *The*

Mystery; Josiah Henson, then lecturing in Europe; and Bibb's New York editor, Lucius Matlack, all served as agents for the *Voice.* By the end of the first year of publication, the paper counted over eleven hundred subscribers.

Bibb laid out the intent of the paper in the first issue:

We expect by the aid of a good Providence to advocate the cause of human liberty in the true meaning of that term. We shall advocate the immediate and unconditional abolition of chattel slavery everywhere, but especially on the American soil. We shall also persuade as far as it may be practicable, every oppressed person of color in the United States to settle in Canada where the laws make no distinctions among men based on complexion and upon whose soil no slave can breathe. We shall advocate the claims of the American slaves to the Bible from which it has ever been withheld. We shall advocate the cause of temperance and moral reform generally. The cause of education shall have a prominent space in our columns. We shall advocate the claims of agricultural pursuits among our people as being the most certain road to independence and self-respect. Our political creed shall be to support that government that protects all men in the enjoyment of liberty without regard to color. We shall oppose the annexations of Canada to the United States to the fullest extent of our ability while that government continues to tolerate the abominable system of slavery. We shall from time to time endeavor to lay before our readers the true condition of our people in Canada, of their hopes and prospects for the future, and while we intend this to be a mouthpiece for the refugees in Canada especially, yet we mean to speak out our sentiments as a free man upon all subjects that come within our sphere, and if others differ with us as they probably will on some subjects, all we shall ask shall be the toleration of opinion and free discussion which is the refutation of error and the bulwark of liberty. We shall make no compromise with wrong or allow personal controversies in our paper, but anything written in respectful language by way of reply or explanation shall always have attention, but we must be the judge of what is suitable to go into our columns.

The *North Star* heralded the new paper:

VOICE OF THE FUGITIVE. This is Henry Bibb's paper, published every other Wednesday, at Sandwich, Canada West.— Terms, one dollar, always in advance. The *Voice of the Fugitive* is to advocate giving "Bibles to the Slaves," and the colonization of "free colored people in Canada," and it will oppose the annexation of Canada to the United States. The first number of the paper is well printed, and gives signs of ability and spirit.

Familiar with the power of the press to sway public opinion, Bibb took a proactive approach when dealing with accusations from Shadd. To present his defense, he sent a letter to *Frederick Douglass' Paper* (after 1851, Douglass had discontinued publication of his *North Star,* merging with the *Liberty Party Paper* to form *Frederick Douglass' Paper).* In June 1852, Douglass printed Bibb's letter but prefaced it by saying, "We have for some time disapproved of the system of begging extensively practiced of late in the name of Canada Fugitives, and the following from Mr. Bibb, who is, himself a Canada Fugitive, will, we trust, have a salutary influence."

Bibb himself condemned begging. He responded to Douglass's comment:

Mr. Editor, I have opposed and shall continue to oppose lying and begging, whether carried on by white or black men, and especially amongst refugees in Canada, with whom I stand identified, and upon whom the whole civilized world are looking to see whether they are capable of taking care of themselves under the anti-slavery government. I know that every man in Canada West, who will work, can make a good living; and it is disgraceful to us as a people, to continue sending agents over the country to beg for a living, when we are just as able to work for it as white men are.

Shadd quickly realized that by addressing the American press, Bibb was generating support for himself and creating an international dialogue. She, too, turned to the "foreign" press to express her point of view. An October 29, 1852, letter written by Shadd to *Frederick Douglass' Paper* was headlined NO MORE BEGGING FOR FARMS OR CLOTHES FOR FUGITIVES IN CANADA, and stated:

"A meeting of the colored citizens of Windsor [Canada West] and vicinity, was held in the barracks in that place, on the evening of Sept. 27, to inquire into the grievances of fugitives, against almoners of donations received from the U.S. and to take measures to put an end, if possible, to the begging system so far as it can apply to them."

One of the resolutions passed at the meeting clearly reflects Shadd's beliefs:

Resolved, That we do not regard the "Refugee's Home Society" as a benevolent institution, designed to benefit a formerly downtrodden people, but as an exceedingly cunning land scheme, the continuance of which, by giving fresh impulse and a specious character to the begging system, will materially compromise our manhood, by representing us as objects of charity, injure seriously the character of this country, and tend to the pecuniary advantage of its agents, and their only.

Frederick Douglass got caught up in the dialogue. In a January 1853 editorial he wrote:

There is an increasing demand in this country for light on the various benevolent schemes in progress for improving the condition of destitute fugitives, who escape from Republican Slavery to British liberty in Canada. The friends of freedom in this country, though severely taxed by the claims of the cause in the States, are, nevertheless, mindful of those who have made good their escape, and they anxiously enquire how they may wisely and beneficially aid them. To this enquiry different and somewhat conflicting answers are returned, showing that the friends of the fugitives in Canada are very much divided among themselves on the subject, and in important particulars point blank against each other.

To his credit, Douglass published letters from each side. Samuel Ringgold Ward, once a Bibb supporter and contributor to the *Voice*, took up the attack on behalf of Shadd, while C. C. Foote supported Bibb and the Refugee Home Society.

Foote's article, "The Colored People in Canada—Do They Need Help?" was published in the *Frederick Douglass' Paper* on January 14, 1853:

Having been frequently in the communities where Mr. And Mrs. Bibb have resided since their removal to Canada, I feel bound to say, they stand as high in the estimation of, and are looked up to more by the refugees than any other persons in the community. Last summer, during the prevalence of the cholera, I spent a short time in Windsor, and during my stay there, Henry B. and wife were thronged with applications for aid and counsel. From morning to night, they were on the move to meet these calls; to get a doctor, to provide watchers, to get a coffin, to send somebody to dig the graves, and to bury the dead. For all these works, the people looked to them as children to parents.

Why the assault is made upon this Society [Refugee Home Society] you will be at a loss to know. Scarcely was it in existence, ere———was writing "bitter things" against it. At first, her objections were confined to the sixth article of the Constitution: "The Society shall give deeds to none but landless fugitives from American slavery." The presence of this article is the source of opposition from the *free* colored people. . . . Look now at the propriety of aiding these people at all. How largely the Bible dwells on the *duty* of aiding the poor! And if these people are not poor, then *none are poor*. If charity should not be extended to *these*, then *there should be an end of charity.*

Foote continued his letter with testimonials from prominent blacks and whites and identified the Michigan officers of the Refugee Home Society and their social standing.

Ward responded but he prefaced his letter by saying that "distinct from their actions in public matters, I have nothing to say against them. My opposition to the Refugee's Home Society, of course is opposition to the official acts of Messrs. Foote and Bibb." Ward outlined his specific objections to the Refugee Home Society, including his belief that the settlers could purchase government land on their own for less than what they might pay the society. He stated that "we do not want boxes and barrels of old clothes, which cost twice as much for transportation as they are worth, nor do we need a set of land-jobbers to beg money to buy land for them." He also argued that the society's agents were begging money on behalf of the settlers, yet keeping 20 percent of what they received.

The Bibbs and the *Voice of the Fugitive* moved to Windsor once it became known that the Great Western Railroad was to terminate there. While the *Voice* reached its peak of subscribers during this time period, editorials in the paper continued to ask the public for support. As with most black newspapers, procuring funding was a constant struggle. Even Frederick Douglass's papers required support from foreign interests and women's groups.

Historian Donald Simpson, with a century of hindsight, has suggested that the "whole struggle over 'the begging system' was a philosophical battle of major importance." He writes:

Most blacks who had self-emancipated to Canada sought autonomy and self-sufficiency and to be let alone. It was difficult then, and it is difficult now, for well meaning whites to grasp the importance of this concept. Some whites through the years moved from the position of doing things "to blacks" to a point of doing things "for blacks." It remained difficult for most, however, to move further to the position of doing things "with blacks" and undertaking projects only if and when they were asked by blacks for assistance.

In 1853, Shadd and Ward announced that they were going to publish the *Provincial Freeman,* also in Windsor. That they would choose to introduce a new paper into a very small marketplace, and to publish it in the same city as the *Voice,* was a clear insult to Bibb.

Bibb and his supporters were outraged and called a protest meeting, where they resolved,

> That as we believe "Union is Strength," and that it is the only way for our elevation, we do not sympathize and have not participated in the discussions, strife, and personal envy that has been fomented by a faction in the village of Windsor, under the cover of opposition to the Refugees' Home Society, and we therefore deprecate and condemn their proceedings as highly injurious to our cause. . . . Resolved, that the *Voice of the Fugitive* was the first standard unfurled on the free soil of Canada, especially devoted to the anti-slavery cause at that trying hour, when the atrocious fugitive slave bill was scattering confusion and dismay over the colored population of the United States. . . . Resolved, That as the *Voice* is not as extensively patronized as its merits demand, there is no necessity for another paper devoted to the interests of the colored people of Canada, and therefore the rival paper about being established to supersede, or divide the interests of the *Voice,* especially as it is the creation of the factionists alluded to above, is unworthy of the support of the well wishers of our race.

Frederick Douglass, still in the fray, was quick to respond. "We think Mr. Bibb and his friends manifest entirely too much sensitiveness and apprehension on account of the proposal to establish a paper in Canada. For our part, we should welcome the establishment of a dozen newspapers in our neighborhood, 'devoted to the interests of the coloured people.' "

For whatever reason, the *Provincial Freeman* did not publish a second issue until its operation was moved to Toronto one year later. Shadd then had her own public platform from which to voice her opinions, but unfortunately her public attacks had created discord among those who sought only to serve the best interests of the fugitives.

Despite the wrangling with Shadd, Bibb was able to publish the *Voice* successfully for three years. "Black views" were presented that had not been allowed in the Canadian white press. Racists like Edwin Larwill could be responded to publicly. Other issues facing black settlers could also get attention: Abolitionism, politics, temperance, education, religion, and the news from the United States all received notice in the *Voice.* And the everyday activities of the settlers were reported as well: Births, deaths, arrival of new fugitives, church activities, women's issues, and women's rights were covered. When William Parker of Christiana resistance fame reached the area, his arrival was covered in the *Voice;* Bibb actually wrote an editorial about him, comparing him to American patriots: "A nobler defense was never made in behalf of liberty on the plains of Lexington, Concord, or Bunker Hill than was put forth by William Parker at Christiana." Advertisements for services and goods of all kinds were also found throughout the paper; many of the ads in the *Voice* were from Detroit businesses, indicating again that blacks on both sides of the Detroit River did not limit themselves to national boundaries.

While the name of the paper, the *Voice of the Fugitive,* seems to indicate Bibb's focus on fugitive slaves emigrating to Canada, the paper covered topics of interest to any new settler. There is some indication, too, that Mary Bibb may have been more involved in the paper than she has been given credit for. Mary was a freeborn black woman, trained in teaching, who had graduated from the Lexington Normal School in Massachusetts. Exactly how much she contributed to the paper is unknown, but it is to be assumed that she took control of the paper during the times when Henry was lecturing throughout the eastern United States. Since she was educated and he, by his own admission, had only three weeks of schooling, it would seem logical that she was very involved in the writing and editing of the articles, if not all the content. Again, because of gender as well as racial constrictions of the day, Mary Bibb is another historical figure who has not received the accolades she deserves. Cooper considers Mary Bibb "the mother of the black press in Canada."

In 1852, at the end of its second year of publication, the *Voice of the Fugitive* was renamed the *Voice of the Fugitive and Canadian Independent,* reflecting, perhaps, Bibb's adoption of Canada as his new home, yet emphasizing that in philosophy, at least, the paper was independent in thought.

In October 1853, in the third year of its publication, the offices of the *Voice of the Fugitive* were burned down; all contents were destroyed as well. In view of the rancorous debate between Shadd and himself, Bibb believed that the fire was the work of an arsonist. It has never been proven who, if anyone, intentionally set the blaze, but white racism could have been at the bottom of it as easily as any detractors from within the black community.

In an attempt to keep the *Voice* alive, Bibb sent out an extra to subscribers and the other black newspapers. In this one-page sheet, he wrote:

> The *Voice of the Fugitive* has been cloven down and partially silenced by the hand of an incendiary, we have reason to believe; and the loss to us has truly been a great one. They have destroyed for us in one night more than all we have accumulated by arduous labor and economy during the last three years. The great question with us now is, not whether we shall suspend the publication of our little sheet or not for the future—for upon this point our mind is fully made up. We shall go forth in the name of outraged humanity, firmly relying on the promises of God and the justice of our cause for success. Our first object in sending forth this Extra sheet is to inform our patrons that the *Voice of the Fugitive and Canadian Independent* is not dead, though crippled, but just as soon as we can repair the breach a little, we assure our readers that the Fugitives in Canada shall be heard from, again, through this paper, regularly.

On August 1, 1854, Henry Bibb died after a brief illness at the age of thirty-nine. Cooper writes, "Bibb rose from obscurity and anonymity to become one of abolition's most well-known and ardent activists. His story was extraordinary. . . ." She notes that his legacy included, "the Refugee Home Society, Canadian Anti-slavery Societies, temperance associations, the Sandwich Baptist Church and, his crowning achievement, the *Voice of the Fugitive.*" His wife of six years, Mary, lived another twenty-three years, continuing to work in the areas of abolitionism and reform.

Word of Bibb's death reached the *Ruby,* a boat filled with Detroit and Canadian area blacks who were cruising the Detroit River in celebration of Emancipation Day. *Frederick Douglass' Paper* related the events:

> The Colored citizens of Detroit being on a pleasure excursion in commemoration of the anniversary of the emancipation of 800,000 human beings from chattel slavery in the British West India Islands, George DeBaptiste, Esq., announced to the assembled company the decease of Henry Bibb, Esq. Which took place at Windsor, C.W., at 3 o'clock this morning, (August 1) and suggested that the excursion party organize themselves into a meeting to express their sentiments in relating to this melancholy event. Where upon, Rev. William C. Monroe was called to the Chair, and J. Theodore Holly was appointed Secretary.

A committee was appointed and resolutions in tribute to Bibb were announced.

> Resolved, That in his death freedom has lost one of its noblest champions, and humanity one of its brightest ornaments.
>
> That we recognize in our deceased companion a true friend and brother, and one who stands among the first on the page of history as the elevator of his race.
>
> That the emancipated bondmen from American slavery, and

the free colored emigrants now in Canada, have lost their chief pillar, and one of their most brilliant advocates.

That to his indefatigable labors is to be chiefly attributed the good repute that Canada and her colored inhabitants are fast gaining all over the world.

That whilst the pleasure of this festive occasion is marred by this melancholy bereavement, yet it was appropriate that such a grand and sublime life, should come to a close on such an eventful day.

That we deeply sympathize with the bereaved widow, disconsolate mother and grief stricken brothers who mourn his loss; but we would comfort them with the recollection of the imperishable legacy that his enduring fame bequeaths to them forever.

After the proceedings, George DeBaptiste, who knew something about working on steamboats, offered thanks to Captain Ward and the officers and crew of the *Ruby* for their good treatment aboard ship. Laura Haviland must have been in Windsor at the time of Bibb's death, as she submitted the following to *Frederick Douglass' Paper:*

Dear Brethern, Josiah Henson, Frederick Douglass, George Carey and Others: In the midst of life we are in death. While we are commemorating the day that disenthralled 800,000, liberates the spirit of one of the most efficient and faithful representatives of nearly 4,000,000 slaves in our United States. The much-lamented Henry Bibb, no more mingles his voice with ours, his faithful pleadings for the enthralled of our land. The slave and his friends have lost a friend, whose melting pathos, in eloquent pleadings for the oppressed, still lives, in the hearts of thousands.

At 3 o'clock this morning, it devolved upon me to perform the sad office of closing his eye in death. No doubt he is now a happy spirit in Heaven. "Blessed are the dead who die in the Lord; yea, saith the spirit, for they do rest from their labors, and their works do follow them."

Mary Bibb did not allow herself to remain in mourning long. Three weeks after Bibb's death, she traveled to the Emigration Convention in Cleveland, Ohio, where Martin Delany acknowledged Henry Bibb's contributions to the abolitionist cause. Mary was elected secretary of the convention, thus remaining active in the abolitionist cause. She continued teaching and later married Isaac Cary, a brother of Mary Ann Shadd Cary's husband, Thomas Cary, making them sisters-in-law. Mary Bibb had no children. She died in the United States in 1877.

Cooper stated: "Though Henry and Mary Bibb, the Michigan abolitionist William King, and others, devised strategies to enable the fugitives to own land, most fugitives went their own way and worked out their destinies themselves, without the aid of 'leaders,' black or white."

Reverend William King established the Elgin Settlement, a free black community in Canada that later came to be known as Buxton. (Photograph courtesy of Western Archives, University of Western Ontario)

Chapter Six

The Elgin Settlement and the Buxton Mission

In 1849, the Reverend William King, accompanied by fifteen former slaves, arrived in Canada West to establish a black settlement. Originally called the Elgin settlement in honor of Lord Elgin, Canada West's governor-general, it became known popularly as Buxton, for Sir Thomas Fowell Buxton, credited with abolishing slavery in the British territories. Of the black settlements in Canada, Buxton can lay claim to being the largest and most successful. Much of the credit for this belongs to the Reverend William King, his leadership skills, and his vision of a "City of God" for fugitive slaves.

King had first set foot on American soil in 1833, in Philadelphia, having been sent from Ireland by his family to sell their potato crop. He was to hold the money from the sale until the rest of the family could emigrate and meet him in New York. From there, they would search for a suitable tract of land to homestead. Like many thousands of other European families during this time, the Kings had been lured to North America by exaggerated promises of cheap and abundant land, covered with lush forests for timber and fertile fields ready for plowing. With

Irish land at a premium, and the economic opportunity created by a small potato crop in America that year, they had decided that the time was right. It was a prescient decision on their part; the next decade would bring a massive potato famine to Ireland.

William had recently graduated from Glasgow University, where he had proven himself a superb classical scholar. Exposed there to the debate of the day, slavery, he began reading the works of pioneering British abolitionists William Wilberforce, Thomas Clarkson, and Thomas Fowell Buxton, and was also inspired by one of his professors to join the Presbyterian Church and become a minister. But his plans for divinity school were put on hold while he helped to settle his family in North America.

King biographer Victor Ullman describes the twenty-year-old émigré William as "just an inch under six feet, broad-shouldered and heavily muscled." King's sisters called him "a boy always sure in stride and motions, a self-reliant and efficient youngster, and even at the age of twenty, ready to assume leadership and to assert it most pragmatically." When he arrived in America, Andrew Jackson had just been reelected president and the era of the common man and the opening of the western frontier were being celebrated. As Ullman tells it, the first sound King heard upon reaching shore was the pealing of the Liberty Bell, followed by the music of a brass band and military drums, part of a parade in honor of the new president. The symbol of the Liberty Bell would be associated with King throughout his life.

He successfully sold the potato crop and moved on to meet his family, arriving in New York in September 1833, just in time to hear the news that Sir Thomas Fowell Buxton had finally succeeded in passing his emancipation bill, abolishing slavery in all British-held lands.

While King's family waited in New York for winter weather to abate, William took the new Mohawk and Hudson Railroad and the Erie Canal across New York to visit a classmate in Ohio. There he went on a land hunt, and eventually he and his brother John agreed upon a tract near Delta, Ohio, in an area called Six Mile Woods. The family purchased 640 acres and began clearing the land for crops. After a year of hard work helping to settle his family, William felt it was time to move on with his own plans; he decided to stay in the United States and teach for several years before returning to Scotland for divinity school.

A classmate from Glasgow offered him a teaching position in Alabama, but the weather did not allow for direct southern travel. He made a detour that changed his plans altogether, arriving in Natchez, Mississippi, amid rumors of slave uprisings incited by northern whites (southerners were still haunted by memories of the Nat Turner uprising in 1831). King declined an offer to stay in Natchez, preferring to move on to Louisiana, where he accepted a job instructing the children of three plantation families. Although he never lied about his abolitionist beliefs, his success in teaching and disciplining the spoiled young men he encountered resulted in the personal friendship and professional support of many influential southern businessmen and wealthy planters, who would aid him in future years.

In 1841, King met and married Mary Mourning Phares, a southern woman who brought two slaves to the marriage as part of her dowry. At that time, the law decreed that, upon marriage, property owned by the wife became the property of the husband. Now the reluctant owner of two slaves, King was conflicted about his situation, but only after the birth of his son, Theophilus, did he begin to admit to himself that it was wrong. In his autobiography, handwritten just years before his death, King wrote: "There was black before me. My boy was now nearly two years and I wished to remove him from the South before he was incapable of knowing between right and wrong. . . . To raise a family of boys under such corrupting influences was almost sure to corrupt their moral principles and ruin them for the life that now is and that which is to come. This danger I could not conceal from my wife who saw it as well as I did."

King continued to gain respect due to his educational prowess. In 1842, he became the rector of Mathews Academy, where his reputation resulted in a dramatic increase in the school's population, and he soon found himself in need of help. He attempted to hire reliable servants, but they all proved untrustworthy, and after trying to employ a slave named Talbert from another owner and being refused, King was finally convinced that he had no recourse but to purchase him. Actually, Talbert, having heard about King's antislavery views, had first approached King about the position. He also wanted to learn to read and write and felt that an opportunity had presented itself.

King realized that he was becoming more and more entrapped. While he wanted to emancipate his slaves, he could not find the way to do so; besides pressure from other slave owners, there were the moral implications of freeing slaves who had nowhere to go and no skills to live by. He and Mary agreed that it was time for him to attend divinity school, get his degree, become a minister, and then return home and find a way to emancipate his slaves. King's father-in-law, considering it unwise for him to drag his wife and son to Scotland, where they knew no one, suggested that King purchase land near his own so that Mary and the child could remain near family in Louisiana until his return. King consented. Unfortunately, as was common, with the purchase of land came slaves, in this case two women and their two children. Before he left for school, King felt compelled to purchase Jacob, another male slave, to help Talbert run the new farm while he was gone. When King set sail for Scotland in 1843, he was a married man with one child and eight slaves, about to enter the New College of the Free Church of Scotland, which was defiantly against slavery.

The school was then under the leadership of Dr. Thomas W. Chalmers, the first moderator of the Free Church of Scotland, whose denomination was Presbyterian. Chalmers was a man dedicated to social reform and charitable work on behalf of the poor. He believed in acting upon one's faith, and envisioned creating a "City of God," a ministry that combined religion and education as two essential elements. His application of this vision to a slum in Edinburgh provided the model and inspiration for King's life work.

The West Port area of Edinburgh was filled with Irish immigrants fleeing the potato famine. Unemployment, overcrowding, and poverty were rampant. King was one of twenty-four students chosen by Chalmers to initiate the mission there. Through their close contact and shared values, Chalmers became not just a teacher to King but also a mentor and lifelong friend. It was through him that King was introduced to the leading philosophers and theologians of the day, including Dr. Lyman Beecher, father of Harriet Beecher Stowe.

After the first year of school, King returned to Louisiana to get his wife and son, but he decided to introduce them to his family in Ohio before returning again to Scotland. En route to Ohio, his son died. Mary also fell ill but regained her health enough to make the trip to Edinburgh. Shortly after their arrival, she gave birth to a daughter, Johanna Elizabeth, but within the year, both Mary and Johanna died, as well. King, now alone, turned his full attention to Chalmers, his work in the slums of West Port, and his faith.

During his time at divinity school, King was almost able to forget that he was a slaveholder. But in 1845, at an abolitionist meeting, he received a harsh reminder in a personal rebuke from none other than Frederick Douglass, recently self-emancipated, whose friends had sent him to Europe to avoid the slave catchers. "The delegation from the United States," King remembered, "had by some means learned that I was a slave owner and was studying in the Free Church for a minister. . . . I was not named but the students all knew that I came from a slave state and that my wife was the daughter of a planter. . . . [I] was advised to say nothing about my [position]."

King wanted to admit his ownership to the church body, but Chalmers advised him that it was sinful to own slaves "if the master did not set his slaves free as the opportunity presented itself." After struggling with his options, weighing them in the context of what he was seeing with his work in the West Port slums, King came to the conclusion that emancipating his slaves would not be enough, that he must also provide them with the skills and education needed to live free. Embracing Chalmers's ideas, he began envisioning his own City of God.

Upon graduating from divinity school, King requested mission work in Canada, having decided that his City of God would be established in a country that had already abolished slavery, where he could set his slaves free and personally provide the religious instruction and education necessary to ensure their successful transition to free citizens.

But first he had to return to take care of his affairs in Louisiana; his father-in-law had recently died, leaving him with many property entanglements. King soon realized that he could not just sell his slaves outright, for the sale might attract attention. If the Presbyterian Church knew he was a slave owner, he might be barred from the ministry. For the time being, he chose to leave his slaves on his land, pay his debts, and move to Canada to begin his ministry. He was assigned to the St. Andrew's Presbyterian Church in Chatham, and began preaching there as well as in Dawn and other Canada West communities. His efforts allowed him to become intimately involved with the black settlements and settlers throughout the area; working among these new freedmen convinced him of the direction he needed to take.

In 1847, King admitted to the Presbyterian Synod that he was a slave owner. While the church members admired and respected him, they felt that under the circumstances they could not let him remain in the ministry, and fired him for lying. Undeterred, King now felt free to proceed to Louisiana and commence plans for emancipating his slaves. He explained later:

> I told them that in two weeks I was going to leave for Canada and would take them with me. The journey was long and I wished them to be ready by that time. They seemed not to understand what was meant by going to Canada. Most of them thought it was some new plantation I had purchased and was going to take them to it. I then explained to them that Canada was a free country, that there were no slaves there, and that when we reached that country I would give them their freedom and place them on farms where they would have to support themselves by their own industry. Until I was ready to start they would have a holiday to visit their friends and to prepare for the journey. . . . The good news seemed to have little effect upon them. They had come to consider that slavery was their normal condition. They did not know what freedom meant. They thought that to be free was to be like their master, to go idle, and have a good time.

One of the slaves, a woman named Harriet, convinced him to purchase her four-year-old son, Solomon, after which King and his group of
fifteen made their way to New Orleans and set sail for Ohio. Upon reaching Cincinnati, he offered the slaves their freedom, explaining that they
were now in a free state. He gave them the option of leaving or continuing
on with him to his family's farm near Delta. They chose to follow him.
Entrusting them to his family, King went to Canada to find land for a settlement.

Word of his actions in leading his slaves to freedom had preceded
him, apparently first reported by the captain of the steamship that had
taken them north from New Orleans. It must have been an unusual sight,
one white man directing fifteen unfettered blacks along the long journey.
Building on his appointed status as a "Moses" leading his people to the
Promised Land, and with the synod now hailing him as a hero, King set
forth his ideas in a treatise called the "King Memorial to the Presbyterian
Synod":

> I believed that these persons who had escaped from slavery, when
> placed in favorable circumstances, were able and willing to support
> themselves and to become respectable members of society and to ac-
> complish that I believed it was necessary to provide them with
> homes where the parents could support themselves by their own in-
> dustry and [provide] their children with the blessings of a Christian
> education. Three things were necessary for that end: land, to place
> the families upon; a church where they could assemble on the Sab-
> bath and hear the gospel; and a day school where the children could
> receive a good Christian education.

King proposed a purchase of two hundred acres to begin the settlement. He stated his belief that this City of God could eventually be a
model for other denominations to appropriate and take to Africa, striking
slavery at its heart. The synod responded positively, if not exactly the
way King had asked. They made what in hindsight was a very wise decision about their support, deciding not to undertake the project them-

selves, but to create an association called the Elgin Association (again named after Lord Elgin) "for the purpose of obtaining subscriptions" to buy land for a settlement for not just King's slaves but for any fugitives reaching Canada. Unlike the other black settlements, which had been built with handouts from wherever the leaders could solicit support, this one was established by obtaining broad-based support up front and thus the first Canadian project on behalf of blacks in Canada's history was created.

A committee incorporating many of the Presbyterian clergy as well as prominent white and black Canadian businessmen was established. King found a nine-thousand-acre tract in Raleigh Township, about fifteen miles east of Chatham and fifty miles north of Windsor. The land was heavily forested and bordered Lake Erie; he thought it would be perfect for the settlement, and wrote his "Prospectus of a Scheme for the Social and Moral Improvement of the Coloured People of Canada." Committee members endorsed the plan and within two months all the stock was sold. King proceeded with his plans to purchase the land, but not before encountering backlash from the local white community, led by Edwin Larwill, editor of the *Chatham Journal*, who had already made his racial views public with attempts to deny aid to black schools. Larwill was not unique in his prejudice against blacks. Despite the legal insurance of freedom given by the British government, most Canadians displayed the same prejudice that most Americans did. The plans for the Buxton settlement seemed to bring this prevailing opposition together under Larwill's direction. He now turned his attention to King's proposed settlement, initiating a petition campaign to stop the land purchase. The petition claimed in part that "the Negro is a distinct species of the Human Family and, in the opinion of your Memorialists, is far inferior to that of the European. Let each link in the great Scale of existence have its place. Amalgamation is as disgusting to the Eye, as it is immoral in its tendencies and all good men will discountenance it."

King was not frightened by Larwill's petition or his implied threats. On several occasions, he publicly stood his ground when confronted. Also, unbeknownst to him, black settlers who feared for his safety would go on "hunting parties" in order to guard him, hiding in the woods and following him to and from his meetings in Chatham. By standing up to Larwill, King earned the respect of more and more white settlers, and thus gained more support for his efforts on behalf of the fugitives. In one last effort to thwart the settlement, Larwill petitioned the government, requesting that "all Negroes be barred from public office and public schools, they be forced to pay a poll tax and they be required to post bond to remain in Canada." It seemed as if he was getting desperate. King ignored the public debate and went on with his work.

The Presbyterian Church of Canada, while deciding not to be economically responsible for the settlement itself, did decide to support a school and church in the Elgin settlement, naming it the Buxton Mission. In 1849, after the land had been purchased, King returned to Ohio, gathered his fifteen former slaves, and led them to the new settlement. They were surprised to find out they were not the first to arrive. Larwill's antics had created headline publicity in both Canada and the United States, attracting the attention of other fugitives who had already found their way to Canada. Awaiting King and his group upon their arrival were Isaac Riley, his wife, Catherine, and their four children, Addison, John, Jerome, and James, who had escaped slavery in Missouri and made their way to St. Catharines. Isaac, who was literate, had read about Buxton and, learning that it was to have a school, decided to move his family to take advantage of it. They were waiting in King's barn when he arrived.

The Elgin Association had divided the land into fifty-acre lots. Settlers were required to purchase at least this amount, at the cost of $2.50 per acre. A down payment of $12.50 had to be paid within a year; the balance was to be paid in nine equal installments at 6 percent interest. Land could not be rented out until paid for. For the first ten years, land could be purchased only by blacks. King established very strict housing standards, which residents were required to adhere to in order to live in the settlement: Each house had to have no fewer than four rooms, and be "at least 24 feet by 18 feet with the roof at least 12 feet high," and had to be "33 feet from the road," with a picket fence and a garden "that must include flowers." Along the driveways, there had to be large side porches, and in front of each house the road had to be cleared and a drainage ditch dug to clear the land of its swampy conditions.

During the time—more than a year—that King's former slaves had lived on his family's farm in Ohio, they had learned to farm, preserve food, and cut down trees, and had been taught to read and write. These skills would prove critical for their new lives. As Ullman mentions, "Their period of indoctrination into the farming ways of the North and Christian education was to prove invaluable in the early years of the Buxton settlement. They set a pattern of industry and avid desire for learning and religion, which was exactly the example King required. They were the nucleus establishing the character of the colony for all the fugitives who were to arrive in Buxton."

While King required much from the new settlers, he required the same of himself and served as the role model for the community, advocating hard work, temperance, and faith. Within the first year, forty-five families had settled in Buxton, and even more had purchased land surrounding the Elgin settlement. After five years, there were more than 150 families living there. Many had already paid off their mortgages, having earned good wages while working for the new Great Western Railroad, then making its way into Canada West.

Word of the new black settlement spread. Throughout its two-decade history, Buxton attracted many visitors, black and white, who wrote about what they observed there. Most of it was positive.

In 1853, Samuel Ringgold Ward toured Canada West on behalf of the Anti-Slavery Society of Canada. The *Provincial Freeman* published his report:

> Buxton, in more points than one, is the model settlement, not only of the colored people, but of Canada. . . . the efforts of those settlers to educate themselves and their children are most praiseworthy. In the day school you find both children and adults, in some instances, parents and children, earnestly intent upon the acquisition of

knowledge. The evening school is attended by parties who walk miles through the forest by torch-light, but they are determined. . . .

In 1854, Benjamin Drew visited and recorded his observations:

The settlers at Buxton are characterized by a manly, independent air and manner. Most of them came into the province stripped of every thing but life. They have purchased homes for themselves, paid the price demanded by the government, erected their own buildings and supported their own families by their own industry; receiving no aid whatever from any benevolent society, but carefully excluding donations of any kind from coming into the settlement. Mr. King having full faith in the natural powers, capacity, and capabilities of the African race, is practically working out his belief, by placing the refugees in circumstances where they may learn self-reliance, and maintain a perfect independence of aid: trusting, under God, on their own right arm.

King's efforts, under the auspices of the Elgin Association, to provide the opportunity for equality and self-sufficiency made moot the whole begging issue. Blacks were in charge of creating their own destinies.

It was not long before the settlers began making money selling their biggest crop, lumber, including oak, hickory, and maple that grew on their land. With the success of the timber industry came other economic opportunities. To get their timber ready for market, a sawmill was needed. Two Canadian businessmen, Henry K. Thomas and Wilson R. Abbott, offered to solicit funds for the endeavor. Thomas had been born enslaved but had escaped and moved to Buffalo, where he had a thriving barbershop; he'd come to Buxton when he no longer felt safe in the United States. Wilson R. Abbott, who had been born free in Virginia, moved to Toronto and became one of the wealthiest blacks in the city, but moved to Buxton to obtain a Christian education for his children. Thomas and Abbott tapped the resources of their wealthy friends in order to raise money, but the project became much larger than originally envisioned. The Canada Mill and Mercantile Association was soon established, its stated purpose to "unite ourselves together in order to establish a sawmill, a grist mill and a good country store, believing that this is the only way for us to become independent and respectable in business transactions." The building of many of the structures was accomplished using the settlers' brick-making skills. Before long, brick making also became a lucrative endeavor for the community, as there was no other such industry in the area. Ullman notes that there "was now a boom in the settlement, getting logs out for the saw mill, clearing land, logging and burning the wood to get ashes to make black salts for the pearl ash factory. . . . [Pearl ash gained from the burning of wood was valuable for making soap and glass, and for washing wool.] The brick yard was also carried on; lumber and brick could now be obtained in the settlement for building purposes, and improvements now began to appear of a more permanent character."

The settlement was becoming self-sustaining and the settlers self-reliant. By 1856, Buxton boasted a two-story hotel, a shoe shop, a savings bank, a post office, and carpenter and blacksmith stores, all located within a central area of the community known as Buxton Square. Buxton's economic success soon brought new privileges. After three years, many of its settlers met the requirements for voting as naturalized citizens. The law stated that voters must own or rent property worth at least twenty dollars, have lived in Canada West for three years, and be at least twenty-one years of age.

It didn't take long for King and the Buxton settlers to use this new political power on their own behalf. Edwin Larwill had become a member of Parliament and was still publicly attacking King and the settlement. But many of Larwill's supporters, having watched the progress of Buxton and having had positive interactions with its settlers through commerce, church, and school, were now opposing his racist views. In 1856, Archibald McKellar, a former Larwill defender and now a Buxton supporter, decided to run against him. In a dramatic show of community support, three hundred eligible male voters from Buxton walked en masse over fifteen miles to Chatham, the nearest polling place, to vote in a bloc for McKellar. Their votes helped unseat Larwill and enabled McKellar to win.

Local Buxton resident and historian Arlie Robbins imagined the voting scene in her 1983 book, *Legacy to Buxton:*

What a day it must have been. Did it rain or did the sun shine? It didn't matter. Was it rough or smooth underfoot? It didn't matter. Were they jeered or were they cheered? It didn't matter. Were they hungry? Thirsty? Tired? It didn't matter. Did these former slaves, as they marched the long miles to Chatham, perhaps remember their former mistresses in the south who were still denied this privilege? That too didn't matter now for it was a glorious and memorable day—one that they would remember with a thrill of pride and joy to the end of their lives. For from that time on the demonstrated political clout of Canada's black citizens would become a recognized factor in Canadian politics. And Buxton's children would talk about "that day the old folks marched to Chatham to vote" for years to come.

Only three short years later, Buxton elected one of their own to represent them. Abraham Shadd, Mary Ann's father, had made his home on the outskirts of the Buxton settlement. In 1859, he was elected to the Raleigh Town Council, the only black to win elective office in Canada West until after the Civil War.

Under King's guidance, the community decided not to accept any outside help, in order to separate themselves from the issue of "begging" that existed in the other settlements. He had convinced them that in order to achieve independence and gain self-respect, they should not depend on others. King later wrote that he'd wanted Buxton to be self-supporting to show "that coloured men, when placed in favorable circumstances, could support themselves and their families as well as the white settlers."

When Boston's Anti-Slavery Society sent boxes of clothing, a meeting was held to discuss whether to accept them. After voting to "accept the gift in the spirit in which it was intended," the settlers wrote in response: "We wish the people in the United States to know that there is one portion of Canada West where the colored people are self-supporting and they wish them to send neither petticoats nor pantaloons to the county of Kent. . . . The few cases of real want which arise from sickness or old age can with a trifling effort be relieved here without making it a pretext for a system of wholesale begging in the United States."

King continued to stress the importance of not accepting outside help for individuals but did accept books and maps for the church and school. And the Buxton citizens made one more exception about accepting outside help. In 1850, King was invited to tour Pennsylvania on behalf of the settlement. Dr. Robert Burns, a member of the Elgin Association board and moderator of the Presbyterian Assembly, accompanied him. The invitation came as a result of positive articles written about Buxton by Martin Delany, then an editor at the *North Star*. King's lectures, sometimes six in one day, took place over a period of three weeks and drew the attention of many other abolitionists. William Lloyd Garrison spread word of the Buxton mission in the *Liberator*. Ullman notes that word also reached Harriet Beecher Stowe, who was working on *Uncle Tom's Cabin*, and who invited King to visit her in Maine. She must have been impressed, as she later used him as the model for the main character in *Dred: A Tale of the Great Swamp*, who is a man named Edward Clayton, "a white who lived on a tidy little exiled farm in the Canadian wilderness." In anticipation of the same sort of backlash she received after publication of *Uncle Tom's Cabin*, this time Stowe provided documentation for her characters, stating that what she had written was "all true of the Elgin settlement, founded by Mr. King."

When King and Burns returned to Buxton, a gift arrived from the free black citizens of Pittsburgh to the newly freed citizen of Buxton, a "Liberty" bell cast by A. Fulton of Pittsburgh and engraved with the inscription "Presented to Rev. Wm. King by the coloured inhabitants of Pittsburgh, for the Academy at Raleigh C. West." An accompanying letter read:

You are now in a land of liberty where the rights and privileges of freemen are secured to you by law. Your future position in society will depend very much on your own exertions. We sincerely hope that by your industry and good conduct you will put to silence those who speak evil of you, and show yourselves worthy of the respect and confidence of the members of the "Elgin Association," who have nobly advocated your cause. . . . We feel a deep interest both in your temporal and spiritual welfare. As a lasting memorial of our kindness, we send to the Rev. Wm. King, a Bell for the Academy, that when we shall be mouldering in our coffins, will call your children to the house of instruction. While your children are brought up under the blessings of a Christian education, we trust that in the land of your adoption you will not forget the God of your fathers. . . .

The bell rang at six in the morning and nine at night. Arlie Robbins notes that it "was erected immediately and the very next Sunday rang out its first call to worship. . . . [It] was rung for every new arrival thereafter [and] . . . still hangs in the steeple of the church [St. Andrew's] and still sends its deep-toned message across the fields of Raleigh, Canada West."

A letter of thanks was sent by the Buxton community, written by Isaac Riley and William Jackson, men who had been enslaved just two years prior.

To the Colored Inhabitants of Pittsburgh Dear Brethren:

We have received your letter dated the 23rd Nov., and the bell presented to the Rev. W. King for the Academy at Raleigh. We are delighted at all times to hear from the friends that we have left in a land of pretended freedom, and although separated in body, we are present with you in spirit; and we fondly hope that our prayers often meet before the throne of God for mutual blessings. We will endeavor to observe and practice the advice, which you have kindly given us, by loving and serving God and obeying the laws of our Sov-

ereign. We will not cease to implore the Divine Blessing on that Government which has given us liberty not only in name but in reality.
The bell has been raised to the place erected for it; by its joyful peals
inviting us to the house of God. We would return to you our sincere
thanks for this memorial of your kindness, and we trust that while its
cheerful peal invites us to the house of prayer, we will then remember
our brethren who are in less favorable circumstances; and our constant prayer will be that the Bible, the gift of God to man, may no
longer be withheld from you by the unrighteous acts of professed
Christian legislators; that the power of the oppressor may be broken,
and that those who have long been held in bondage may be set free.

In 1854, Frederick Douglass visited Buxton and was moved to state
that it was "one of the most striking, convincing, and gratifying" pieces
of evidence that black men, "can live, and live well, without a master,
and can be industrious without the presence of the blood-letting lash to
urge [them] on to toil." He also offered a public apology to King in front
of the St. Andrew's congregation for the remarks he had directed at him
in Edinburgh in 1845. According to Ullman, upon his return home
Douglass printed the apology in the *North Star* and sent a copy to King's
former Presbyterian church in Scotland, in order to exonerate him and
publicly voice his support of him and the Buxton settlement.

Much of Buxton's success can be credited to the educational model
King adopted. Unlike those of Dawn and Wilberforce, which had been
based on a vocational school model, training new refugees in the trades
and domestic arts, Buxton's schools used a classical education model,
with the teaching of Greek and Latin in addition to math, reading, and
writing in preparation for college entrance. King believed that to teach
only the trades would be a "tacit admission that Negroes were to be forever condemned to work of the hands, that work of the mind and spirit
was beyond their potentiality." He had heard these arguments about the
capabilities of blacks before, in the slavocracy of the South as well as the
slums in Edinburgh. He did not believe them and was determined to
prove them untrue. Ullman explains: "[King] believed that his own 'City

of God' was to be a demonstration of the intellectual as well as the economic capacities of the Negroes. With their own land, they were freed from economic bondage. With their own church, they were freed from spiritual poverty. With equal intellectual opportunity, they would be completely free."

King's faith in the capabilities of the new freedmen was revolutionary for the time, and though not everyone in Buxton became classical scholars, many did. He was eager to display their success. Visitors to the settlement were astounded when ten-year-old Jerome Riley recited excerpts from Virgil's *Aeneid* in Latin and afterward translated the text into English and interpreted it for his audience. It was also not uncommon to hear recitations of the catechism memorized by the young students.

Word of the success of the Buxton schools spread quickly. John Scoble, who had been sent by the British and Foreign Anti-Slavery Society to the British American Institute in Dawn to save the scandal-ridden school, visited Buxton and reported his findings to the Canadian Anti-Slavery Society:

> I am not the advocate for exclusively coloured schools; I believe that one mode of breaking down the prejudice which exists against colour will be educating the children of all complexions together. An important fact came to my attention at Buxton, which illustrates this point. At this interesting settlement an excellent school was opened by the Rev. Mr. King, at which superior education was imparted, and the result was that the white school in the neighborhood was given up, and the children transferred to the coloured school where I had the pleasure of seeing them distributed through the various classes, without distinction, and found that they studied harmoniously together.

If the Buxton schools were not the first in Canada to be integrated, they were certainly among the first to succeed in this egalitarian endeavor. Integration was not accomplished through legislation, but through excellent educational opportunities.

Though King had begun the Buxton Mission with the backing of the Presbyterian Church, he was not so naïve as to think that all the settlers would be comfortable with his approach to religion. He recognized that many had grown up in more expressive Baptist or Methodist settings. In order to support continued religious involvement by the newly arriving settlers, he and members of St. Andrew's helped erect three Baptist churches and an African Methodist Episcopal church in the community.

Buxton shared its success with neighboring communities. Its schools were open to students from all over Canada and the United States, and attracted both black and white pupils desiring the quality of education offered. Also, besides building churches for various denominations, Buxton provided needed business services, overcoming the prejudice fostered by whites such as Larwill simply by being successful.

In 1856, the Buxton community held a celebration, with speakers from Toronto and guests from England, including the future Earl Spencer and John Probyn, a member of the British House of Commons. Over a thousand Buxton settlers hosted the same number of white guests, most of them from nearby Chatham. Ullman describes the scene:

> The guests sat crowded into a pavilion made of lumber from Buxton's own sawmill. It was 120 feet long, covering the entire lawn in front of St. Andrews [sic] Church, was 14 feet deep and was shielded from the sun by an arbored ceiling 12 feet high. There were flowers everywhere, from Buxton's gardens, on the long trestle table and on the tables hurriedly set up on the lawn to accommodate the overflow. Flowering climbers grew high on the church walls, following ropes produced in Buxton's own rope-walk.
>
> They dined on venison and wild turkey, both hunted in Buxton's own forests. They also had a choice of beef, mutton, and pork from Buxton's own herds and drank milk from Buxton's two hundred milk cows. They ate bread baked from flour ground in Buxton's own gristmill out of wheat raised on the one thousand acres of land cleared and under cultivation only seven years after the first Negroes

arrived. The vegetables came from approximately two hundred front yard gardens of two hundred homes in Buxton.

Ideas of self-reliance were applied to self-government as well. A "court of arbitration" was established early on in the settlement to handle disagreements. When elections for its five-member board were held, King declared himself ineligible, believing blacks should govern themselves and their community. Throughout the following years, this court became the governing body of the settlement, taking over responsibility for the well-being of new fugitives and fielding complaints as well as organizing celebrations. On one occasion, the court took on the issue of profanity, which became a moot point when the man in question, an Irishman working on the railroad, moved out of the area. The issue of liquor was also decided by the community. King had seen the damage done when liquor became a part of the lives of poor people and had established that the Elgin lands were to be liquor-free. However, a man from outside the community opened a grocery store on the outskirts of the Elgin property, initially selling liquor as well as groceries. Settlers basically boycotted the man's store until he quit selling liquor, at which time they once again became customers. No temperance society was necessary to regulate drinking. Community-instilled values did not require any external pressure. To this day, liquor has never been sold in Buxton.

Another example of learning independence came with the establishment of the savings bank. Again, there was no requirement that the settlers use the bank, but handling their newly earned money became a badge of honor among them. The bank was open every Tuesday and Friday evening from six to seven o'clock. Again, the settlers themselves were the bank trustees. King might have established the bank's rules, based on well-known banking regulations found successful elsewhere, but he turned its management over to the settlers themselves.

Nor did he limit his efforts to those fugitives who found their way to Buxton. On several occasions, King became an "emergency" Underground Railroad conductor. Certainly he had knowledge of the people and stations of the Railroad, as many of the Buxton settlers had made their way to Buxton by following its routes. Once, when King was riding a train back to Canada after a lecture tour in the States, a white man escorted a young black man aboard and seated him next to King. The young man, an escaping slave, was given a ticket and instructed to act as King's manservant. The ruse succeeded, in part because King's intuition told him to get off the train they were on and catch a different one into Canada before they could be stopped and questioned. King also aided a man named Shadrach in his quest to return to the South, find his wife and children, and return with them to Buxton, where he had already settled.

King used his good judgment when it came to giving his support to causes he felt were not in the best interest of the Buxton-area settlers. He was not invited to John Brown's Chatham convention, but he certainly knew what was going on, since Buxton men—Abraham Shadd, Ezekiel Cooper, William Howard Day, and Thomas Stringer—had all attended the convention. King also knew that at least one meeting had been held at Abraham Shadd's home in Buxton, but he had the foresight to see that Brown's plan would not work.

At a West Indian Emancipation Day celebration on August 2, 1858, King revealed his sentiments: "A spirit of uneasiness is manifesting itself. The fugitive slave bill, the Dred Scott decision and the Kansas aggressions are the symptoms of an incurable disease. . . . Hate and a festering sense of undeserved injury, prompting to revenge, together with a despair of attaining to its end by lawful means, will goad on to some lawless, desperate act of wide-spread rebellion, in which the planter and his property will perish together."

Ullman, claiming King's influence, states: "It was Dr. Martin R. Delany, a Negro, who made the famous Constitutional Convention in Chatham possible on May 8–10, 1858. It was Rev. William King, a white man, who made the invasion of Virginia by Canadian ex-slaves impossible in October, 1859."

King and Delany would later join forces with a plan to attack slavery in Africa. According to Ullman, "King believed that slavery would be

ended by ending the African slave trade. . . . Delany believed that slavery might be ended by creation of a black Israel in Africa."

At the time Delany was proceeding with his Niger Valley expedition
in the hope of creating a black settlement, King was preparing missionaries for the foundation work. Historian Donald Simpson, writing that
"the backbone of the team was to come from the Buxton boys who had
graduated from college," describes their joint effort: "It was to be an international peace corps which would send a cadre of specially trained
young blacks from North America to assist the natives in establishing viable Christian colonies. The hope was that the black emigrants would be
able to teach the Africans some techniques of self-help and some new
agricultural procedures that would allow them to find greater profits in
cotton and sugar than they would in supplying slaves to the European
slavers. Slavery was to be destroyed at its source." But the dream Delany
and King shared was never realized. The date set for the expedition was
June 1861. In April of that year, the Civil War began.

Dramatic stories of slavery, escape, and survival could have been told by
any of the early Buxton settlers. But it was William Parker who came to
epitomize militant black resistance in the years following the 1850 Fugitive Slave Act. His description of the Christiana resistance, narrated in
his two-part autobiography, stands with Osborne Anderson's record of
the events at Harpers Ferry as an important eyewitness account told by a
black participant.

In 1851, William and his wife, Eliza Parker, formerly enslaved, were
living in Christiana, Pennsylvania, where they rented a two-story brick
home from Levi Pownell, a Quaker. Eliza's sister Hannah and her husband, Alexander Pinckney, lived there with them. The men ran a horse-
drawn threshing machine. Pennsylvania's shared border with the slave
state of Maryland created many problems for both free blacks as well as
fugitives. Kidnappings were frequent. Parker described them as so common "that we were kept in constant fear. We would hear of slaveholders
or kidnappers every two or three weeks; sometimes a party of white men

would break into a house and take a man away, no one knew where; and again, a whole family would be carried off. There was no power to protect them, nor prevent it."

Just before dawn on the foggy Thursday morning of September 11, 1851, Edwin Gorsuch, a Maryland slave owner, approached the Parker house, accompanied by a posse of eight armed with guns and a search warrant. Gorsuch and his men had first traveled to Philadelphia to have the U.S. commissioner there swear out the warrant. The 1850 Fugitive Slave Act gave him the legal right to take possession of four slaves, George Hammond, Noah Buley, Nelson Ford, and Joshua Hammond, who had escaped from his farm in Maryland over a year before. He'd had word that the four had been sighted at the Parker residence in Christiana, Pennsylvania. A mere forty miles separated Gorsuch's slaveholding plantation in Maryland from Parker's residence in the free state of Pennsylvania. The free blacks and fugitives who reached the area were well aware of the danger they faced living so close to a slave state. But Parker and his friends had taken steps to protect themselves by establishing their own self-defense organization. They were prepared to stand their ground and fight for their freedom if need be. In his memoir, Parker wrote, "[We] formed an organization of mutual protection against slaveholders and kidnappers. [We] resolved to prevent any of our brethren being taken back into slavery, at the risk of our own lives." Parker further defended his stance on self-defense in view of the prevalence of slavery and the violence perpetrated against blacks: "The frequent attacks from slaveholders and their tools, the peculiarity of our position, many being escaped slaves, and the secrecy attending these kidnapping exploits, all combined to make an appeal to the Lynch Code in our case excusable, if not altogether justifiable. Ourselves, our wives, our little ones, were insecure, and all we had was liable to seizure."

Unbeknownst to Gorsuch, a tavern owner named Samuel Williams, a member of William Still's Philadelphia Vigilance Committee, was watching him closely. After getting the specifics, Williams left to warn the Parker household. Logistical problems getting the posse together resulted in a day's delay in Gorsuch's attempt to serve the warrant.

Williams reached the Parkers and other blacks in the area in time to warn them.

Much of what is known about the incident comes from Parker's written account. The warning brought by Williams "spread through the vicinity like a fire in the prairies." Besides the Parkers and Pinckneys, a friend, Abraham Johnson, and two of the fugitives slept at the Parker home the night of September 10. They had expected the raid to occur that night, but when it didn't, one of the fugitives left early the next morning to go to work. Meeting the posse at the end of the lane, he recognized Gorsuch and went running back to the house and up the stairs, screaming that the kidnappers had arrived and, in his haste, leaving the front door open. Gorsuch, with Deputy Marshal Henry H. Kline, who was notorious for his slave-catching activities and who had been directed to head the posse, followed him into the house, where they encountered William Parker standing at the top of the stairs. Parker began bantering with the posse below him. Gorsuch wanted to climb the stairs and take the fugitives, telling the marshal that he wanted to go up and "claim his property," a refrain he would use many times during the encounter. The sound of guns being loaded upstairs could be heard. As Gorsuch began climbing, someone from upstairs threw something at him. Marshal Kline read the warrant and demanded that the group surrender. While Gorsuch kept talking about his "property," the marshal threatened to burn the house down. Parker replied, "You can burn us, but you can't take us; before I give up, you will see my ashes scattered on the earth."

Eliza had climbed to the roof and began blowing a horn. "It was a custom with us," Parker wrote, "when a horn was blown at an unusual hour, to proceed to the spot promptly to see what was the matter." Eliza continued to blow the horn, despite the fact that the posse began firing shots at her. Gunshots were exchanged; one of them grazed Gorsuch. There are differing stories as to who fired first.

Gorsuch and Parker bandied back and forth, each quoting Scripture. "Where do you see it in Scripture, that a man should traffic in his brother's blood?" Parker asked. "Do you call a nigger my brother?" Gorsuch asked in return. "Yes," Parker replied. The stalemate continued.

It was then about seven in the morning. A large number of white men had begun appearing from all directions, and the marshal was deputizing as many as he could. In the house, Pinckney and his wife, Hannah, wanted to surrender. Parker told his brother-in-law that if he tried to, he would have to "blow out his brains." "Don't believe that any living man can take you," he said. "Don't give up to any slaveholder." Eliza Parker, angry at the weakness of her sister who also wanted to surrender, "seized a corn-cutter, and declared she would cut off the head of the first one who should attempt to give up." Johnson stood his ground, declaring, "I will fight till I die."

The commotion was now drawing the attention of their neighbors. Elijah Lewis, a Quaker storekeeper and the local postmaster, had been told that kidnappers were at the Parkers'. He and Castner Hanway, another local Quaker, arrived at the Parkers' about the same time that some armed blacks were also arriving. Another of Gorsuch's fugitives was in the group. A cheer went out from the house. The Gorsuch group thought the blacks were cheering the arrival of white sympathizers, when in actuality they were cheering the arrival of more blacks. Depending on who later told the story, the numbers of blacks and whites who responded varied. Most accounts state that fifteen to twenty-five blacks were involved in the incident.

Marshal Kline showed the warrants to Lewis and Hanway and asked them to assist him. He had every right to believe that they would do as the Fugitive Slave Law required them to do, and was surprised when they both refused, on the grounds that "the colored people had a right to defend themselves."

While they were talking, Parker had come downstairs and continued to verbally confront Gorsuch. Again, there are disagreements over what transpired next. Shots were fired from both sides. According to Parker, one of Gorsuch's slaves "struck him the first and second blows; then three or four sprang upon him, and when he became helpless left him to pursue others. *The women put an end to him.*" (The italics are Parker's, in his original autobiography. It is not stated what actions they took.)

A shot passed through Parker's hat. Gorsuch's son, Dickinson, fled to the cornfields, having suffered over eighty "squirrel shots." It appeared to all that he would die. The marshal and the rest of the white posse had already run from the scene, chased by the black resisters. The incident, from start to finish, lasted only an hour.

Parker recalled: "Having driven the slavocrats off in every direction, our party now turned towards their several houses. Some of us, however, went back to my house, where we found several of the neighbors. The scene at the house beggars description. Old Mr. Gorsuch was lying in the yard in a pool of blood, and confusion reigned both inside and outside of the house."

Edward Gorsuch was dead and his son critically wounded; a nephew had been shot in the wrist, shoulder blade, and back, and had a black eye and scalp wounds; a cousin had been "knocked silly"; Marshal Kline and two neighbors who arrived on the scene later had escaped without injury. Two of the black men had gunshot wounds, but neither was seriously injured. That evening, Levi Pownell, Jr., son of the owner of the Parker house, discovered there many hidden letters from fugitive slaves, which he destroyed in order not to implicate Parker or divulge any secrets they held. It is presumed that the letters might have revealed Parker's Underground Railroad activities.

On Friday, September 12, Marshal Kline filed charges against fifteen blacks and two whites, Lewis and Hanway, for "aiding and abetting in the murder of Edward Gorsuch." When Hanway and Lewis heard about the warrants, they turned themselves in. Several newspapers reported "a local reign of terror" gripping the area as both vigilantes and those dutifully assigned the task sought to arrest those charged. A letter from Baltimore reported that in Gorsuch's neighborhood, "the feelings of some have led to a deep-seated and burning desire for revenge. . . . Numbers of young men have left, with the avowed purpose, it is said, of proceeding to the locality of the outrage, and capturing, at all hazards, the perpetrators and instigators of the dreadful act."

Involved in the hunt were forty-five marines and forty policemen from Philadelphia, who, when asked what they were doing, said, "We are going to arrest every nigger and damned abolitionist in the country."

One of those rounded up and arrested was Cassandra Warner, Eliza and Hannah's mother. There are differing accounts of her arrest. One claims that she turned herself in and begged to be returned to her "master." An interview printed in the *Liberator* offered a different story, in which she admitted that after being arrested, she told authorities she wished to go back to slavery, "but said she was terrified by their violence and threats and feared a worse fate, if she refused to go. . . . 'I thought I might as well go back as to live so. But now,' she said with a woebegone look, 'I don't want to go back; O, I don't want to go back.' " Both reports indicate that she asked to see her grandchildren before being taken back, a request the commissioners refused. Cassandra Warner was never to see her children or grandchildren again. In a more recent account, historian Dr. Ella Forbes suggests that Cassandra's actions can be explained as a mother's last gift, a deflection of attention away from her escaping daughters and their husbands.

While others to be charged in the Christiana affair were being rounded up, William Parker, Alexander Pinckney, and Abraham Johnson were running. Parker had been warned that he would soon be arrested if he did not move quickly. He later wrote:

> I determined not to be taken alive, and told them so; but thinking advice as to our future course necessary, went to see some old friends and consult about it. Their advice was to leave, as, were we captured and imprisoned, they could not foresee the result. Acting upon this hint, we set out for home, when we met some female friends, who told us that forty or fifty armed men were at my house, looking for me, and that we had better stay away from the place, if we did not want to be taken.

Reluctantly, Parker left his family behind, realizing that to escape with a large group would be next to impossible. He, Pinckney, and Johnson arrived at the home of Frederick Douglass in Rochester two days later. It would have been logical to seek help from the leading abolitionist of the day, but it is interesting to note that Parker and Douglass had already known each other when both were enslaved. Douglass wrote about his involvement in their escape: "The work of getting these men safely into Canada was a delicate one. They were not only fugitives from slavery but charged with murder, and officers were in pursuit of them. . . . The hours they spent at my house were therefore hours of anxiety as well as activity."

Douglass and his friends succeeded in putting the three aboard a steamer bound for Canada later that day. Historian Thomas Slaughter has written that "Parker presented his friend [Douglass] with the pistol that had fallen from the hand of a dying Edward Gorsuch as a 'memento of the battle for liberty at Christiana.' "

Upon arrival in Canada, Parker and Johnson heard that Governor Johnston of Pennsylvania was going to attempt to extradite them to the United States. Instead of hiding, the two went to Toronto and asked to see Lord Elgin, the governor-general, who had already received Johnston's request for extradition. Elgin proceeded to question Parker "as to whether he was a fugitive from slavery or from justice." Parker explained his situation to Elgin, stating that he would "not be taken back alive" to the United States. Elgin assured Parker that he would not, in his opinion, be required to return. Elgin had no intention of supporting Parker's extradition back into slavery, as Canada had abolished slavery decades earlier. When other business interrupted their conversation, Elgin asked Parker to return later that afternoon. When he did, the message waiting for him from Lord Elgin was "You are as free a man as I am."

When the three arrived in St. Catharines, they were aided by Hiram Wilson, who gave Parker a letter of introduction to carry to Henry Bibb of the *Voice of the Fugitive* in Windsor, who was to help them the rest of the way to Buxton:

> *Dear Brother Bibb,*
>
> *It gives me pleasure to introduce to you the bearer, Bro. Wm. Parker, who was the hero of the Christiana battle for freedom and protection against the hellish slave hunters. He is bound for the Elgin Settlement with his family, and in company with quite a number of others, who are*

destined to the same place. As they are short of means, please have the
kindness to favor them when they arrive in Windsor, with such advice
and encouragement as may be in your power to render. I have favored
them what I could; they deserve our sympathy and ought to have assis-
tance. Yours truly, Hiram Wilson.

It was recorded that during this time Eliza and Hannah had been arrested, but then escaped when given permission to go back and get Hannah's baby. Eliza and Hannah would arrive in Canada two months after
their husbands. Their older children had been left behind with friends
until they could get settled.

Parker and Johnson moved on to the town of Kingston, where they
worked while waiting for their families. They got to Buxton in April
1852. Word of their arrival in Canada was celebrated in the abolitionist
press. Henry Bibb welcomed them with an editorial in the *Voice of the
Fugitive* that was also carried in *Frederick Douglass' Paper:*

This man in our estimation deserves the admiration of a Hannibal, a
Touissaint L'Ouverture or a George Washington. A nobler defense
was never made in behalf of human liberty upon the plains of Lexington, Concord or Bunker Hill than was put forth by William
Parker at Christiana. . . . We bid him with his family and all others
from that hypocritical republic welcome to this our glorious land of
adoption where no slave hunter dare to step his feet in search of a
slave.

Five years after Parker arrived in Canada, Mary Ann Shadd Cary, in a
letter of defiance and victory, publicly praised Parker in an editorial:

A NOBLE FELLOW

We had the pleasure on last Saturday, of taking by the hand, Mr.
William Parker, the hero of Christiana. The memory of that conflict
of five noble bondmen, unarmed [*sic*] in protection of their wives
and children, against an armed gang of thirty wretches in the em-

ployment of the United States, with the hireling Kline of Philadelphia, and old Gorsuch or Gorsuch, and son, slaveholders of Maryland at the head, will never be effaced.

Mr. Parker is a slender man, rather tall, mild and forgiving in expression and character, but as decisive as death, as determined as a
hurricane, and as brave as a Dessalines. A hundred such villains as
Kline of Pennsylvania would be made to tremble and quake before
the masterly eye of such a man as Mr. Parker. Grant, that his manly
arm could have reached the cowardly breasts of the whole thirty
who assailed him at the time, instead of only two! His ever faithful
wife suffered many privations till she reached him; but they are now
happy in their own domestic abode, under the protection of the
British Lion.

In 1857, Frederick Douglass, lecturing at a West Indies Emancipation
Day celebration, referred to "Parker and his noble band of fifteen, who
defended themselves from the kidnapper with prayers and pistols, [and]
are entitled to the honor of making the first successful resistance to the
Fugitive Slave Bill." At an Emancipation Day celebration held in Christiana a year later, William Wells Brown reported that "there is an impression in Christiana that a slaveholder will never come there again in
pursuit of fugitive slaves."

Among the abolitionist community, William Parker became a folk
hero. It is not mentioned whether he was one of those attending John
Brown's Chatham convention held in 1858, just a few short miles from
his home in Buxton. But in 1859, John Brown, Jr., having returned to the
Chatham area to follow up on his father's recruitment efforts, wrote:

At (B-n) I found *the* man, the *leading spirit* in that "affair," which
you, Henri, [Kagi] *refered* [sic] to. . . . After viewing him in all
points which I am capable of, I have to say that I think him worth *in
our market* as much as *two or three hundred average men,* and even at
this rate I should rate him too low. For *physical capacity,* for *practical
judgment,* for courage and moral tone, for *energy and force and will,*

for *experience* that would not only enable him to meet difficulty, but give *confidence* to overcome it, I should have to go a long way to find his equal, and in my judgment, he would be a cheap acquisition at almost any price.

In 1866, Parker's narrative of the Christiana affair appeared in *The Atlantic Monthly.* His editor for the article wrote a preface:

The manuscript of the following pages has been handed to me with the request that I would revise it for publication, or weave into its facts a story which should show the fitness of the Southern black for the exercise of the right of suffrage. . . . It is written in a fair, legible hand; its words are correctly spelled; its facts are clearly stated, and—in most instances—its sentences are properly constructed. Therefore, it needs no revision. On reading it over carefully, I also discover that it is in itself a stronger argument for the manhood of the Negro than any which could be adduced by one not himself a freedman; for it is the argument of facts, and facts are the most powerful logic. Therefore, if I were to imbed these facts in the mud of fiction, I should simply oblige the reader to dredge for the oyster, which in this narrative he has without the trouble of dredging, fresh and juicy as it came from the hand of nature—or rather, from the hand of one of Nature's noblemen—and who, until he was thirty years of age, had never put two letters together—This man is a doer, not a writer; though he gives us—particularly in the second part— touches of Nature and little bits of description, which are perfectly inimitable—

As expected, almost immediately claims were raised that Parker had not, nor could he have, written this. But historian Jonathan Katz reveals that an old ledger belonging to Abraham Shadd was found indicating that the narrative was already in progress in 1858, and that Abraham Johnson, Parker's friend and coresistor; Alexander Augusta, a local doctor; Anderson Abbott, son of one of the first Buxton leaders; and Mary

Ann Shadd's brother Joseph had all collaborated on the piece. The explicit facts in the narrative certainly indicate that Parker was directly involved in writing it and that the narrative, if not solely his, was a group effort to claim a piece of history they were proud of.

Victor Ullman seems to have had no concerns about Parker's ability to write the article. He writes that "the story about the Christiana riot probably would have been lost if not for William King's adult classes in which Parker enrolled. He was thirty years old when he reached Buxton and could neither read nor write. Within a few years, Frederick Douglass' Kent County correspondent for the *North Star* was William Parker, and he was writing many of the communications for the Court of Arbitration [in Buxton]."

Much has been written about Christiana. It has been labeled a "riot," "the battle for liberty," an "affray," a "tragedy," and more recently described as an act of "resistance." Frederick Douglass wrote of the event just five days after spiriting Parker and his friends to Canada: "Everybody seems astonished that in this land of gospel and light and liberty men had been found willing to peril even life itself to gain freedom and avoid slavery. Pro-slavery men especially are in a state of amazement at the strange affair. That the hunted men should fight with the biped bloodhounds that had tracked them, even when the animals had a *'paper'* authorizing them to hunt, is to them inexplicable audacity."

While blacks in the States were vocalizing their support for Parker's actions, encouraging more of the same, the government was preparing to prosecute the defendants for treason. Antislavery attorney Thaddeus Stevens was among the lawyers for the defense. Marshal Kline was to be the chief prosecution witness. A grand jury indicted thirty-six black men and five white men for treason against the United States; Castner Hanway was to be tried first. After the prosecution rested its case, the jury deliberated only fifteen minutes before bringing back a decision of "not guilty." The government did not succeed in gaining even one conviction with any of the charges brought against any of those arrested, not even on the lesser charges of murder and riot.

William Still would later write:

[It] was doubtless the most important trial that ever took place in this country relative to the Underground Railroad passengers, and in its results more good was brought out of evil than can be easily estimated. The proslavery theories of treason were utterly demolished, and not a particle of room was left the advocates of the peculiar institution to hope, that slave-hunters in future, in quest of fugitives, would be any more safe than Gorsuch. The tide of public sentiment changed. . . . Especially were slave-holders taught the wholesome lesson, that the Fugitive Slave Law was no guarantee against "red hot shot. . . ." In every respect, the Underground Rail Road made capital by the treason.

Many historians now claim that the Christiana resistance was the opening battle of the Civil War.

Buxton was the last black settlement to be developed in Canada. By 1859, ten years after its inception, its population numbered thirteen hundred, its largest ever recorded, and its area encompassed nine thousand acres. If William King provided the original leadership to ensure its success, it was the settlers of Buxton themselves who can be credited with proving to the world that blacks could achieve the same as whites when given freedom and equal opportunity. Indeed, when President Abraham Lincoln first thought about emancipating American slaves, he sent members of the newly formed Freedmen's Bureau to Buxton as well as to other communities in Canada West to investigate a successful model.

At the end of the Civil War, the exodus of blacks to the United States resulted in a dramatic decline in the population of Canada West's black settlements. Buxton was no exception. In 1874, some of those who had stayed established North Buxton on lands in the northern part of the original Elgin settlement. North Buxton remains a community today of fewer than one hundred people, many of them descendants of the original Elgin settlers, many still farming the lands of their ancestors. The community celebrates its heritage with a museum, an original school-house, and a church.

First Buxton Settlers
(compiled from Arlie Robbins, Legacy to Buxton)

1. Talbert, the twenty-year-old bought by King to help him run his school
2. Fanny, included with King's purchase of land near his father-in-law
3. Peter, Fanny's eight-year-old son
4. Molly, also included with King's land purchase
5. Sarah, Molly's eight-year-old daughter
6. Jacob, twenty-two, purchased by King to help run the farm with Talbert
7. Amelia, seven, included in Mary King's wedding dowry
8. Eliza, thirty, Amelia's mother, also included in the dowry
9. Ben, inherited from King's father-in-law's estate
10. Emaline, same inheritance
11. Robin, same
12. Ise, same
13. Stephen, same
14. Harriet, same
15. Solomon, Harriet's son, purchased at her request by King
16. Isaac and Catherine Riley and their children, Addison, John, Jerome, and James

William Wells Brown, famed abolitionist, speaker, and author of the
novel *Clotel*. (Illustration courtesy of the Ohio Historical Society)

Chapter Seven

Niagara Region

L ess than one mile separates Buffalo, New York, from Fort Erie, Ontario. Between them lies the Niagara River, which is actually a strait—the word *Niagara* is Iroquois for "strait"—connecting Lake Erie to Lake Ontario. From 1746 until 1949, ferries linked the two cities, and during the period before the Civil War provided a sea route for the Underground Railroad.

Like the distance from Midnight to Dawn, that from Buffalo to Fort Erie was immeasurable; to those seeking freedom, it was a step from the past toward the future, a step that has been commemorated by both countries. On the American side, in Broderick Park at the foot of Ferry Street, in what was once the town of Black Rock and is now part of Buffalo, a marker titled UNDERGROUND RAILROAD RIVER CROSSING explains, "From this site and from other places along the Niagara River escaping slaves were conducted across the boundary from the United States to freedom in Canada." In Fort Erie, a plaque on a large, flat boulder is labeled "The Crossing," and reads, in part: "At this former ferry crossing landing hundreds of escaped slaves experienced freedom for the first time."

In the early 1800s, the area surrounding both sides of the Niagara River was called the Niagara Frontier. Once held by the French, and then by the British, the region had been divided between the Americans and the British after the American Revolution, with the Niagara River as the international boundary. Today, the Canadian area includes the cities of Fort Erie, Niagara Falls, Queenston, Niagara-on-the-Lake, and St. Catharines; the American side includes Buffalo and the American town of Niagara Falls.

The falls themselves are shared by the two countries, the much larger Horseshoe Falls in Canada and the smaller American Falls in the United States. Historically, the falls have been considered a natural attraction to exploit for tourism as well as a problem to solve for trade and travel. The steamship created new possibilities for both throughout the Great Lakes region, but there were navigational problems to overcome, the falls being just one.

Buffalo, originally a small village known as New Amsterdam, was part of Niagara County, which had been incorporated in 1832. Many of the War of 1812 skirmishes between the United States and Great Britain took place there. In 1813, Americans crossed into Canada and burned the town of Newark (now Niagara-on-the-Lake); in retaliation, the British burned Buffalo and Black Rock, two towns that had been in competition to become the western terminus of the Erie Canal. An amazing engineering feat, the canal, which was completed in 1825, ran the length of New York State—almost four hundred miles—and was initially referred to as "Clinton's Big Ditch," after Governor De Witt Clinton, its initiator. Albany, on the Hudson River, was the natural choice for its eastern terminus, but the location of the western terminus became for some time a political hot potato. Both Black Rock and Buffalo wanted the economic stimulus the canal would surely bring. Wrangling over the site continued after the war, until the canal commissioners finally chose Buffalo, and Governor Clinton's 1816 prediction came true: "Buffalo is to be the point of beginning and in 50 years . . . will be next to New York in wealth and population."

William Hamilton Merritt, a local merchant in St. Catharines, was one in a long string of advocates for the creation of a canal to solve the next problem—the necessity for a long portage around the falls. Merritt's original, simplistic design was soon eclipsed by a much grander scheme, and the Welland Canal, built on the Canadian side of the Niagara River, opened in 1829, linking Lake Erie to Lake Ontario and creating a water detour around the falls. The successful completion of both the Erie and Welland canals opened up trade and began the westward migration in Canada as well as in the United States.

The climate of the Niagara area, mild due to the "lake effect," which creates harsh snowstorms south and east of the lakes during the winter, yet provides a natural form of air conditioning during the spring and summer, made the area even more attractive. As far back as the eighteenth century, southerners from the States came to escape the stifling heat and humidity of their long summers. Southern tourists, often accompanied by their enslaved black servants, kept company with southern Loyalists who had moved to Canada after the Revolution. Visits to the falls were combined with stays at the Cataract House in Niagara Falls, New York, or spa vacations to St. Catharines, home of many natural springs. Newly freed blacks, though they were not allowed to stay at the hotels or use other amenities provided by the resorts, found employment there, often as waiters. Southerners who vacationed at the Stephenson House, the Clifton House, or the Welland House must have been surprised to find themselves waited on by fugitives who had found freedom in Canada.

Escaping slaves crossed the Niagara River by any means at their disposal. Sympathetic ferry captains gave them free passage, and after 1851, they could walk or take the train across the new suspension bridge over Niagara Falls. In one dramatic instance, a fugitive being chased had little time to plot his escape. Searching for the quickest way to cross the river, he found a gate and attempted to use it as a raft. The current eventually carried him into Lake Ontario, where the Canadian steamship *Chief Justice Robinson* rescued him and took him the rest of the way to freedom.

When Lieutenant Governor John Graves Simcoe first arrived in Upper Canada in 1792, he had anticipated promoting a legislative agenda that would include his own strongly held abolitionist beliefs, but he soon realized that there were many constituents who were adamantly opposed to abolishing slavery, chief among them the American Loyalists, some of them slave owners who had brought their "property" with them into Canada. Because they'd already forfeited land and other possessions when they fled the United States, they would not easily be persuaded to give up slave "property" as well.

A few slaveholders acted to sell their slaves before being required to free them. Perhaps this is what prompted William Vrooman, a white Loyalist who had fled to Canada after the Revolution and was living in Queenston, a small village on the Niagara River just north of Niagara Falls, Ontario. In 1793, Vrooman bound and carried a screaming Chloe Cooley, his "property," to the shores of the Niagara River, where he placed her in a boat, rowed her across, and sold her to a waiting American slaveholder. The episode was observed by Canadian Peter Martin, a free black man, who related the story to the Executive Council governing the area, which included the newly arrived Lieutenant Governor Simcoe.

After Peter Martin testified, he buttressed his own observations with the eyewitness account of William Grisley, a white man, who claimed that "in the evening he saw the said Negro girl tied in a rope that afterwards a boat was brought and the said Fromond [Vrooman] with his brother, . . . forced the said Negro girl into it . . . that the said Negro girl was then taken and delivered to a man upon the bank of the river by Fromond, that she screamed violently, and made resistance, but was tied in the same manner, as when the said William Grisley first saw her, and in that situation delivered to the man."

Council members were outraged, and Simcoe was appalled to discover later that Vrooman's actions were entirely legal. Chloe Cooley was never heard from again, but the "Chloe Cooley incident," as it became known, is credited with motivating Simcoe to enact Upper Canada's first antislavery legislation, the 1793 Emancipation Act.

One of the earliest black settlers in the Niagara Region was Richard Pierpoint, who had gained recognition serving with Butler's Rangers. While contemporary with Chloe Cooley, Pierpoint had a different perspective on the black experience in early Niagara, having earned his freedom during the American Revolution, after which he used his status as a freeman to challenge the status quo for blacks constantly.

When the Treaty of Paris ended the Revolution and the boundary lines between the United States and Canada were set, thousands of British Loyalists were pushed back across the river to land on the western shore. Those who had fought for the British were given land grants; Pierpoint's two hundred acres in the Niagara region now sit in the center of the town of St. Catharines. One grantee described the land: "The whole country was forest, a wilderness that had to be subdued by axe and toil. For a time we had a regular Robinson Cruso [sic] life with a few poles and brushwood, formed our tents on the Indian plan. As the clearances enlarged, we were supplied with some agricultural implements, for we brought nothing with us but a few seeds."

The Chloe Cooley incident proved the discrimination and uncertainty blacks were living with in the Niagara region at the time. In 1794, nineteen black men petitioned Simcoe's government:

That there are a number of Negroes in this part of the Country many of whom have been Soldiers during the later war between Great Britain and America, and others who were born free with a few who have come into Canada since the peace—Your Petitioners are desirous of settling adjacent to each other that they may be enabled to give assistance (in work) to those amongst them who may most want it, . . . if your Excellency should see fit to allow them a Tract of Country to settle on, separate from the white settlers, your Petitioners hope their behavior will be such as to shew, that Negroes are capable of being industrious, and in loyalty to the Crown they are not deficient.

Despite Simcoe's personal belief in the equality of all races, he turned down the request. Perhaps he did not want to push black issues again so soon after he had succeeded in passing the Emancipation Act of 1793.

Pierpoint was not heard of again until the War of 1812. At sixty-eight, he understood the significance of this war for blacks: An American victory could mean a return to slavery for those now enjoying freedom. Convinced of the loyalty of his fellow black citizens, many of them ex-slaves, as well as his knowledge of their capabilities, he petitioned General Sir Isaac Brock to raise an all-African military unit, "that all may stand and fight together."

Several months after Pierpoint's request, a "Company of Coloured Men" was created under the leadership of a Capt. Robert Runchey, a white man. About thirty blacks, including Pierpoint himself, joined the unit. In October 1812, when an American force attacked the village of Queenston, it was successfully stopped with units that included Runchey's Coloured Company.

In 1820, Pierpoint and other fellow soldiers received word that they were to be rewarded with land in the Oro Township, though discrimination was evidenced in the disparate treatment of white soldiers, who received two hundred acres, and blacks, who received one hundred. Title to the land was not to be granted until ten acres had been cleared and a home built. Pierpoint's land was located in Garafraxa Township in the Queens Bush area in the central region of Ontario. Pierpoint (known also as "Captain Dick"), who had somehow lost title to his original two hundred acres, realized that clearing land at his age would be a great obstacle, and sought instead to return to his native homeland. In 1821, he once again petitioned the government:

The Petition of Richard Pierpoint, now of the Town of Niagara, a Man of Colour, a native of Africa, and an inhabitant of this Province since the year 1780.

Most humbly showeth,

That your Excellency's Petitioner is a native of Bondou in Africa; that at the age of Sixteen years he was made a Prisoner and sold as a Slave; that he was conveyed to America about the year 1760, and sold to a British officer; that he served his Majesty during the American Revolutionary War in the Corps called Butler's Rangers; and again during the late American War in a Corps of Colour raised on the Niagara Frontier.

That Your Excellency's Petitioner is now old and without property; that he finds it difficult to obtain a livelihood by his labour; that he is above all things desirous to return to his native Country; that His Majesty's Government be graciously pleased to grant him any relief, he wishes it may be affording him the means to proceed to England and from thence to a Settlement near the Gambia or Senegal Rivers, from whence he could return to Bondou . . .

Pierpoint never heard back regarding his request. He moved to his land in Garafraxa and began the arduous process of clearing and setting up a homestead. Apparently he fulfilled the requirements to receive title to his land, as records indicate, in 1825. A will dated 1828 left all his possessions to a farmer, Lemuel Brown, and indicated that Pierpoint had no living blood heirs. There is no record of Pierpoint's personal thoughts as to his life and legacy. Oral history has it that he served as the griot, or keeper of the stories, of the Niagara black community. As he traveled back and forth from the Niagara River region to the Queens Bush land, probably stopping along the way at the homes of his acquaintances, he told stories of the early Niagara Frontier. But despite his contributions to African Canadian history, it has only been in recent years that his life story has been uncovered and celebrated. Richard Pierpoint, African, Black Loyalist, soldier, and citizen, died in 1838 at the age of ninety-four.

———

Eight years before Pierpoint's death, in 1830, a sympathetic ship captain took Josiah Henson and his family to Buffalo and then paid for their passage across to Canada. While Henson's story has been told in conjunction with the British American Institute in Dawn, it should be noted that he began his life in freedom in the Niagara region and that his escape was aided by black seamen on Lake Erie and the Niagara River. Wilbur Siebert, in his 1898 historical record of the Underground Railroad, wrote about the "waterway extensions of secret lines," identifying many "safe boats" or "abolition boats" on the Great Lakes: the *Illinois,* the *Arrow,* the *United States,* the *Bay City,* and the *Mayflower,* all boats "plying between Sandusky and Detroit," as well as the *Forest Queen,* the *Morning Star,* and the *May Queen,* running between Cleveland and Detroit. Siebert also noted the routes on the eastern end of Lake Erie that "joined Toledo, Sandusky and Cleveland to Amherstburg and Detroit at one end of the lake, and Dunkirk, Ashtabula Harbor, Painesville and Cleveland with Buffalo and Black Rock at the other end. . . ."

West African sailors had brought their navigational skills with them from home, where they had long piloted up and down the coastal waterways. Gravitating toward the familiar, free blacks were often employed on steamships and other boats on the Great Lakes as well as on the Atlantic seaboard. Dubbed "Black Jacks" by seaman and historian W. Jeffrey Bolster, these sailors "established a visible presence in every North Atlantic seaport and plantation roadstead between 1740 and 1865." Indeed, it was this visibility that allowed Frederick Douglass to escape bondage in 1838 by borrowing a black seaman's credentials and wearing the typical clothes of a sailor.

Black Jacks provided more than just camouflage, however; often they were the communication link between free blacks in the North and the enslaved in the South, much to the consternation of southern slave-owning whites. In 1822, Denmark Vesey, a slave who had bought his freedom after winning the South Carolina lottery, plotted an uprising in

Charleston. He might have succeeded, but he was betrayed by one of his conspirators. Vesey was hanged along with thirty others, though not before Charlestonians realized that he had relied on his former connections as a sailor to aid him. As a result, the legislature of South Carolina passed the Act for the Better Regulation and Government of Free Negroes and Persons of Color, which required free persons of color working any of the ships coming into the Charleston harbor to be "confined in jail until said vessel shall clear out and depart from this State." Other southern states enacted similar laws.

In 1829, David Walker, a northern free black, reignited these fears of slave insurrection with the publication of a pamphlet entitled *Walker's Appeal*, addressed to the "Coloured Citizens of the World." It was aimed directly at those still enslaved and was meant to rile and incite:

> Having travelled over a considerable portion of these United States, and having, in the course of my travels, taken the most accurate observations of things as they exist—the result of my observations has warranted the full and unshaken conviction, that we (coloured people of these United States), are the most degraded, wretched, and abject set of beings that ever lived since the world began . . . Are we MEN!!—I ask you, O my brethren, are we MEN? Did our Creator make us to be slaves to dust and ashes like ourselves? . . . The whites have always been an unjust, jealous, unmerciful, avaricious and blood-thirsty set of being, always seeking after power and authority. . . . I count my life not dear unto me, but I am ready to be offered at any moment. For what is the use of living, when in fact I am dead. But remember, Americans, that as miserable, wretched, degraded and abject as you have made us in preceding, and in this generation, to support you and your families, that some of you, on the continent of America, will yet curse the day that you ever were born.

Not long after its publication, the pamphlet was circulating among southern blacks, distributed to them by black seamen from the North.

When discovered, the crackdown was immediate. If black sailors provided the means for covert communication, as Siebert documented, in many cases they also provided the means of covert travel. From the ports of New York all the way down to Cuba, black sailors were often banned from coming ashore.

One of the more famous of these Black Jacks who made his way to the Niagara Frontier was a fugitive named William Wells Brown, who had escaped from his owners in Missouri in 1834 and made his way to Cleveland, where he found employment on steamships sailing Lake Erie, from Cleveland to Buffalo or Detroit.

Much of what is known about Brown comes from his own memoir, *Narrative of William W. Brown, a Fugitive Slave*, which he published in 1847. Early in his life, he had been put to work on steamships plying the waters of the Mississippi River. He remembered those days as some of the most "pleasant time for me that I had ever experienced." When not sailing, Brown was often hired out to others. In one case, he was sent to the St. Louis publisher Elijah P. Lovejoy. "My work, while with him, was mainly in the printing office, waiting on the hands, working the press, & C. Mr. Lovejoy was a very good man, and decidedly the best master that I had ever had." What Brown did not reveal, however, is that Elijah Lovejoy was an abolitionist whose presses were on several occasions destroyed by mobs. In one final instance, in 1837, while protesting the lynching of a free black in Alton, Illinois, Elijah P. Lovejoy was assassinated.

Brown continued to be hired out to work on other steamships up and down the Mississippi, from St. Louis to as far south as New Orleans, where he often witnessed the sale of the slaves who had been chained and transported on his ships. After a failed attempt to escape with his mother to Canada, he was returned to slavery and his mother "sold south" (a common expression used to mean being sold to the Deep South, where cotton and sugar were harvested under often brutal conditions). Brown's mother left him with these words: "My child, we must soon part to meet no more this side of the grave. You have ever said that you would not die a slave; that you would be a freeman. Now

try to get your liberty! You will soon have no one to look after but yourself!"

Brown, again enslaved, was put aboard another steamship to work,
but his mother's admonitions and his own dreams of freedom remained. "I would dream at night that I was in Canada, a freeman, and
on waking in the morning, weep to find myself so sadly mistaken."
With his owners plotting to marry him off to try to keep him happy,
Brown states, "the next day was the first of January [1834]. I had looked
forward to New Year's day as the commencement of a new era in the
history of my life. I had decided upon leaving the peculiar institution
that day." After arriving in Ohio, Brown made his escape in the hustle
and bustle of the ship unloading its cargo. He walked for four days before he met an "old man walking towards me, leading a white horse. He
had on a broad-brimmed hat and a very long coat . . ." This man, a
Quaker named Wells Brown, took William into his home for several
weeks. When he asked William his full name, William replied that not
only had he no last name but that even his first name had been changed
upon occasion to suit the whims of his owners. Wells Brown informed
him that as a freeman, he needed two names, and in an act of deep respect, William gave the old Quaker the privilege of naming him. The
old man said, ". . . I shall call thee Wells Brown, after myself." Brown's
Narrative is dedicated to this man:

> Thirteen years ago, I came to your door, a weary fugitive from
> chains and stripes. I was a stranger, and you took me in. I was hun-
> gry, and you fed me. Naked was I, and you clothed me. Even a
> name by which to be known among men, slavery had denied me.
> You bestowed upon me your own. Base, indeed, should I be, if I
> ever forget what I owe to you, or do anything to disgrace that hon-
> ored name!
>
> As a slight testimony of my gratitude to my earliest benefactor,
> I take the liberty to inscribe to you this little Narrative of the suf-
> ferings from which I was fleeing when you had compassion upon
> me. In the multitude that you have succored, it is very possible

that you may not remember me; but until I forget God and myself,
I can never forget you.

Your grateful friend, William Wells Brown.

Before Brown wrote his autobiography, he married, and in 1836 he and his wife moved to Buffalo. As the new terminus for the Erie Canal and steamboat lines sailing the Great Lakes, the city provided many opportunities for black seamen, and thus had a large black population and many black-owned businesses that catered to canal workers and sailors near the docks. Though fugitives reaching Buffalo were still in danger of being caught by slave catchers who roamed the area, this was one location where blacks knew they might find support and safe passage. One of the most colorful of these places of refuge was Dug's Dive, a saloon in the basement of the Union Block, a three-story building that housed black residences and businesses. As a founding member of the local Temperance Society, William Wells Brown would probably not have frequented Dug's, but he would have been aware that at least some of the fugitives he was aiding across the river or lakes were familiar with the place. Another, more staid location noted for its historical connections to fugitives was Buffalo's Michigan Street Baptist Church, dating back to 1845. Oral tradition has it that the cubbyholes in the church basement were hiding places for those waiting to cross into Canada.

William Wells Brown wrote that while he was working on the Lake Erie steamboats, he actively aided those escaping: "I found many opportunities of helping their cause along." According to his own recollections, "In the year 1842, I conveyed, from the first of May to the first of December, sixty-nine fugitive[s] over Lake Erie to Canada. In 1843, I visited Malden [Amherstburg], in Upper Canada, and counted seventeen, in that small village, who owed their escape to my humble efforts."

If Buffalo provided Brown with a port to call home, it also allowed him to be close to the abolitionist activities gaining support in the area. In 1843, the city hosted the National Convention of Colored Citizens as well as a national antislavery convention. It was while attending these sessions that Brown would have met Frederick Douglass and others who had begun to take charge of the Negro Convention Movement. Brown was inspired by the rhetoric of abolitionists such as Henry Highland Garnet, a former student at Oneida and a supporter of the Liberty party, a new political party supported by free blacks calling for the immediate end of slavery. Garnet, in his "Address to the Slaves of the United States of America," described Denmark Vesey's insurrection as a "blast of the trumpet of freedom" and Nat Turner's rebellion as "noble and brave." He concluded his remarks by shouting, "Let your motto be resistance, resistance, resistance! . . . if hereditary bondsmen would be free, they must themselves strike the blow." Frederick Douglass and Brown both thought Garnet's speech to be a "call to violence" and persuaded the convention members to reject him.

Brown soon became renowned as an antislavery speaker in his own right. On his lecture tours, he often carried a copy of *Original Panoramic Views of the Scenes in the Life of an American Slave,"* that included twenty-four scenes he had painted to illustrate his years of slavery. But he seems to have focused his lectures on what his audiences wanted to hear—the horrors of slavery and the Middle Passage. According to W. Jeffrey Bolster, "Brown honored the relationship between blacks, ships and slavery but neglected the [often heroic] story of the black sailors," although he himself was one.

Several times he participated in the rescue of fugitives whose owners had attempted to grab them and return them to bondage. And he was hardly the only person engaged in such activities; in one case, a fugitive couple named Stanford and their baby were recaptured and attempts were made to return them to Tennessee. When blacks in Buffalo heard about the abduction, an armed posse of fifty was organized, which seized the Stanfords by using their superior numbers to intimidate the slave owners. They then put the couple on board a ferry to Canada. In another case, Brown and other abolitionists retained Millard Fillmore as an attorney for an alleged fugitive. This was the same Millard Fillmore who would later become president and sign the 1850 Fugitive Slave Act.

In 1849, Brown began a lecture tour of England; he remained abroad until 1854, reveling in the limelight among British abolitionists, and protecting himself against the Fugitive Slave Act, which had been put into effect since his departure from the States. A letter written by a Londoner to William Lloyd Garrison, and reprinted by William Still under the title "Fugitive Slaves at the Great Exhibition," notes, "Fortunately, we have at the present moment, in the British Metropolis, some specimens of what were once American 'chattels personal' in the persons of William and Ellen Craft, and William W. Brown." The Crafts had gained notoriety after escaping from Georgia disguised as mistress and servant, Ellen being fair enough to pass for white. When their former owners attempted to return them to bondage, the Vigilance Committee in Boston, where they were living, took immediate action and proactively sued the owners on charges of slander. Meetings were held; resolutions passed. In one, they resolved, "That as South Carolina seizes and imprisons colored seamen from the North, under the pleas that it is to prevent insurrection and rebellion among her colored populations, the authorities of this State, and the city in particular, be requested to lay hold of, and put in prison, immediately, any and all fugitive slave-hunters who may be found among us, upon the same ground, and for similar reasons."

According to the letter Garrison received from London, several antislavery people took the Crafts and Brown and walked arm in arm with them through the World's Fair's Crystal Palace. With many southerners in attendance, "[t]o see the arm of a beautiful English young lady passed through that of a 'nigger,' taking ices and other refreshments with him, upon terms of the most perfect equality, certainly was enough to 'rile,' and evidently did 'rile' the slave-holders who beheld it . . . It was a circumstance not to be forgotten by these Southern Bloodhounds. Probably, for the first time in their lives, they felt themselves thoroughly muzzled."

In another instance, the same English abolitionists took a figure entitled *Virginia Slave*, as drawn in their satirical magazine *Punch*, and placed a model of it at the exhibit of the *Greek Slave*, by an American,

Hiram Powers, one of the most popular statues of the nineteenth century and prominently displayed at the fair. The letter makes no reference to how the "Southern Bloodhounds" felt about Josiah Henson's lumber exhibit, which they must also have come across.

While abroad, William Wells Brown wrote several books, including *Clotel*, which, until the recent discovery of Hannah Crafts's *The Bondwoman's Narrative*, was the first novel written by an African American. *Clotel* tells the story of Thomas Jefferson and the daughter and granddaughters he fathered with Currer, his slave. (It wasn't until a century later that the very similar Sally Hemmings story surfaced.)

British abolitionists eventually purchased William Wells Brown's freedom so he could safely return to the States. In 1861, he toured Canada West to promote James Redpath's Haytian Emigration Bureau, which was acting on behalf of the Haitian government to encourage black migration to Haiti. Brown's observations were printed in *Pine and Palm*, the bureau's official newspaper. While he was only one of several writers to tour black communities in Canada in the early to middle decades of the nineteenth century, his observations, written in 1861, depict the black settlements in Canada West at the height of their development just before the Civil War, when many living in these communities returned to the United States.

Of St. Catharines, he wrote:

Only ten miles from the American side of the Niagara river, and the principal depot for fugitive slaves who escape by way of New York, Philadelphia, Harrisburg, and Buffalo, St. Catharine's has long been an important place for the oppressed, and consequently has become the home of many of these people. In the village and its environs, there are not far from eight hundred colored people, representing every Southern State in the late American Union. . . . Out of the eight hundred in St. Catharines, about seven hundred of them are fugitive slaves. . . . Among them I found seventeen carpenters, four blacksmiths, six coopers, and five shoemakers. Two omnibuses and two hacks are driven by colored men.

These reports were later compiled in a book, *The Colored People of Canada*. In the introduction, Brown wrote:

No section of the American Continent has been watched with so much interest, both by the oppressor, the oppressed, and the friends of freedom and civilization, as the Canadas. The only spot in America, where every child of God could stand and enjoy freedom, and the only place of refuge for the poor whip-scarred slave of the Southern plantation, it has excited the malignant hate of all slaveholding Americans, while it shared the sympathy and approving interest of the friends of the African race everywhere.

Blacks finding refuge in Canada found freedom under British law but were always wary of the possibility of kidnappings and illegal extradition back into slavery. In 1833, Upper Canada passed legislation entitled the Fugitive Offenders Act, providing for the extradition of any persons wanted for crimes in other countries. The act gave broad leeway to the governor in council to judge each case as they saw fit, though it didn't satisfy persons on either side of the fugitive issue. American senator Thomas Hart Benton believed that it proved the abolitionist leanings of the British government, while British abolitionists saw it as requiring Canadians to be slave catchers.

There were two famous cases that involved the new act. In 1837, a fugitive named Solomon Moseby escaped from Kentucky by stealing a horse; when his owner filed suit, an arrest warrant for horse stealing was issued in Kentucky and Moseby was jailed in Niagara. The lieutenant governor of Upper Canada eventually ruled that Moseby should be extradited back to Kentucky, but blacks in the area would not hear of it and more than two hundred came to Niagara to guard him. Under arms, Moseby was taken to a wagon to be transferred for extradition back to the States. But a riot ensued, two men were killed, and in the melee Moseby escaped and was never heard from again. A similar case soon followed in which the act was used to resolve the case in favor of the fugitive. This case involved Jesse Happy, who also stole a horse, although he left it at the border and even wrote a note to his former master to tell him where to find it. The master still filed charges, but the case was eventually satisfied in favor of Happy, who was set free under the defense that he had used the horse to escape and not for theft, and since slavery didn't exist in Canada, neither could the crime of escape. In the future, the defense maintained, evidence in such requests had to be gathered in Canada, so that if it proved to be false, it might be subject to charges of perjury.

In 1854, a meeting was convened at the African Methodist Episcopal Church in St. Catharines to discuss the refusal by drivers working for local resort hotels to accept black passengers, many of whom worked as waiters in these same hotels. Mr. Dyke, headwaiter at the American Hotel, urged others to follow him in quitting his job. Mr. Morris, headwaiter at St. Catharines House, appealed to those present "to respect themselves, and their rights as a people, and submit no longer to such degrading treatment."

"Man is man," the group resolved, "without respect to the colour of his skin," and "we, as men, will not submit to degrading terms of service, nor see our brethren treated with indignity by public conveyances, or excluded therefrom, without showing a manly spirit of resentment."

They also resolved that "as waiters, at the public hotels of St. Catharines, we will not continue in the service of our present employers, unless, in the management of their conveyances, they henceforth treat ourselves and our people with that respect and civility, to which we are entitled, as men."

The work stoppage succeeded. Within six months, the hotels changed their rules. Blacks could now also frequent the establishments they worked for.

That same year, Mary Ann Shadd visited Niagara and reported in the *Provincial Freeman* that "Niagara is a beautifully situated town, very healthy and rapidly rising into importance. The colored citizens are prosperous. Nearly every family possessing a homestead. There is no prejudice. Lots can be had on reasonable terms and tradesmen, labourers, etc. are on active demand."

By that time, blacks on the American side of the river had also become more active on their own behalf, the 1850 Fugitive Slave Act having driven to militant action even former believers in nonviolence and "moral suasion" (the belief that slavery could be eliminated by appealing to a slaveholder's Christian morality). Samuel Joseph May, a Unitarian minister and pacifist, wrote to the *North Star*, "We must trample this infamous law under foot, be the consequences what they may. Fines, imprisonment shall not deter me from doing what I can for the fugitive, and the sooner and the oftener we have trials of this law, the better."

May got his wish. Several instances of slave abduction were brought to court in the early 1850s. In each case, abolitionists, white and black, mobilized to rescue those being abducted; when necessary, they also provided legal defense to those who had been brought to trial.

A man who would live out the rest of his days as minister of St. Catharine's Zion Baptist Church provided the most dramatic challenge. Anthony Burns had escaped slavery in Virginia in 1854, but his owner traced him to Boston and took out a warrant for his arrest. The case became one of Boston's most famous legal battles, pitting Richard Henry Dana—abolitionist lawyer, seaman, and author of the autobiographical book *Two Years Before the Mast*—against the prosecution. The Burns case produced the same outcry among blacks and sympathetic whites in Boston and the northern United States as had the Moseby and Happy cases. Abolitionists held a meeting at historic Faneuil Hall—where Samuel Adams, John Hancock, and others had plotted the American Revolution—to argue against the Fugitive Slave Act. On the same day, Congress approved the Kansas-Nebraska bill, which would permit each new state to decide for itself the issue of slavery. The passage of this bill further inflamed those supporting Burns and pushed even more citizens to the activist side of the antislavery movement.

The meeting attracted over two thousand Bostonians. Samuel Gridley Howe offered a resolution stating "that as the South has decreed, in the late passage of the Nebraska bill, that no faith is to be kept with freedom; so, in the name of the living God, and on the part of the North, we declare that henceforth and forever, no compromises should be made with slavery." More fiery rhetoric ensued from other speakers, until the crowd was incited to take matters into their own hands. They marched to the courthouse to try to free Burns, but their attempts did not succeed and the trial took place as scheduled. Expecting the worst, federal officials took action to prevent violence. Troops from Fort Independence and a force of marines were brought in to keep order. President Pierce, hearing of the use of federal troops, wired the officials, "Your conduct is approved. The law must be enforced."

After a ruling that Burns would be returned to slavery, attempts were made to transfer him to a ship in the harbor. Both sides were ready. At half past two in the afternoon, he was taken down a route, accompanied, as has been noted by Jane and William Pease, "by one of the most formidable escorts a slave ever had. Leading the procession was a detachment from the National Boston Lancers. After them came a company of United States infantry. They were followed by a company of marines. Next came Burns, inside a hollow square composed of sixty volunteer guards and flanked by another company of marines. At the rear followed a six-pound cannon, loaded and ready for use, and a final company of marines."

While marines and state troopers moved Burns to the ship, more than fifty thousand Bostonians lined the streets in support of him. A coffin was hung from the statehouse with a sign declaiming THE FUNERAL OF LIBERTY. News of the case rippled throughout the abolitionist world. In Toronto, the *Provincial Freeman* gave a lengthy account, printing Burns's request, "To All the Christian Ministers of the Church of Christ, in Boston: Brothers, I venture humbly to ask an interest in your prayers and those of your congregations, that I may be restored to the natural and inalienable rights with which I am endowed by the Creator, and especially to the enjoyment of the blessings of liberty, which, it is said, this Government was ordained to secure." *Freder-*

ick Douglass' Paper responded to a sermon given by the Reverend Theodore Parker: "MR. ANTHONY BURNS. We like this feature of Mr. Parker's sermon. It speaks of the man returned to slavery, not as 'Anthony,' not 'Burns,' not the 'fugitive,' not the 'colored man,' or the 'Negro,' but he is called 'Mr. BURNS,' just as he would be called were he a white man." The *Provincial Freeman* also printed a letter, by abolitionist and feminist Angelina Grimke Weld: "The arrest of fugitives . . . [and] the shedding of human blood is utterly abhorrent to my mind, as barbarous and unchristian, yet the tame surrender of a helpless victim up to the fate of the slave is far more abhorrent; as slavery is equally, if not more, abhorrent to Christianity, than murder . . . we are compelled to choose between two evils, and all that we can do is to take the lest, and baptize liberty in blood . . . I confess that I would rather see twenty men killed than one poor fugitive returned into bondage."

Eventually, on March 16, 1854, the *Frederick Douglass' Paper* printed a story under the title "Anthony Burns in Boston": "This gentleman has, at length, been redeemed from the clutches of Slavery. Thirteen hundred dollars were paid for his ransom. He can now preach the gospel in peace. We hope Dr. Nehemiah Adams will go and hear him occasionally, and get his impression of the South Side View of Slavery." Members of the Twelfth Baptist Church, where Burns had been a member, had paid his ransom.

After attaining his freedom, Burns went on to study for the ministry at Oberlin College, and in 1860, he moved to St. Catharines to become the minister of Zion Baptist Church. Unfortunately, his struggles contributed to an early death. Two years after arriving, Burns died and was buried in Victoria Lawn Cemetery. His weathered limestone grave marker, now protected, reads "In Memoriam, Rev. Anthony Burns/ The fugitive slave of the Boston Riots, 1854/ Pastor of Zion Baptist Church/ Born in Virginia, May 31, 1834/ Died in the triumph of faith in St. Catharines, July 27, 1862.

———

"Refuge and Rest! These are the first ideas which arise in my mind in connection with the town of St. Catharines. . . ." Benjamin Drew's words reflected the desire for sanctuary sought by refugees as they moved farther inland from the border, to a town that provided a home for hundreds of blacks in the middle of the nineteenth century.

St. Catharines was appealing to fugitives; the building of the Welland Canal had created an economic boom there as the Erie Canal had done for Buffalo, and blacks as well as Irish immigrants moved there to participate. The Irish, however, who had brought their religious animosities with them, and who were laboring under living conditions fraught with disease, injury, and death, began fighting among themselves in 1849. The Battle of Slabtown ensued, with Protestants supportive of British rule and Catholics still struggling against British domination. (Slabtown was a region near the Welland Canal, so named because of the shanties built to house these workers.) Black soldiers were brought in to keep the peace, but were seen as representative of British domination and became targets of the violence, as well. Still, their peacekeeping service is credited with stopping the battle and allowing the successful completion of the canal.

Hiram Wilson, after resigning from Dawn's British American Institute under scathing attacks on his management skills, moved to St. Catharines and continued his work among the refugees there. In 1851, in keeping with his educational mission, he started another school for blacks. Wilson remained in St. Catharines the rest of his life, continuing to serve as a lightning rod for many of the issues surrounding blacks in Canada, especially in regard to the "begging question," posed by Mary Ann Shadd.

In a *Provincial Freeman* editorial after a visit to St. Catharines, Shadd wrote:

During my stay . . . I had frequent opportunities of examining the general improvements of the place, and was in no way more gratified than when viewing the snug homesteads of the colored people. . . . their success is a standing refutation to the falsehood that begging is needed for the fugitives of St. Catharines. The African Methodist Episcopal Church, too, for which the Rev. Hiram Wilson is now a paid Agent, is a fine building; by the way, the Rev. Hiram Wilson is erecting a large brick mansion for his own house in the suburbs, which, when completed, must, from its adornments, cost several thousand dollars. Mr. Wilson has long resided in St. Catharines, and, like other enterprising Americans, has profited by his change of position; having but little of this world's goods on his arrival in Canada, he has, by superior skill, as a missionary, to fugitives, for many years, and latterly as a preacher to the canal sailors, Agent for the African Church, etc. etc. become possessed of some valuable town lots, Mr. Wilson's prosperity only confirms one in the irresistible conclusion, that no missionary field is more profitable than that in which the fugitives of Canada are the victims. . . .

Benjamin Drew apparently had a much more positive view of Wilson after meeting him in St. Catharines on his 1855 tour:

a distinguished, self-denying philanthropist . . . With him the refugee finds a welcome and a home; the port stranger is pointed by him to the means of honorable self-support, and from him receives wise counsel and religious instruction . . . I have seen the Negro—the fugitive slave, wearied with his thousand miles of traveling by night, without suitable shelter meanwhile for rest by day, who had trodden the roughest and most unfrequented ways, fearing, with too much cause, an enemy in every human being who had crossed his path; I have seen such arrive at Mr. Wilson's . . . I have seen such waited on by Mr. And Mrs. Wilson, fed and clothed, and cheered, and cared for. . . .

In 1851, the most recognizable figure in Underground Railroad history sought sanctuary in St. Catharines, for herself as well as her family.

From 1851 until 1857, Harriet Tubman, the "Moses" of her people, made the community her base of operations and her home. While her place in the pantheon of historic black figures is assured, Tubman's Canadian connections are largely ignored. Yet without the safety of living in a country that guaranteed her legal freedom, she might never have been able to achieve some of her success.

Tubman was born on a plantation in Dorchester County, Maryland, circa 1820. Named Araminta Ross, she was the fifth of nine children born to enslaved parents, Harriet, or "Rit," Green and Ben Ross, who were owned by different masters. Araminta, who in her twenties took the name Harriet (probably in honor of her mother), often worked as a field hand. She was described by William Wells Brown as "a black woman of medium size, upper front teeth gone, smiling countenance, attired in coarse, but neat apparel, with an old-fashioned reticule, or bag, suspended by her side, and who, on taking her seat, would at once drop off into a sound sleep." Historian Milton Sernett described her as "[l]ess than five feet tall but with a muscular build," and wrote that "she excelled at physical labor and often performed astonishing feats of strength. Her father was a timber inspector who was responsible for cutting and hauling lumber to Baltimore's shipyards. On occasion, Harriet helped him with this work, and she could cut half a cord of wood in one day." The Reverend Samuel May said, "She seemed to know no fear and scarcely ever fatigue." Others would describe her personal attributes: "A nobler, higher spirit or a truer, seldom dwells in human form," Frederick Douglass said, and addressing her, he noted, "Excepting John Brown, of sacred memory, I know of no one who has willingly encountered more perils and hardships to serve our enslaved people than you have. Much that you have done would seem improbable to those who do not know you as I know you. . . ."

Tubman was enslaved almost thirty years before liberating herself. Always enterprising and an extremely hard worker, she preferred fieldwork, away from the eyes of the mistresses in the homes; often she hired herself out to other plantations and was the recipient of abuse. In one episode that affected her mentally and physically the rest of her life, she was hit—mistakenly—on the head with an iron weight an angry overseer had thrown at an escaping slave. For the rest of her life, Tubman had spells where she seemingly dropped off to sleep and lost consciousness, though after a few moments she awakened and continued her conversation as though never interrupted. According to Tubman biographer Kate Clifford Larson, the head injury was also the beginning of the "religious enthusiasm and dreams" that Tubman claimed allowed her to foretell the future. This religious expression fit into the context of the Second Great Awakening, which was sweeping the country in the decades between 1820 and 1850. As a counter to rationalism, it was often evidenced in camp revival meetings lasting from day into night. Dynamic preachers moved participants to express their dedication to God outwardly through shouts, screams, laughter, and rolling on the ground. Charles Finney, the movement's leading preacher, stated that "religion is the work of man, it is something for man to do," emphasizing that dedication to God also required social action. Elizabeth Cady Stanton, the future women's rights leader, attended one of Finney's revivals: "I can see him now, his great eyes rolling around the congregation and his arms flying about in the air like those of a windmill. One evening he described hell and the devil and the long procession of sinners being swept down the rapids, about to make the awful plunge into the burning depths of liquid fire below, and the rejoicing hosts in the inferno coming up to met them with the shouts of the devils echoing through the vaulted arches."

Placed in this religious context, Tubman's own version of religious mysticism does not seem too out of the ordinary. Perhaps, as has been intimated, she was influenced by her African roots. According to Earl Conrad, another Tubman biographer, legend told of her Ashanti African heritage. As this particular tribe was known for their resistance and courage, it would seem that Tubman took strength from her ancestry.

Historian James McPherson described how the Second Awakening impacted slavery: "This evangelical enthusiasm generated a host of moral and cultural reforms. The most dynamic and divisive of them was abolitionism." The Awakening prompted the women's movement as well. The two came together with the appearance of free black women preachers such as Maria Stewart, who had a religious conversion and dedicated herself to the personal uplift of blacks, perhaps influenced, in part, by the fiery rhetoric of her husband's business associate, David Walker, whose *Appeal* had been so widely circulated in the South. She often voiced her views in the pages of Garrison's *Liberator*, under the heading "Ladies Department." Jarena Lee and Zilpah Elaw, as well as other women, preached on the Eastern Shore camp-meeting circuit. Both Lee and Elaw "made female self determination an important theme," as Kate Larson has written. It is possible that Tubman attended and was influenced by these camp revivals, much as Shadd had been influenced by the enlightened spiritual view of women embraced by the Quakers.

In 1849, discovering that some of her family members might be sold, Harriet Tubman and her two brothers made an attempt to escape. She had married John Tubman, a free black, around 1844, but John, understandably in no fear for his own life, did not join them. Fearing capture and certain reprisal, Tubman's brothers soon returned; Tubman followed them back but made another attempt several months later, and this time succeeded in reaching freedom in Pennsylvania. There she began making plans to emancipate the rest of her family, and hopefully convince her husband to come with them. But when she returned to Maryland, she discovered that he had taken a new wife and didn't want to leave. Tubman didn't let this stop her; she made the best of the situation and left with a group of others instead.

But the Fugitive Slave Act of 1850 affected her as it did every other black person living in freedom in northern states. By 1851, Tubman realized that she was no longer safe in the North, and neither were any of the fugitives she was helping to escape. Wilbur Seibert quotes her as saying, "I wouldn't trust Uncle Sam wid my people no longer." She moved to Canada and settled in St. Catharines, where she lived until 1857. But as John Brown later stated, she was an "active" abolitionist, not just one who talked abolitionism. Tubman made approximately

thirteen trips south to rescue the rest of her family as well as other people. According to some records, the figure is at least seventy, or, as often
quoted, upwards of three hundred. Although the numbers vary greatly
in the telling and mythologizing of Tubman's story, the fact is that she
risked her life continuously to return to slave states to lead others to
safety. Historian Afua Cooper indicates that the term *trans-border* figure might be as applicable to Tubman as it is to Henry Bibb.

Tubman was interviewed on numerous occasions, including by
Benjamin Drew in 1855, who quoted her as saying:

> I grew up like a neglected weed, ignorant of liberty, having no ex-
> perience of it. Then I was not happy or contented; every time I saw
> a white man I was afraid of being carried away. I had two sisters
> carried away in a chain gang; one of them left two children. We
> were always uneasy. Now I've been free, I know what a dreadful
> condition slavery is. I have seen hundreds of escaped slaves, but
> never saw one who was willing to go back and be a slave. I have no
> opportunity to see my friends in my native land. We would rather
> stay in our native land, if we could be as free there as we are here. I
> think slavery is the next thing to hell. If a person would send an-
> other into bondage, he would, it appears to me, be bad enough to
> send him into hell, if he could.

She was not exaggerating. In one instance, she had given directions
to a certain Samuel Green, Jr., for his escape to Philadelphia, where he
was to be assisted further by conductor William Still. Green's father, a
friend of Tubman and possibly a relative, a Methodist minister who
had been able to purchase his own freedom, stayed behind, along with
his wife. The father risked a visit to his son in Canada, but upon his return to Maryland, according to accounts by Still printed in the *Provincial Freeman,* "the enemy was lurking in ambush." Slave catchers had
been watching Green for a long time and believed him to be aiding
fugitives. They searched his home one night and found a map of

Canada, several schedules of routes to the North, and a letter from his son in Canada, as well as a copy of *Uncle Tom's Cabin*. After the first indictment against him failed, he was found guilty of the following: "In the case of the State against Sam Green (Free Negro) who was tried at the April term of the Circuit Court of this county, for having in his possession abolition pamphlets, among which was *Uncle Tom's Cabin*, [defendant] has been found guilty by the court, and sentenced to the penitentiary for the term of ten years . . ."

There are many stories about Tubman's heroism. She was often rumored to have carried a gun to ensure that the fugitives she was leading would not back out. She is quoted as saying she "never lost a passenger." Tubman is credited for her uncanny ability, especially in one who never learned to read or write, to traverse the foreign terrain and geography of the eastern seaboard. When William Wells Brown interviewed her family and friends about her amazing successes, their opinion was that "whites can't catch Moses cause you see she's born with the charm."

On her travels to Canada, Tubman often crossed the suspension bridge spanning the Niagara River. It must have been a majestic, if frightening, sight, crossing over the rushing waters below, not being able to hear because of the roar of the falls. On one occasion, a scared "passenger" crossed the bridge but refused to look down. Upon reaching the Canadian shore, he told Tubman that he was not taking any more trips, except perhaps to heaven. Tubman replied, "You might have looked at the Falls first and then gone to Heaven afterwards."

Tubman's actions placed her in the center of a very tight network of abolitionists who knew, or at least knew of, one another. When in need, they relied on this network. John Brown tapped into it, knowing that Tubman had much to offer with regard to his own plans, especially given her knowledge of geography. Tubman gathered family and friends to hear him, but though he succeeded in garnering her verbal support and encouragement, she did not show for an agreed-upon meeting with him at the train station when he was leaving. Nevertheless, Brown went forward with his plans. He crossed back into the

States, gathered his recruits, and then went back to Canada for his constitutional convention in Chatham.

While Brown's plans for Harpers Ferry were put on hold due to the leak by Hugh Forbes, Tubman continued her work of aiding family and friends in St. Catharines. It was around this time that she became acquainted with Franklin B. Sanborn, Brown's friend and one of his Secret Six. Over a period of several years, Sanborn met with Tubman and conducted interviews. He later compiled his notes into a biographical essay (the first biography of Tubman to be published), which appeared in 1863 in the antislavery newspaper *Boston Commonwealth*.

In 1857, noting her parents' failing health and their desire to get away from Canadian winters, Tubman was provided a home near Auburn, New York, by the abolitionist William H. Seward, from whom she later purchased the property. After moving her parents there, she continued to solicit funds for herself and her family, for the refugee community in St. Catharines, and for John Brown. Brown commenced his plans for Harpers Ferry, but Tubman never arrived there as he had hoped. No reason for her absence has ever been recorded. Tubman herself never spoke of it; nevertheless, she continued to express her deepest admiration for Brown. She made the following remarks after his hanging: "I've been studying and studying upon it and its clar [sic] to me, it wasn't John Brown that died on that gallows. When I think how he gave up his life for our people, and how he never flinched, but was so brave to the end; its clar to me it wasn't mortal man, it was God in him. When I think of all the groans and tears and prayers I've heard on the plantations, and remember that God is a prayer-hearing God, I feel that his time is drawing near." Tubman would later say of Brown, "He done more in dying, than 100 men would in living."

Along with Brown's capture and death came incriminations for any who might have been involved with him. It is believed that Tubman, too, as well as members of the Secret Six, all moved to Canada for a time. When she felt it was safe, she continued lecturing, soliciting funds for her various philanthropic endeavors. When she had first moved to St. Catharines, Tubman had funneled fugitives and support to Hiram Wilson, who was already there aiding refugees. But controversy had followed Wilson from Dawn, and in St. Catherines, he was verbally attacked once again for mismanagement of funds. Tubman, apparently sharing this distrust, became an executive of the Fugitive Aid Society of St. Catharines, which was organized in 1861.

When the Civil War broke out that year, Tubman felt that her job was now to assist Union forces in the South. In May 1862, she moved to Beaufort, South Carolina, to work at Port Royal Island among the "contrabands," slaves fleeing and seeking shelter behind Union lines. Tubman provided service as a seamstress, cook, nurse, and washerwoman. She also served as a scout, spy, and recruiter of former slaves for the Second South Carolina Volunteers, a unit under the command of Col. James Montgomery, a friend of John Brown, who had also been involved in the Kansas skirmishes. In 1863, Tubman advised Montgomery and accompanied him on an armed river expedition that succeeded in destroying Confederate torpedoes and stashes of food and munitions. Along the way, watching the slaves coming out from the fields toward the river, she remarked that it reminded her of a biblical scene: "the children of Israel, coming out of Egypt."

In April 1865, Tubman's friend William Seward, who had been secretary of state under Lincoln, as well as a contributor to and a signer of the Emancipation Proclamation, was stabbed in his home the evening of Lincoln's assassination by a coconspirator of John Wilkes Booth. Tubman had turned to Seward to seek help obtaining the back pay she was owed for her service to the Union army. Seward tried to help but was not successful.

Money remained Tubman's biggest problem, until in 1868 Sarah H. Bradford published *Scenes in the Life of Harriet Tubman,* a biography that focused public attention on Tubman as an historical figure. Bradford turned over the royalties to Tubman, thus allowing her to pay her debts and support her family. In 1869, Tubman married Nelson Davis, a Union soldier and boarder at her Auburn home. When he died in

1888, at the age of forty-five, Tubman filed for widow's benefits based on Davis's Civil War service. After much bureaucratic hassling, she was finally awarded a pension of twenty dollars—eight dollars per month as widow's benefits and twelve dollars for her service as a former Civil War nurse. Her services as a spy and a scout for Union forces were not acknowledged by the government.

In 1896, Tubman finally achieved a long-held dream, purchasing land adjacent to her property in Auburn for a home for aged and infirm African Americans. The home, which included her original house and another building, was officially opened in 1908 and named the Harriet Tubman Home. Tubman herself called the brick building in the conclave John Brown Hall. Throughout the rest of her life, she continued to focus her energies on seeking funds for this home, though she also turned her attention to suffrage for women, a new movement now surfacing, taking the stage with such famous suffragettes as Susan B. Anthony. While Tubman is known historically for her abolitionism, and Anthony for her work with women's suffrage, they were each involved, at least to a certain extent, in both movements. Emma P. Telford, in an unpublished manuscript, wrote: "(Harriet) is a personal friend of Susan B. Anthony's and is often seen by her side when suffragists are in session. At the Twenty Eighth annual convention of the New York State Woman Suffrage Association in Rochester, Miss Anthony appeared on the rostrum leading Harriet by the hand, introducing her to the audience as a faithful worker for the advancement of her race who had reason to revere President Lincoln." Telford quoted the *Rochester Democrat*:

> The old woman was once a slave and she stood before the assemblage in her cheap black gown and coat and big black straw bonnet without adornment, her hand held in Miss Anthony's; she impressed one with the venerable dignity of her appearance. Her face was black and old and wrinkled and strongly marked with her race characteristics, but through it all, there shows an honesty and true benevolence of purpose which commend respect. She bowed modestly as Miss Anthony presented her, and when she commenced to

speak her voice low and trembling at first rose gradually as she warmed to her subject till it was plainly heard throughout the hall.

An excerpt from Anthony's diary provides this reference to Tubman:

Tried to interest myself in a sewing society; but little intelligence among them . . . attended Progressive Friends' meeting; too much namby-pamby-ism . . . Went to colored church to hear Douglass. He seems without solid basis. Speaks only popular truths . . . Quilted all day, but sewing seems to be no longer my calling . . . I stained and varnished the library bookcase today, and superintended the plowing of the orchard . . . The last load of hay is in the barn; all in capital order. Fitted out a fugitive slave for Canada with the help of Harriet Tubman . . .

In 1911, Tubman herself, now approximately ninety years of age, entered the Harriet Tubman Home, where she died in 1913 of pneumonia. St. Catharines honors her with a plaque in front of the British Methodist Episcopal Church, Salem Chapel, on the corner of North and Geneva Streets, rumored to be Tubman's place of worship. It states:

HARRIET ROSS TUBMAN c. 1820–1913

A legendary conductor on the Underground Railroad, Harriet became known as the "Moses" of her people. Tubman was born into slavery on a Maryland plantation and suffered brutal treatment from numerous owners before escaping in 1849. Over the next decade she returned to the American South many times and led hundreds [sic] of freedom seekers north. When the Fugitive Slave Act of 1850 allowed slave owners to recapture runaways in the northern free states, Tubman extended her operations across the Canadian border. For eight years she lived in St. Catharines, and at one point rented a house in this neighbourhood. With the outbreak of the Civil War, she returned to the U.S. to serve the Union Army.

UNCLE TOM'S CABIN;

OR,

LIFE AMONG THE LOWLY.

BY

HARRIET BEECHER STOWE.

VOL. I.

BOSTON:
JOHN P. JEWETT & COMPANY.
CLEVELAND, OHIO:
JEWETT, PROCTOR & WORTHINGTON.
1852.

Uncle Tom's Cabin book jacket.

Chapter Eight

Detroit Frontier

Before the nineteenth century, the Detroit Frontier, like the Niagara Frontier, encompassed an area on both sides of a river that would later become an international boundary. The Detroit River became a "fluid border," at once separating and connecting Canada and the United States. Many blacks as well as whites crossed and recrossed the river and became, like Henry Bibb and Harriet Tubman, "trans-border" citizens, whose lives were entwined with both countries. For blacks seeking freedom, the Detroit River was a door swinging in both directions.

The French, attempting to control the fur trade, were the first to make their way by ship across the Great Lakes to the Detroit River. In 1679, explorer Robert Cavelier La Salle, describing the area at its mouth, wrote:

> The islands are the finest in the world. They are covered with forests of nut and fruit trees, with wild vines loaded with grapes. From these we made a large quantity of wine. The banks of the Straight are

vast meadows and the prospect is terminated with some hills covered with vineyards, trees bearing good fruit, and groves and forests
so well arranged that one would think that Nature alone could not
have laid out the grounds so effectively without the help of man, so
charming was the prospect. . . . The country is well stocked with
stags, wild goats, and bears, all of which furnish excellent foods.

Father Louis Hennepin, a missionary traveling on the *Griffin*, La
Salle's ship, writing of the scenery as he passed the seventeen islands
along the twenty-five-mile journey of the Detroit River, called the strait
"finer than Niagara," and the banks "vast meadows."

In 1701, French explorer and trader Antoine Cadillac began building
a fort to protect French fur-trading interests from the encroaching westward expansion of the English. Cadillac named the area (now called Detroit) Ville d'Etroit, City of the Strait, or Narrows. To build their new
colony, French settlers were offered a spade, an ax, a plow, a large wagon,
a small wagon, and seed, as well as a cow and a pig. By 1760, over 2,500
people, mostly French, lived on both shores of the Detroit River.

The English, also realizing the potential of this new land, were not going to cede it without a fight. In 1760, under the command of Sir Jeffrey
Amherst, they captured Detroit, although they didn't hold it for long:
the success of the American Revolution transferred control of the Great
Lakes area, including Detroit, to the Americans.

At that point, the international boundary between America and
British North America was set, dividing the Detroit River down the
middle and forcing the British to remove their western fort from Detroit
to the opposite shore of the river, where they established Fort Amherstburg, later called Fort Malden. The British had been preparing for this
day. Beginning in 1788, members of the Royal Engineers had been surveying the area and had already chosen the site because of its location at
the mouth of the Detroit River at Lake Erie, where the distance between
shores was less than four miles and the channels ran deep. The choice enabled the British to control access to the river. The fort was to serve not

just as a military garrison but also as headquarters for the British Indian Department, led by men such as Matthew Elliott, a veteran of the American Revolutionary War. It was their task to build alliances with the various Indian tribes in the area. One of the ways they did this was to initiate an annual gift-giving ceremony. Reference to this ceremony is made in an 1855 book *Sketches of the City of Detroit:* "Annually in the month of June, thousands of Indians come from the Upper Lakes on their way to Malden to receive presents from the British Government, who stopped and lined the beach with their birchen canoes and pitched their tents beneath the shade of those trees [pear trees brought and planted by the French]. . . ." Some historians cite the British allegiances with the Indians as one of the major factors behind the War of 1812.

Relations between Great Britain and the United States had been simmering since the American Revolution, but it was the impressment of over ten thousand American sailors by British ships that resulted in the declaration of war on June 18, 1812. While the conflict was carried on predominantly in the Atlantic, it also extended to the Great Lakes region. American Brigadier-General William Hull, stationed at Fort Detroit, easily crossed the border and captured the shoreline town of Sandwich. But faced with a lack of supplies and the reinforcements he had requested, and concerned about the fact that the British forces had now been joined by over five hundred Indians led by the great chief Tecumseh, Hull felt compelled to retreat with his men back to Fort Detroit. Tecumseh had already shown his strength and abilities by fighting two small skirmishes with the Americans and preventing supplies from reaching Fort Detroit; Hull was leery of facing him again. Hull's troops, however, were outraged that they did not march on and take Fort Malden after taking Sandwich. He almost had a mutiny on his hands.

Tecumseh and Gen. Isaac Brock, head of the British forces in this area, were both men of action. When Hull did not agree to Brock's demand for surrender, they implemented an ingenious strategy to invoke fear. Tecumseh marched his men across the Detroit River and surrounded the fort, using a deceptive technique of moving his men in and out of the forests to create the illusion that he had many more forces than he really had. Brock and his men, meanwhile, bombarded the fort with cannon fire from across the river.

The sight of hundreds of Indians surrounding the fort, the sounds of artillery exploding in and near, the knowledge that a British force lay waiting to cross the river, and the war cries of Tecumseh's men left Hull scared and incapable of taking action. Hoisting a white sheet, he surrendered the fort without a fight. The capture of Fort Detroit provided a great moral victory for the British. Over two thousand Americans surrendered and the Michigan Territory once again changed hands. General Brock became a hero in both Britain and Canada because of his victory, while General Hull later faced court-martial for his decision to surrender. Tecumseh, who received little credit for his efforts on behalf of the British, continued to do battle with the Americans. But at the Battle of the Thames in Upper Canada the next year, the American army, led by William Henry Harrison, defeated the British and Indian forces. During the battle, the British were forced to retreat, leaving Tecumseh and his men to fight alone. Tecumseh was killed. The 1813 Battle of the Thames was the largest land battle of the War of 1812.

Only one month before, the British fleet had suffered their greatest naval defeat at the Battle of Lake Erie, within sight of Fort Malden. Commodore Oliver Hazard Perry, assisted by vessels manned by black sailors, commanded the American forces. On defeating the British, Perry sent his now-famous message to his commander, "We have met the enemy and they are ours." American soldiers took Fort Detroit back two and a half weeks later, but it would be another year and many more battles before the Americans would claim victory in the War of 1812. With international borders once again restored to their prewar designations, national attention could be focused on more important issues facing the new country—continued westward expansion, business and industry, and, by default, the problem of slavery.

The transportation industry took off first, spurred by demand. Roads and turnpikes were built, connecting towns, harbors, and cities; canals

were dug and the steamship was invented, creating navigational high-
ways; and soon came the railroads, completing the system.

The War of 1812 ended, once and for all, Britain's claim to the Northwest Territory, which included Detroit. In essence, the war ended as a
stalemate; no lands were accessed or ceded by either side. Detroit, which
had been coveted and controlled at times by each side, was once again an
American city. Those wanting to remain loyal to the Crown now moved
across the river to settle.

Earlier, two towns had developed along the riverfront across from
Detroit. Sandwich, designated to be the local seat of government, was begun on a one-mile square of land, originally inhabited by the Ottawa,
Potawotami, Wyandot, and Chippewa tribes and sold to the British in
1788. Many Detroit merchants wanting to remain loyal to Great Britain
moved across the river to Sandwich when Detroit passed to the Americans. To maintain memories of their former home, city planners and sur-
veyors laying out the town of Sandwich mirrored the layout of the city
streets of Detroit. Neighbors who'd lived side by side in Detroit now
lived side by side in Sandwich.

Amherstburg, the second town, named for Gen. Lord Jeffrey
Amherst, the successful British commander in the French and Indian
Wars, was situated at the mouth of the Detroit River at Lake Erie and
was originally designed as a garrison town supporting Fort Malden.
During the American Revolution, when Col. Matthew Elliott, a Loyalist, was assigned to Fort Malden to serve as the Indian liaison, he brought
with him fifty to sixty slaves he had kidnapped on raids conducted
throughout Kentucky, with the intention of having them work on his
2,500-acre estate near Amherstburg. There are no accounts of how Elliott treated his slaves, but oral-history accounts make mention of settlers
in the area seeing a "lashing ring" attached to a tree in his yard.

Legend has it that during the War of 1812, Tecumseh met Gen. Isaac
Brock at the Elliott home, and was invited to sleep there overnight.
Tecumseh refused a bed in the house itself, preferring to sleep behind the

house in a stone structure later dubbed "Tecumseh's barn." The North American Black Historical Museum in Amherstburg notes that the Elliott house was the site where the last British-held slaves were set free following the passage of the 1833 British Emancipation Act.

After Matthew Elliott's death, his widow and children became active in the antislavery movement. They built a large brick home on the original property and became stationmasters on the Underground Railroad, aiding newly arriving fugitives as they entered Canada near Amherstburg, one of the closest locations to the United States.

Blacks had begun migrating to the area when soldiers returning after the War of 1812 took back stories of free blacks and the "land of freedom" near Fort Malden. Historian Andrea Moore notes that in 1820, "a group of slaves led by Henry Brown, John Hubbs, and Willis Jackson, calling themselves the 'Close Communion of Baptists,' " began holding church services in the Sandwich area. The group must have grown, because they were able to build a log church by 1840. In that same year, Sandwich's First Baptist Church and Amherstburg's First Baptist Church and Second Baptist Church, under Detroit's William Monroe, formed the Amherstburg Regular Missionary Baptist Association. In the 1850s, the continued growth of the black population and a commensurate increase in church membership allowed for the construction of a brick church, with each family contributing a certain number of bricks and aiding personally in the project.

Black settlers in the area also addressed the issue of education. Though there are few records to that effect, those that do exist suggest that the growing black population was determined to build an infrastructure for themselves and those who were to follow. Sandwich was granted town status in 1858.

Mention must be made of one other influential person in the lives of blacks during this time period. Isaac Rice, a Presbyterian minister associated with the American Missionary Association and the Canada Mission group, came to Amherstburg in 1838. He and his wife worked hard

to meet the needs of the fugitives, but their efforts received mixed reviews. Levi Coffin, after his visit in 1844, raved about Rice:

> He had labored here among the colored people, mostly fugitives, for
> six years. He was a devoted self-denying worker, had received very
> little pecuniary help, and had suffered many privations. He was well
> situated in Ohio, as pastor of a Presbyterian church and had fine
> prospects before him, but believed that the Lord called him to this
> field of missionary labor among the fugitive slaves who came here by
> hundreds and by thousands, poor, destitute and ignorant, suffering
> from all the evil influence of slavery. We entered into deep sympathy
> with him in his labors, realizing the great need there was here for
> just such an institution as he had established.

But Rice was seen differently by many of the black population, who
began attacking him for "begging" on their behalf.

In the next decade, the begging issue would take on a life of its own
when Mary Ann Shadd and Henry Bibb entered the scene. Rice may
have been the first to be denounced for such actions, but he certainly was
not the last. Questions of begging versus self-reliance and assimilation
versus segregation came rushing to the forefront and even the most well-
intentioned efforts were often perceived negatively by those wanting to
control their own lives. Whether Rice deserved the attacks or not, he was
just one of many who would get caught in the cross fire.

There are some indications that Harriet Beecher Stowe traveled to
Amherstburg while researching *Uncle Tom's Cabin* and that she visited
the Elliott homestead during this time period. Curators at the Stowe
Center state that they have no record that she was ever in Ontario; never-
theless, she does have a connection to the area in the true story of Eliza
Harris, a fugitive slave from Dover, Kentucky.

The young mother of a two-year-old child, Eliza made her escape in
1838, after hearing that she was to be separated from her son and sold

south. Without help, in the dead of winter, and with slave catchers close on her heels, she ran to the frozen Ohio River, and, with bare feet, jumped across the drifting cakes of ice, all the while cradling her son. She reached the opposite shore at Ripley, Ohio, about fifty miles east of Cincinnati, but only eight miles from Maysville, Kentucky, a major trading center for tobacco and slaves. Reaching Ripley, Eliza was aided by the famous white Presbyterian minister and abolitionist John Rankin, one of many free black and white men and women who had settled this area and ran the local Underground Railroad station.

Rankin's home, built on a cliff overlooking the Ohio River and separated from the slave state of Kentucky by only the width of the river, was in a perfect position to aid fugitives. A boarded stairway of about one hundred steps had been built into the cliff and led down to the riverbank. From Ripley, Eliza was sent via the Underground Railroad to Sandusky, where, by differing accounts, she was taken across Lake Erie to either Point Pelee or Amherstburg. Curators at the North American Black Historical Museum state that she rested at the Elliott homestead before moving on to Chatham.

Eliza's story was passed down by locals for generations. Harriet Beecher Stowe must have heard it somewhere, because she fictionalized Eliza's harrowing escape in *Uncle Tom's Cabin,* even naming her character Eliza, although the fictional Eliza, much like Uncle Tom, was a composite. Defending her characters and incidents in her *Key to Uncle Tom's Cabin,* Stowe referred to the story: "Last spring while I was in New York, a Presbyterian clergyman of Ohio came to me and said, 'I understand they dispute that fact about the woman's crossing the river. Now, I know all about that myself for I got the story from the very man that helped her up the bank. I know it is true, for she [Eliza] is now living in Canada.' " Additionally, in the early 1900s, Judson Smith, a local entrepreneur, published a picture postcard of the Elliott home and labeled it "Eliza's Cabin." Years later, in a 1938 interview, an elderly Windsor man showed a reporter a plank from "Eliza's Cabin" that he had procured before the Elliott house had fallen to ruin.

Levi Coffin, the "president" of the Underground Railroad, related further news of Eliza in his book, *Reminiscences:*

In the summer of 1851, I was on a visit to Canada, accompanied by my wife and daughter, and Laura S. Haviland, of Michigan. At the close of a meeting which we attended, at one of the colored churches, a woman came up to my wife, seized her hand, and exclaimed: "How are you, Aunt Katie? God bless you!" etc. My wife did not recognize her, but she soon called herself to our remembrance by referring to the time she was at our house in the days of her distress, when my wife gave her the name of Eliza Harris, and by relating other particulars. We visited her at her house while at Chatham and found her comfortable and contented.

While there is no record of Eliza's death, Chatham historian Gwen Robinson suggests that she might be buried in Oberlin, Ohio, where her son George is buried. While her dramatic flight might have been fictionalized in *Uncle Tom's Cabin,* its underlying facts remain true.

British abolitionist Charles Stuart lived in Amherstburg from 1817 to 1822. During that time, he actively aided newly arriving fugitives, and wrote that he had become "more or less acquainted with them all and found them quite equal to any class of laborers in the county." According to historian Donald Simpson, Stuart attempted to provide homes for the fugitives "on a small tract of land in the rear of the village where the refugees became his tenants." Simpson cites a British surveyor who saw this while working on establishing the international boundary: "The Negro village and the clearances were then but just begun. As it was a very rainy season, the land seemed to be a swamp and the huts very indifferent affairs, but were thought to be palaces by the freemen who inhabited them. Subsequently heavy crops were obtained from their farms. Captain Stuart had the goodness to walk over some of them with me; and I am glad that I had the discernment to cheer him on in his difficult undertaking." Stuart's efforts appear to be the first organized attempts to help fugitives in the area.

Benjamin Lundy, touring Upper Canada in 1832, reported that there were three hundred blacks in the Amherstburg area. In his paper, the *Genius of Universal Emancipation,* he gave a positive report of his findings about blacks in Canada but added this caveat to his recommendation: "I would not urge, I would not ask a single free man to go, who is not so disposed. My business is to give him information." Lundy was already aware that the American Colonization Society's plan to send blacks to Africa was of concern to many blacks, who believed they were being forced out of their country.

Several other travelers to southwestern Canada published their impressions of the early days of Sandwich and Amherstburg. Patrick Sherriff, a British farmer, traveled throughout North America in 1833 in order to report on the agricultural potential of the area for those farmers wishing to emigrate. "Amherstburg is one of the oldest places in Canada," he wrote, "situated in its finest climate, the best British post on Lake Erie, and in beauty and healthiness of situation, inferior to no place in America; yet every thing, with exception of two handsome residences below the town, seems in a state of listless decay. I have no doubt there are better days in store for Amherstburg."

Anna Jameson, an established travel writer, Victorian feminist, and friend of such notable writers as Elizabeth and Robert Browning, toured the area as well. In 1837, while attempting to reconcile with her husband, who had already relocated there, Jameson traveled around Lake Huron and wrote her impressions in *Winter Studies and Summer Rambles in Canada.* The book remains one of the most important examples of early travel writing. Her descriptions of Amherstburg are also not too flattering: "[It] contains about six hundred inhabitants, has a good harbour, and all natural capabilities; but here also progress is lacking. There is a wretched little useless fort, commanding, or rather *not* commanding, the entrance to the Detroit River on our side, and memorable in the history of the last American war as Fort Malden."

Sherriff and Jameson both thought little better of the town of Sandwich, Sherriff observing that it was "also on the Detroit, sixteen miles above Amherstburg, and derives its only importance from being the county town. The houses compose an irregular street, running along the river, and chiefly occupied by French. The trade of Sandwich is more limited than that of Amherstburg, and I do not think it has the same chance of progressing." Four years later, Jameson wrote that although Sandwich was the chief place in the Western District, she saw nothing to convince her that it had made any progress.

The geography of the area surrounding Sandwich and Amherstburg was influential not just because of its prime location on Lake Erie and the Detroit River, which made it a desirable travel destination. Inland from the riverfront towns lay the hardwood forests; Jameson traveled the Thames River toward Chatham and described them:

> We plunged at once into the deep forest, where there was absolutely no road, no path, except that which is called a blazed path, where the trees marked on either side are the only direction to the traveler. How savagely, how solemnly wild it was! So thick was the overhanging foliage, that it not only shut out the sunshine, but almost the daylight; and we traveled on through a perpetual gloom of vaulted boughs and intermingled shade. . . . The timber was all hard timber, walnut, beech, and bass-wood and oak and maple of most luxuriant growth.

In addition to the timber, the soil was apparently conducive to growing tobacco. Joseph Pickering, another visitor to the area, wrote in 1826 that "black slaves, who have run away from their masters in Kentucky, arrive in Canada almost weekly, where they are free and work at raising tobacco; I believe they introduced the practice. One person will attend and manage the whole process of four acres, planting, hoeing, budding, etc., during the summer." (One of those blacks moving into the area was Josiah Henson, who arrived with his family in 1834 and settled for a time in Colchester, a small community south and east of Amherstburg.)

If the towns of Amherstburg and Sandwich were not "progressing" during the 1830s, the area directly across the river from Detroit was certainly beginning to benefit from its location. Rowboats, dugout canoes, and flat-bottomed boats that had been used to cross the river gave way to horse-powered side-wheelers such as the *Olive Branch,* described as "a sort of cheese-box on a raft, not much longer than it was wide." By 1831, the area was being called Sandwich Ferry in order to distinguish it from the town of Sandwich and to indicate its usage as a ferry port. It did not take long for Sandwich Ferry to overtake Sandwich in importance.

"About a mile and a half above Sandwich is the ferry at Detroit," Sherriff noted, "at which there are fifteen or twenty houses on the Canadian side of the river, and several brick buildings were being erected at the time of my visit. This place will soon eclipse Sandwich, and may rival Chatham. Detroit is the great market of Western Canada, and the ferry possess advantages, in proximity and access during winter, above every other situation." Sandwich Ferry continued to grow. In 1836, town officials decided to disengage themselves from any connections to Sandwich by naming their town Windsor.

With the Industrial Revolution came dramatic changes in business, industry, and transportation; expectations of economic prosperity grew with the advent of the steamship and the railroads. Windsor, in a position to reap the benefits, was chosen over Sandwich in 1852 as the site for the western terminus of the Great Western Railroad, and Sandwich, like the town of Black Rock on the Niagara River, continued its gradual decline and was eventually annexed to the incorporated town of Windsor.

With the invention of the railroad, the phrase "to take the train" took on a new meaning. According to historian R. Alan Douglas, "long before the coming of the railroad, of a winter's day one could take 'the train' from Windsor to Chatham, but what was meant was a train of sleighs, coupled together and drawn by horses on the ice. From 1854 onward, to travel by rail one took 'the cars.' " It was about this time that another term was coined, the *Underground Railroad,* which took on a meaning of its own.

In 1840, when the British Parliament passed the Act of Union, unifying the Canadian provinces and renaming Upper and Lower Canada as Canada West and Canada East, a new national identity, separate from the United States, was formed. But the Detroit border area remained porous, especially to those seeking safety and freedom.

The Erie Canal, finished in 1825, provided the water highway from the East Coast to the West and opened up the Detroit Frontier via water. Steamboats had already been transporting people and goods across Lake Erie as early as 1818. One was hailed in a New York City newspaper: "The swift Steamboat, *Walk-in-the-Water*, is intended to make a voyage early in the summer from Buffalo on Lake Erie, to Michilimackinac, on Lake Huron, for the conveyance of company. The trip has so near a resemblance to the famous Argonantic expedition in the heroic ages of Greece, that expectation is quite alive on the subject. Many of our most distinguished citizens are said to have already engaged their passage for this splendid adventure." Other boats also began scheduled routes across the lake, linking Buffalo to Detroit, with stops at port cities in the United States and Canada such as Sandusky and Amherstburg. By the end of the 1830s, almost forty different ships had regularly scheduled routes crossing Lake Erie. More ships would be added when the railroad lines from the East were extended to the West. The two modes of transportation connected at the port cities of Buffalo, Detroit, Toledo, Chicago, and New York, providing a natural water extension to the canal and railroad lines that crisscrossed the country. It soon became possible to purchase tickets that included both rail and steamboat travel.

Transportation across the country was now not just accessible, but also became affordable. According to the *Buffalo Spectator*, in 1836 the cost of passage from Buffalo to Detroit, with a cabin that included meals, cost eight dollars and took thirty-six to forty hours on average. For those who could not afford a cabin, there was steerage or deck passage, which did not include a bed or meals and which cost only three dollars for the same passage.

It has already been mentioned that black sailors were a large part of the sailing community on the eastern seaboard. This black maritime employment extended to the Great Lakes, as seen with sailors such as William Wells Brown. He was certainly not alone. As the lines and modes of transportation were extended, more and more blacks took advantage of the opportunities, whether building railroad lines or working as waiters or deckhands.

That these sailors would use their positions to aid fugitives is not surprising. According to Great Lakes marine historian John Polacsek, "the Underground Railroad was not built from scratch, but was [often] an extension of the communication and transportation networks of the day." Polacsek has documented several connections among specific vessels, their captains, and abolitionist activities. In one instance, Polacsek shows a probable relationship among a merchant ship owner named Richard Sears, of Buffalo, his schooner *Commerce* under the command of Capt. John Burnham, a documented October 1830 cargo loading in Sandusky, and the escape of Josiah Henson. Henson's autobiography supports this. He states that a sympathetic ship captain named Burnham had hired him to load cargo on his ship for free passage for himself and his family, who were en route from Sandusky to Buffalo, from which they reached Canada on October 28, 1830.

Polacsek has documented other such connections among ship agents, ship owners, ships, free blacks, and fugitives on the Great Lakes, maintaining that there was indeed a "nautical branch of the Underground Railroad." Wilbur Siebert corroborated this in his book, *The Underground Railroad: From Slavery to Freedom:* "Abolitionists found it desirable to have waterway extensions of their secret lines. Boats, the captains of which were favorable, were therefore drafted into the service when running on convenient routes." Siebert cited specifically a General Reed, whose boats included the *Sultana,* the *Madison,* the *Missouri,* the *Niagara,* and the *Keystone State,* as involved in aiding fugitives out of Racine, Wisconsin. He named Captain Steele, also out of Racine, and his vessel the *Galena,* as well as Captain Kelsey and the *Chesapeake,* both used by abolitionist A. P. Dutton to transport fugitives. He also listed the *Arrow,* the *United States,* the *Bay City,* and the *Mayflower,* mentioned by fugitives in interviews as providing transportation from Sandusky, and the *Forest Queen,* the *Morning Star,* and the *May Queen,* traveling from Cleveland to Detroit, as ships that also carried fugitives.

Michigan was admitted to the Union as a free state on January 26, 1837. Following the precedent set by the Northwest Ordinance, which originally governed the territory, slavery was forbidden there by the state's first constitution. The northwestern location and access to navigational waters and proximity to Canada attracted many free blacks, fugitives, and antislavery whites to the state, establishing it as an important center for abolitionist activity.

Michigan was involved in a number of cases of attempted abductions of fugitives, but the black community, supported by some sympathetic whites, were for the most part successful in rescuing them and getting them across the river to Canada. In one case, Kentucky slave owners planned a raid into Cass County, Michigan, and even sent a spy to learn where the abolitionists and fugitives lived. The man handed out antislavery newspapers while operating in disguise, but his southern drawl put the community on alert and he was run out of town—not, however, before he was able to draw a map, which he gave to the Kentucky slave owners. Thirteen members of a Kentucky "protective association" rode into town, purportedly to buy a washing machine. They succeeded in rounding up eight blacks, but the Quaker community quickly realized the ruse and went into action. They surrounded the slave owners, holding them as prisoners. It must have been an amazing sight, a group of thirteen Kentucky slave agents and the eight blacks they thought they had captured, surrounded by more than three hundred abolitionists walking alongside the group, making sure they arrived at the Cassopolis courthouse safely to face their own charges.

At the hearing, the Kentuckians defended their right to claim their "property," while lawyers representing the former slaves issued their own warrant, accusing the raiders of kidnapping, trespassing, and assault and battery. The Kentucky slave agents were found guilty and the blacks were set free and taken to Canada. The incident made national news. Henry Clay, upon hearing of it, denounced Michigan on the Senate floor as a "hotbed of radicals and renegades."

Shortly after, the 1850 Fugitive Slave Act was passed. Michigan, however, stayed true to its antislavery origins with a Personal Liberty Law in 1855, making the capture of fugitives in the state a crime. County jails could not be used to house possible fugitives and prosecuting attorneys were ordered to defend any Negroes brought in front of them. But while Michigan was legislatively supportive of freedom, individual actions told a different story.

Against this backdrop, certain individuals, both black and white, rose to meet the needs of fugitives coming to the area. Some had made their way to freedom in Michigan, only to have to make one last stand for freedom; some, already free, aided others in achieving theirs. Some stayed on the Detroit side of the river to conduct their abolitionist activities; others, especially after the 1850 Fugitive Slave Act, moved across the river to continue their work under the protection of the British flag. Individuals such as Thornton and Lucie Blackburn, Henry and Mary Bibb, Laura Haviland, William Lambert, George DeBaptiste, William Webb, and Seymour Finney each played a role in establishing Detroit as "Midnight" on the Underground Railroad.

In 1833, four years before Michigan's admission to statehood, the city of Detroit had its first race riot, its focus a self-emancipated couple from Kentucky. Lucie and Thornton Blackburn, like many other fugitives seeking freedom, had made their way to Detroit in 1831. Thornton found work and was praised publicly by a weekly newspaper, the *Detroit Courier,* as a "respectable, honest and industrious man and considerably superior to the common class of Negroes."

Two years later, slave hunters came to Detroit to seize the Blackburns after having been tipped off that they were living in the community. As their former owners sought to return them to bondage in Kentucky, the Detroit black community "prepared to protect" the Blackburns.

The couple was arrested and taken to jail, and a hearing to determine their freedom was held. When they could offer no proof of their freedom, such as a certificate some blacks were now carrying, the court upheld that the Blackburns' Kentucky owner could rightfully claim his "property" and take them back into bondage.

The black community responded to this hearing by gathering near the jail with clubs, and, as reported in the Detroit *Courier* of June 19, 1833, "exhibiting a determination to attempt a rescue, and continued there until the departure of the steamboat in the evening." According to historian David Katzman, blacks had even crossed the river from Malden and other Canadian towns in order to aid the Blackburns.

That evening, Lucie was visited in the jail by Mrs. George French, a local woman. After her visit, Mrs. French was seen leaving the jail and making her way to the river. It was not until the next day that the jailor realized that Mrs. French had exchanged clothing with Mrs. Blackburn and that the woman who left the jail the previous evening was Lucie Blackburn herself. It was Mrs. French now sitting in the jail cell, while Lucie was safely across the river in Canada.

Others in the black community, armed with clubs, stones, and pistols, had responded to the increased tension of the situation by remaining a visible presence around the jail and near the wharf. While they were not hiding their intentions, the *Courier* apparently did not take them seriously, calling their actions an "impulse or braggadocio threat." Thornton Blackburn was taken from the jail, but before he could be placed in the prison carriage he whipped out a pistol and shouted, "Get back, damn you!" The sheriff panicked and ran back to the jail, while Blackburn was placed in a dray owned by two blacks known in the community as "Sleepy Polly" and "Daddy Walker." They drove off with Thornton and took him to the river, where he too was removed safely to Canada to meet up with his wife.

In the meantime, the sheriff, beaten severely by the crowd, sustained multiple wounds, including a skull fracture. He would die less than one year later. One source states that whites stood on the street corners and shouted, "The niggers have risen and the sheriff is killed," further inciting the fears of white crowds now gathering. Authorities responded by arresting any blacks they thought might be involved in the "conspiracy." They later tried to reinstitute black codes regulating black freedom in Detroit.

The mayor ordered all blacks who could not produce a certificate of free-dom to leave town. A committee appointed to investigate the riot deter-mined that the black community was all at fault: "Neither their habits, nor their morals, with a few exceptions, make them a safe or desirable addition to our population. Indeed—but a small number of the colored people seen in our street can be considered as residents of the city. The greater portion are vagrant and transient persons, who are continually shifting their quar-ters from one side of the river to the other, as they find employment, or it is to be feared, for the greater convenience of carrying on their depreda-tions against the property of our citizens."

The committee recommended that the black code of 1827 be en-forced, that there be a nine o'clock curfew placed on the black popula-tion, and that no blacks be allowed to land boats on the Detroit shore. For the next two weeks, federal troops patrolled the city streets. The event has since been called the Blackburn Riots of 1833.

After their successful escape, the Blackburns moved to Toronto, where Thornton started the first cab business in Upper Canada. He called his taxicab "the City." Respected throughout the area, Thornton later served on the board of the Canada Mill and Mercantile Association established by the Elgin settlement. The couple remained active in aboli-tionist activities until the end of their lives.

By 1840, there were more than seven hundred blacks living in the state of Michigan. While the largest cluster (over two hundred) lived in Detroit, the rest had chosen rural settlements in which to begin their new lives. Some of them must have been delighted upon arrival in southeast-ern Michigan to encounter the Raisin Institute, a school run by Laura Haviland, a former Quaker abolitionist.

Haviland and her husband had left their traditional Quaker commu-nity to join the Wesleyan Methodist church because it seemed a closer fit for their abolitionist beliefs. Laura was said to have been inspired in this direction in part by her meeting with Elizabeth Margaret Chandler, a young poet and author who had been working with Benjamin Lundy, also a Quaker, on his abolitionist newspaper, the *Genius of Universal Emanci-pation*. It was Haviland, along with Chandler, who organized the Logan

Female Anti-Slavery Society in Lenawee County, Michigan's first women's antislavery society. Chandler died at the early age of twenty-six, but Haviland was committed to carrying on with their shared vision of black emancipation.

She had organized her Raisin Institute on the Oberlin model of racial integration, opening it to blacks as well as whites, making it the first integrated school in Michigan. The Raisin Institute was progressive also in that it was open to young women as well as men. Despite the prevailing prejudice against blacks, the school attracted white students from as far away as a hundred miles, due to its quality education.

Haviland was not content just to open up an integrated school; she also became one of Michigan's foremost Underground Railroad conductors. That she has received such little historical notice may be due to her gender, but in her memoir, A Woman's Life-Work, she carefully documented her courageous activities on behalf of fugitives and made clear the religious and spiritual inspiration for her work. She indicated that she often had prophetic dreams and visions, which places her in that category of nineteenth-century female religious individuals, such as Tubman, who found guidance and inspiration for their abolitionist activities through their spirituality.

Haviland and her husband, Charles, had eight children, but in one year alone, 1845, her husband, sister, mother and father, and a child all died. It is amazing to consider what she achieved after this, as a single mother of seven in an age when women were expected to be at home, not in the public arena. As an Underground Railroad conductor, Haviland often traveled by herself to the South to aid fugitives, stopping frequently at the Levi Coffin home for rest and conversation, "one conductor to another."

By 1852, Haviland's reputation had preceded her. She was asked to go to Windsor, Canada, to begin a school for fugitives. There she conducted a school for children as well as adults, and taught Sunday school as well. Of her Sunday school, Haviland stated, "an old couple, past eighty, were among the most regular attendees." Her life was hardly easy while there; the winters were harsh and her accommodations poor. Haviland awakened one winter day to find snow on her face and up to half an inch on her bed.

Haviland returned to the States and continued her caregiving activities until her death, providing aid to Union troops who were imprisoned in the South during the Civil War, and becoming an agent for the Freedman's Aid Commission after the war's end. She worked extensively in Kansas among the war refugees and was later honored by the naming of a town for her: Haviland, Kansas.

Haviland wrote her memoir in 1881; it went through five editions, and despite its religious and almost mystical overtones, sold very well. She is remembered as a founder of not just the Logan Female Anti-Slavery Society but also the Women's Christian Temperance Union in Michigan. She died at the age of eighty-nine, while living with her brother in Grand Rapids, her popularity noted by the four funerals held for her. Eleven years after her death, in 1909, the Adrian Women's Christian Temperance Union and the Haviland Association erected a full-size statue of her in Adrian, Michigan, one of the few statues erected at that time to honor a woman in history. While the sides of the base of the statue listed her accomplishments, a drinking fountain sculpted at her feet was inscribed, "I was thirsty and ye gave me drink."

The Underground Railroad Monument at the water's edge of Detroit portrays a group of fugitives being directed across the river to freedom in Canada by a central character who is pointing the way. This man, chosen to represent the Detroit Underground Railroad, is George DeBaptiste, considered to be the "president" of the Detroit Underground Railroad community. DeBaptiste, William Lambert, considered the "vice president, or "secretary," and Laura Haviland, the "superintendent," were among the most well-known abolitionists in the Michigan territory.

William Lambert was the first to arrive in Detroit. Born in New Jersey circa 1817 to a free mother and enslaved father, he was employed as a cabin boy on Great Lakes ships in his youth. He moved to Detroit around 1840 and became a prominent businessman, with his own tailoring and dry-cleaning business. But it was his abolitionist activities that brought him historical notice.

In 1843, Lambert, considered at that time the leading black abolitionist in Detroit, put out a call for a statewide black convention, following up on the National Negro Convention held earlier that same year in Buffalo. The call was published in the local newspaper, the *Detroit Daily Advertiser*, as well as in the *Signal of Liberty*, an antislavery newspaper published in Ann Arbor. His words were stirring:

> For as we are an oppressed people, wishing to be free, we must evidently follow the examples of oppressed nations that have preceded us. For history informs us that the liberties of an oppressed people are obtained only in proportion of their own exertions in their own cause. Therefore in accordance with this truth, let us come up, and like the oppressed people of England, Ireland, and Scotland, band ourselves together and wage unceasing war against the highhanded wrongs of the hideous monster, Tyranny!

The convention was held on October 26–27, 1843, at Second Baptist Church in Detroit. Lambert was elected chairman pro tem. The members, including William Monroe, pastor of Second Baptist, and Henry Bibb, composed a letter to the "People of the State of Michigan":

> We the representatives of the oppressed of this State will continue to write, publish, cry aloud, and Spare not, in opposition to all political injustice . . . until the first and second article of our State Constitution shall cease to conflict with each other. . . . [T]he Declaration of Independence is the textbook of this nation and without its doctrines be maintained, our government is insecure.

The convention called for "the immediate abolition of American slavery" and approved Henry Bibb's resolution, which was "never to consent to emigrate or be colonized from this, our native soil, while there exists one drop of African blood in bondage in these United States."

Much of what we know of Lambert comes from an interview he granted the *Detroit Tribune* on January 17, 1886, when he was almost seventy years old. In it, he revealed much about his Underground Railroad activities, including membership in a secret society alternately referred to by him as the African-American Mysteries, or by fellow member George DeBaptiste as the Order of the Men of Oppression.

When interviewing Lambert at his home about this secret society, the reporter watched as Lambert "took from a desk where *Walker's Appeal* . . . and the letters of Mr. John Brown, Lloyd Garrison, Wendell Phillips and Lucretia Mott were carefully preserved, two books bound in sheep, and of the pattern called memoranda books in the trade. In Lambert's own handwriting was the ritual, the names of the degrees, the test words, grips, descriptions of emblems and lessons." Lambert stated that every fugitive brought to Detroit by the Underground Railroad was initiated into the secret society and taught a specific dialogue:

> Question: Have you ever been on the railroad?
> Answer: I have been a short distance.
> Question: Where did you start from?
> Answer: The depot.
> Question: Where did you stop?
> Answer: At a place called Safety.
> Question: Have you a brother there? I think I know him.
> Answer: I know you now. You traveled on the road.

Both Lambert and DeBaptiste described the order similarly, saying it had three degrees, "Captives, Redeemed, and Chosen," with the first degree also having an added step specifically for Underground Railroad agents, entitled "Confidence." Lambert explained that the "Chosen" degree had five stages or levels the initiate could achieve: "rulers, judges, and princes, chevaliers, sterling black knight and knight of St. Domingo." The last stage had elaborate rituals detailing the principles of freedom.

John Brown historian Jean Libby writes:

The African Mysteries were an important part of African American militant antislavery efforts and retention of African culture through internal social structure. The origin is the curriculum of ancient Kemet [Egypt] called the Mysteries, which were studied to obtain wisdom. The fields included mathematics, science, literature, astronomy, and medicine. Many people think that enslaved Africans lost their heritage in the Middle Passage, but John Brown's friend and convener of the Chatham Convention Martin Delany published a periodical in Pittsburgh in the 1840's which was called "The Mystery" after this system.

Liberty Leagues were self-defense groups among African Americans in the South, (both free and enslaved) who assisted fugitives and maintained order and culture among the group. Like the African Mysteries of the North, they were established on African principles of organization and philosophy. . . . Both these organizations are militant self-defense groups who are the black operatives of the Underground Railroad.

It is not merely coincidental that Lambert and DeBaptiste organized an Underground Railroad secret society in Detroit; both of them were already members of a separate secret society, the Prince Hall Masons, as were many of the others who met with John Brown in Chatham. The relationship Brown, Lambert, and DeBaptiste had was close, if not always exactly what Brown wanted. It was William Lambert who assisted Brown by putting out the call for the Chatham convention. While DeBaptiste did not attend, Lambert and fellow Detroit Underground Railroad conductor William Monroe both did; Monroe served as presiding officer at the convention. Monroe was also a Prince Hall Mason, as were Chatham convention participants Martin Delany, Thomas Kinnard, and Thomas Stringer. Allies for Freedom, a John Brown research group, explains:

John Brown was building alliances with free blacks who were willing to fight for freedom and were connected with the abolition and emi-

grationist movements. These free Africans were members of the independent black congregations, were part of the Underground Railroad, and were Prince Hall Masons. They were consistent delegates
to Black Conventions. . . . John Brown knew that this black infrastructure existed because of his own organizational activities for
self-defense among fugitives, and recruited support among its most
militant members.

Lambert explained in his interview that fugitives would be fed and
sheltered and kept hidden until they could be put aboard rowboats hidden
underneath the docks, then safely rowed across the river under the cover
of night. He specifically mentions Seymour Finney, a white businessman
who owned a hotel and livery stable near the wharf. In recent newspaper
interviews, Finney descendants have confirmed the story that the elder
Finney would be hosting slave catchers at his hotel at the same time he was
hiding fugitives in his stables. It was an inside joke among the Detroit
abolitionists as well. Around "midnight," when the slave catchers would
still be carousing in his hotel, or sleeping, the fugitives would be taken
from his barn and secreted in the waiting rowboats. There have been several suggestions as to where Detroit got its code name, "Midnight," including this reference to hiding fugitives in Finney's barn. Thus far, no
other explanation has surfaced.

Another of Lambert's memories was of how the group used the Mc-
Kinseyites to aid them on the Underground Railroad. This "band of cut-
throats" were known terrorists running through the Southwest at that
time. Their technique involved stealing slaves from plantations, selling
them to other slave owners, then stealing them again and taking them to
Detroit where they would be handed off to Lambert and his Underground Railroad group. The McKinseyites were in it only for the money.
Lambert understood their motives but he said:

It was a long time before we could make up our minds to use these
scoundrels, but we at last concluded that the end justified the
means. Indeed we went further than that before we got through our

work, and held that the effort to secure liberty justified any means to overcome obstacles that intervened to defeat it. . . . Our association with the McKinseyites was from the very necessities of the case of short life. They were sure to be caught sooner or later, and at last some more daring robbery than usual brought some of them to prison and dispersed the rest.

Lambert boasted of the organization of the Detroit Underground, telling the reporter that "we could put through an invoice of freight by our own road from the [Ohio] River to the Lake [Erie] in ten to eleven days. If the war had not come we would have had thirty-three per cent of the 3,000,000 slaves of the South in Canada by the year 1865."

If William Lambert was one of the two main pillars of the Detroit community in the nineteenth century, George DeBaptiste was the other. He was born of free parents in Virginia circa 1815, and early in his life learned the trade of barbering. He then became known as a trustworthy manservant and was hired by a prominent southerner to travel with him. DeBaptiste married and in 1838 moved with his wife to Madison, Indiana, where he became active in the local Underground Railroad and became the stationmaster of a safe house. However, his activities brought him unwanted attention. Authorities trying to thwart his efforts demanded that he comply with an 1831 Indiana black code requiring that blacks post bonds in order to remain in the state. DeBaptiste decided to fight the law. While he did not succeed on overturning the black code, the court did rule that he could stay in the state.

While living in Madison, DeBaptiste also drew the attention of William Henry Harrison, a local citizen and war hero. Harrison had served as governor of the Indiana Territory and succeeded in opening up the Indian-held lands of the Northwest to settlers pushing westward. He had led his troops in the Battle of Tippecanoe, and successfully broke Tecumseh's Indian confederacy. While it was this battle that brought Harrison his fame, he also led the charge in the Battle of the Thames, in which his troops defeated the British and Indian forces and killed Tecumseh.

Harrison hired DeBaptiste as his personal valet after the two met in Indiana. DeBaptiste served in this capacity throughout Harrison's successful presidential campaign of 1840. When "Tippecanoe and Tyler Too" were inaugurated as president and vice president, DeBaptiste moved into the White House as Harrison's steward. Unfortunately, the elderly Harrison, who was elected to the presidency at age sixty-eight, died a month after his inauguration. It was noted in DeBaptiste's obituary that at the time of Harrison's death, DeBaptiste had been by his side and "supported the General's head in his arms when he breathed his last, and was one of the sincerest mourners at the General's funeral." DeBaptiste returned to Indiana briefly but moved his family to Detroit in 1846. There he joined with William Lambert and Henry Bibb to lead the black community's abolitionist efforts.

Throughout his life, DeBaptiste had several successful careers. In addition to his service as a personal valet, he bought a bakery in Detroit and ran a catering business for several years, even winning first prizes for his wedding cakes in the 1873 Michigan State Fair. He had earlier served as a steward on the steamship *Arrow*, which traveled between Sandusky and Detroit. According to historian Ronald Palmer, DeBaptiste was specifically singled out by passengers on the inaugural voyage of the *Arrow*, who praised the ship and the officers and crew: "They also tender their thanks to George DeBaptiste, the Steward, for his unremitting attention to their comfort. Dated, June 29, 1848."

DeBaptiste later purchased the *T. Whitney*, a steamship that ran the same route, often stopping in Amherstburg supposedly to "get lumber." Although blacks were not allowed by law to be licensed to run steamboats, DeBaptiste hired a white man, Captain Atwood, to run the boat. Polacsek suggests that DeBaptiste and Lambert implemented a division of labor regarding their Underground Railroad activities. DeBaptiste ran the "water routes" in this area, while Lambert ran the "land routes."

Obviously DeBaptiste purchased his boat, in part, to aid him in his work as an Underground Railroad conductor. Sandusky was well known as one of the ports where fugitives could find a sympathetic ship captain to ferry them to Canada. DeBaptiste's boat would pick fugitives up in

Sandusky and either take them directly to Detroit or drop them off in Amherstburg. Siebert identified four ships using this route as an extension of the Underground Railroad: the *Arrow,* the *United States,* the *Bay City,* and the *Mayflower.* Ship registries indicate that Atwood captained the *Arrow* before he was hired to captain DeBaptiste's *T. Whitney.* DeBaptiste had hired a proven abolitionist as his boat captain.

One year after the Chatham convention, John Brown arrived in Detroit with some of his followers, bringing twelve (some accounts give the figure of fourteen or nineteen) fugitives he had emancipated from Missouri. On their trek, a child had been born to one of the fugitives; the parents named the child John Brown. Stopping briefly in Chicago, the group was aided by famed detective Allan Pinkerton, who solicited funds for the rest of their journey. They reached Detroit on March 12, 1859. Brown escorted them safely across the river, then returned to Detroit to hold a secret meeting at the home of leading Detroit businessman William Webb. Webb owned a grocery store. He is described by his descendant, family historian Leslie Williams, as a "black man with a fair complexion. He could pass as a white man. He would dress in disguise and go into taverns and listen to the slave catchers conversations and then go back and report so they would know how to change the routes of the Underground Railroad. He led a dangerous life. That's what we [our family] always talk about, [his] courage."

Lambert, DeBaptiste, Monroe, and several others attended the meeting at Webb's home. Whether by advanced agreement or by happenstance, Frederick Douglass was in Detroit that evening, giving a lecture at City Hall. He was invited to the meeting, as well.

The attendees had differing responses to what they heard. DeBaptiste, perhaps tongue in cheek, argued for even more severe actions. He suggested blowing up fifteen southern churches on a Sunday when slaveholders would be attending services, but Brown said that that would hurt too many innocent people. Douglass expressed his doubts as to the potential success of Brown's plan but did offer to contribute money. It is not known how the others responded at the meeting, but none of them followed Brown to Harpers Ferry.

Over a decade later, in April and May of 1870, DeBaptiste granted three interviews to the local Detroit newspapers, hoping perhaps to set the historical record straight regarding his own experiences with the Underground Railroad and with John Brown. The first was entitled, "The Gideon of God's Enslaved: The Secret History of the John Brown Harpers Ferry Raid." DeBaptiste described the Detroit John Brown meeting:

> Ossawatomie's counsel finally prevailed, and the only favor, besides money and advice, that he asked of his Detroit friends was to furnish one man, which they did—a Chathamite [Osborne Anderson]. The news of the disturbance at Harper's Ferry, which took the nation with so much surprise, was perfectly well understood by the colored people of this city. . . . These facts, however, have been kept with sworn secrecy until lately, by the colored men of Detroit. The particulars have never been published.

In another interview, DeBaptiste tried to correct the prevailing opinions regarding John Brown:

> [T]he object of the John Brown raid was not, as has been supposed, to incite insurrection in the South. It was designed as a vast emigration scheme, to lead the slaves of Virginia to Canada in organized bodies, partially armed, by companies and regiments, in such masses that the ordinary machinery of the Fugitive Slave Law could neither stop them, nor . . . dare interfere with their march. The first step was the organization throughout the North, of Secret Societies, the whole known as the "Order of Emigration."

DeBaptiste related that in addition to the use of a secret society, a cipher or numerical code was developed to enable the Underground Railroad conductors to make use of the telegraph to send messages. Since the telegraph had become popular in the 1840s, it seems likely that the conductors made use of it.

DeBaptiste often used his public persona to provide him a platform from which to present his views. He was an occasional correspondent to the *North Star* as well as to the *Liberator.*

After Brown was arrested, tried, and hanged, a Senate investigating committee, led by Senator Mason, the same southern senator who had drafted the 1850 Fugitive Slave Act, attempted to subpoena a John De-Baptiste from Michigan. The subpoena was later changed to George De-Baptiste, not John. Since several persons knew of a John, there is speculation that DeBaptiste may have used an alias in his Underground dealings.

State politicians had advised the Senate committee investigating Harpers Ferry against calling DeBaptiste as a witness. They were concerned that this would give him a public platform from which to voice his views and convey a black perspective. The Detroit sheriff, whose task it was to serve the warrant on DeBaptiste wrote to the committee: "Knowing the caste and character of DeBaptiste my first impression on receiving the summons was that if Senator Mason knew the facts he would not desire the summons to be served, even if I should find DeBaptiste here. . . . If DeBaptiste were summoned, there is no probability that he would obey—for being a fugitive slave, claiming to be one, he would no doubt go over to Canada to avoid further process. I beg that you will be kind enough to confer with Senator Mason on this subject and advise me what further actions I shall take in the matter." The committee must have agreed with the sheriff's assessment, as the summons was never served.

George DeBaptiste died on February 22, 1875 (his age given by one paper as "about fifty-seven"). Both the *Detroit Post* and the *Detroit Advertiser and Tribune* posted lengthy obituaries detailing his work on behalf of the Underground Railroad, his connection to President William Henry Harrison, and his successful career as a businessman. The *Advertiser* stated, "Yesterday morning at a quarter before eleven o'clock Mr. George De Baptiste [*sic*], one of the most prominent colored men of Detroit, and a resident of this city for nearly thirty years, died at his residence. . . . Mr. De Baptiste was well known in this city, having been in business here for many years, a portion of the time as a caterer, where he was brought into intimate acquaintance with many of our citizens."

While certain locations such as the Raisin Institute, Finney's barn, and Webb's house have been mentioned in connection with the Detroit Underground Railroad, there is one site that has yet to be noted. The Second Baptist Church of Detroit, located at 441 Monroe Street, is the oldest African American congregation in the Midwest. Second Baptist dates its inception to 1836, when thirteen former slaves separated from the First Baptist Church of the city due to discrimination and a desire to aid escaping fugitives without the knowledge of the white community. Among the original congregants were Mr. and Mrs. George French and Mr. and Mrs. Madison J. Lightfoot, both couples who had been directly involved in the Thornton and Lucie Blackburn escape. William Monroe, who would later put out the call for John Brown's Chatham convention and serve as its presiding officer, was selected as the first pastor of the church.

Monroe left a carefully detailed history of the church. "My work was threefold: preaching, teaching and 'railroading.' Detroit and Second Baptist Church were known for slave smuggling," he wrote. He cited several Underground Railroad routes through Michigan, indicating the "Detroit River as Route No. 1; Second Baptist Church No. 2." Monroe wrote of having "the unique honor of being a station master, hiding, feeding and instructing the passengers during the day, then taking them to the waiting barges and canoes during the night. On several occasions we paused at a marker of the city's whipping post at [Woodward and Jefferson]." By 1841, membership at Second Baptist included most of the abolitionist community of Detroit. William Webb, William Lambert, and George DeBaptiste were all on the roll. In that same year, Pastor Monroe put out a call to all Baptist churches of Canada West to meet in Amherstburg:

> Believing that the time is now come that we should form ourselves
> into an Association because we cannot enjoy the privileges we wish

as Christians with the white churches in Canada; centuries having rolled along since our fathers were organized as a church; and believing that many of our fathers have gone down to the grave not enjoying their just privileges and rights in the Christian churches among the whites, we invite all the Christian churches of the same faith and order to unite with us in the great Celestial Cause. Union is strength. United, we stand; divided, we fall. Come up, brethren, from all parts of the province and let us see what we can do for ourselves and our children.

The Canadian churches responded. Joining together with their Detroit brethren, they founded the Amherstburg Regular Missionary Baptist Association. Monroe gives a very specific reason for his desire to combine the Baptist churches of Detroit and Canada West: "to provide a haven for fugitives and freedmen crossing the River."

As well as becoming the focal point for the black community, providing sanctuary for fugitives and a place for religious worship, churches also offered sites for education. Second Baptist, with William Monroe as its first pastor, led the way. Monroe ends his reminiscences by saying:

> Detroiters knew me as Father Monroe. I am proud to be connected with the progress of this city and of my people. It pleases me greatly to read in the Board of Education's archives my quoted statement: "Although I am a preacher first, my interest in helping Detroit children to gain a good education has long been a passion with me." Among my prized souvenirs is this note from one of my members, "Pastor, tomorrow night at our 8:00 meeting let's read Exodus 10:8." That meant in Underground language, "Conductor No. 2 will be arriving at 8:00 p.m. with 10 slaves, 8 men and 2 women."

On January 6, 1863, Second Baptist Church hosted a meeting to discuss the recently issued Emancipation Proclamation. At this meeting, the attendees passed a resolution "stating black readiness for military service."

In March of the same year, Detroit suffered its second race riot, this time precipitated over the purported molestation of two young white girls. Black businessman William Faulkner was accused, convicted, and sentenced to life in prison. Whites, including Irish and German immigrants competing with blacks for jobs, used this accusation as an excuse to riot against the black community, destroying over thirty black homes and injuring dozens of people. In effect, the Detroit riot was one of a larger pattern of draft riots occurring throughout the North as a result of the newly passed Enrollment Act requiring compulsory military service. Wealthy men could avoid the draft by hiring a substitute for three hundred dollars, so the draft burden fell unfairly on those who could not buy their way out, immigrants and blacks. Newly arriving immigrants had no desire to fight a war on behalf of the very population group with whom they were competing for jobs. A Pennsylvania newspaper summed up their sentiments: "Willing to fight for Uncle Sam, but not for Uncle Sambo." In New York, where the largest riot occurred, the Union army was sent in and more than a thousand people were killed or wounded. The black community in every city was always hardest hit. Detroit was no exception.

DeBaptiste took a leadership role during the racial tensions by trying to calm the black community down and encouraging them to volunteer for the Union army. Second Baptist once again took a prominent position, becoming the first Michigan-area black recruitment center when the War Department finally authorized black troops. DeBaptiste, Martin Delany, and Mary Ann Shadd all served as recruiters for the Union army from this area.

In 1867, one of the young women who had accused Faulkner of rape confessed that he was innocent of the crime. Faulkner was freed and given enough restitution by the City Council to begin a restaurant. There is no record of an apology by anyone in the white community. One of DeBaptiste's friends, a Col. Fred Morley, had publicly defended Faulkner throughout the trial and afterward. In gratitude for his support, DeBaptiste gave Morley a copy of William Henry Harrison's inaugural speech, which had been given to him by the former president.

The *Detroit Tribune* noted the celebration, held in Detroit on April 7, 1870, of the ratification of the Fifteenth Amendment. George DeBaptiste hung a sign on his building, stating, "Notice to Stockholders, Office of the Underground Railway, This office is permanently closed. Hereafter Stockholders will receive dividends according to their desserts. For further information apply to Senator Revels, Washington."

Historian David Katzman describes the scene: "One hundred and fifty Union League members carried a banner commemorating Crispus Attucks; fifty members of the Youths' Mental Improvement Club carried a portrait of Charles Sumner; on the obverse side was the slogan: 'Equal Privileges to All.' Spotted in the procession were pictures of Thaddeus Stevens and Frederick Douglass . . . Portraits of Presidents Grant and Lincoln, Senator Hiram Revels, and John Brown swept by."

The procession included over fifteen hundred black citizens on foot and in carriages, including fifty members of the 102nd United States Colored Infantry, "fully armed and equipped . . . united under their old regiment flag."

William Lambert chaired the celebration and offered a prayer; his son, Toussaint L'Ouverture, read the Fifteenth Amendment aloud to the crowd. The Governor of Michigan was introduced and George DeBaptiste made some humorous remarks. James Madison Bell, a participant and the host to John Brown during the Chatham convention, as well as a renowned poet, read a poem he had written for the occasion. The celebration concluded in the afternoon with the singing of William Lambert's song, "The Martyr's Triumph."

By 1870, great numbers of people were again crossing Detroit's borders, but this time in the opposite direction. Blacks were returning to the home of their birth with great hopes for the future.

Frederick Douglass, famed abolitionist, orator, and writer.
(Photograph couresy of the Ohio Historical Society)

Chapter Nine

The Civil War and Reconstruction Years

I n the three decades before the Civil War, more than thirty thousand blacks, some freeborn, others self-emancipated, found sanctuary in Canada. During this time, they bought land, felled timber, built homes, were educated, raised families, started businesses and newspapers, and became politically active. They lived as free men and women under the legal protection of the British government. Nevertheless, despite finding freedom in their new country, for the majority, Canada was not home.

Notwithstanding the entreaties of staunch Canadian emigrationists such as Henry Bibb and Mary Ann Shadd Cary, most blacks who had migrated to Canada still longed for an American homeland, where familiarity, climate, and family beckoned them back. When the opportunity to return "home" presented itself, at least two-thirds began the return migration southward.

The opportunity they were looking for did not come immediately on the election of Abraham Lincoln, or after the firing on Fort Sumter and the secession of the southern states. None of these events singularly offered any real assurances to fugitives. Even the words from the new president did not give them hope. In Lincoln's first inaugural address, he declared that he had "no purpose, directly or indirectly, to interfere with slavery in the States where it exists."

In the spring of 1861, the Reverend William King had been watching the unfolding events in the United States closely, while in cooperation with Martin Delany he was preparing his group of young men to go to Africa as missionaries, to expand on his City of God concept. As he explained, he anticipated that the Civil War would eventually have to embrace the issue of slavery:

> While I was corresponding with the Society in London about sending the young men out, the southern states seceded and war was declared. I then wrote to the Society in London that the sword had been drawn from the scabbard and would not be returned until liberty was proclaimed for the captives. The market for slaves as far as the U.S. was concerned would come to an end with the war. The young men who intended to go out to Africa to colonize the West Coast were prepared to go south to fight for liberty as soon as the opportunity would be given to them to enter the northern army.

King later wrote that the years between 1862 and 1863 were the "darkest period" for Buxton settlers. All were waiting and watching to see if the Civil War would be fought, not just to preserve the Union but also to free the slaves.

While Lincoln personally hated slavery, as president he felt that his first duty was to preserve the Union of the United States. It was fortuitous then that those still enslaved in the South gave Lincoln and abolitionists in the North and Canada the opportunity they were looking for. Slaves began to cross battle lines, requesting asylum of Northern troops fighting in the South. Initially, many Northern generals returned the slaves to their owners, but it soon became apparent that an opportunity existed to weaken enemy forces. Perhaps remembering British actions during the American Revolution, in 1861 Congress passed the Confiscation Act, which gave "contraband" status to any slaves who had been used by the Confederates in support of their war efforts. (Union general and abolitionist Benjamin Butler is credited with first designating such slaves as "contrabands of war.") Word passed quickly. On hearing of this avenue for freedom, slaves began escaping to Union lines in great numbers.

Noting that the war was going badly for the North and that not all Northern generals were enforcing the Confiscation Act, Horace Greeley, editor of the *New York Tribune,* the North's preeminent newspaper, and a radical antislavery supporter, wrote an open letter to President Lincoln in August 1862, demanding enforcement by his generals: "We must have scouts, guides, spies, cooks, teamsters, diggers and choppers from the blacks of the South, where we allow them to fight for us or not, or we shall be baffled and repelled." Lincoln responded to Greeley with the famous words that made abolitionists in the North and in Canada still leery of his intent:

My paramount object is to save the Union and not either to save or destroy slavery. If I could save the Union without freeing any slave, I would do it; and if I could save it by freeing all the slaves, I would do it; and if I could save it by freeing some and leaving others alone, I would also do that. What I do about slavery and the colored race, I do because I believe it helps to save this Union; and what I forbear, I forbear because I do not believe it would help to save the Union. . . . I have here stated my purpose according to my view of official duty, and I intend no modification of my oft-expressed personal wish that all men everywhere could be free.

Greeley did not know that Lincoln was already laying the groundwork for the emancipation of Southern slaves; the year 1863 was to be pivotal. With the war going longer and more poorly than planned, Lincoln told members of his cabinet that emancipation was a "military necessity" if the North was to win the war. On January 1, 1863, he issued the Emancipation Proclamation, freeing all slaves in those states rebelling against the Union. Border slave states and parts of Confederate states now controlled by Union armies were exempt.

Canadian blacks remained cautious, given the fact that Lincoln's decree freed slaves from the Southern states only. But Lincoln took two other steps that finally convinced them that he could be trusted to include slavery in the war agenda. He was aware that thousands of slaves had fled to Canada and were now living in freedom. Before freeing thousands more from the South, he wanted to know how the Canadian blacks fared in their new status as free men and women. Under the auspices of the Freedmen's Inquiry Commission, he authorized Samuel Gridley Howe to tour Canada West, interview the fugitives, and report back.

Lincoln must have known of Howe's credentials and realized that he would be welcomed in Canada; a physician, Howe had been one of John Brown's Secret Six, was married to Julia Ward Howe, author of the "Battle Hymn of the Republic," and was active in many abolitionist causes. In 1863, he began his tour of Canada West, stopping at the towns where blacks had settled in large numbers, including St. Catharines, Hamilton, London, Toronto, Chatham, Buxton, Windsor, Malden, and Colchester.

Howe spent considerable time interviewing many of the settlers, recording his findings in a report, *The Refugees from Slavery in Canada West*. In the preface, he stated:

> It is commonly said that the Canadian refugees are "picked men;" that the very fact of their escape from slavery, is proof of their superiority; and therefore, however well they may succeed in taking care of themselves, it does not prove that ordinary negroes can do the same . . .
>
> No! the refugees in Canada earn a living, and gather property; they marry and respect women; they build churches, and send their children to schools, they improve in manners and morals,— not because they are "picked men," but simply because they are *free men.*

Howe's findings addressed the fact that many fugitives wanted to re-turn to the United States if conditions were safe. "The local attach-ments of the slaves are very strong. They cling far more fondly than whites do to the 'old place.' They want to be free; and have a strong, though vague feeling, that freedom will, somehow, and at some time, come to them."

Howe's report was organized under headings that included the his-tory of emigration; the physical condition of the emigrants, including climate; the material condition of the settlers; their mental and moral condition including churches and schools; and, as he worded it, "the inferences to be drawn from the experiences of the colored people in Canada, as to the future condition of those in the United States." He in-terviewed over one hundred fugitives during his tour, and stated that it was "impossible to ascertain the number of exiles who have found refuge in Canada since 1800 but according to the most careful esti-mates, it must be between thirty and forty thousand."

Howe concluded with his opinion that the abolition of slavery in the United States would impact dramatically the population of fugitives in Canada:

If slavery is utterly abolished in the United States, no more colored people will emigrate to Canada; and most of those now there will soon leave it. There can be no doubt about this. Among hundreds who spoke about it, only one dissented from the strong expression of desire to "go home." In their belief, too, they agreed with Rev. Mr. Kinnard, one of their clergy, who said to us, "if freedom is es-tablished in the United States, there will be one great back streak, reaching from here to the uttermost parts of the South."

Antiblack prejudice in Canada was also addressed. One interviewee said, "The prejudice against colored people is growing here. But it is not a British feeling; it does not spring from our people, but from your people coming over here. There are many Americans here, and great deference is paid to their feelings." Howe summed up the discussions on prejudice by saying, "The truth of the matter seems to be that, as long as the colored people form a very small proportion of the population, and are dependent, they receive protection and favors; but when they increase, and compete with the laboring class for a living, and especially when they begin to aspire to social equality, they cease to be 'interesting negroes,' and become 'niggers.' "

About the issue of economic independence, Howe compared the Canadian fugitives to those who had been colonized to Africa:

> There is a most striking contrast between these exiles—penniless, unaided in a cold climate, amid unsympathesizing people,—and those who were sent, at great expense, across the ocean to an African climate, then supported entirely for six months, and afterwards aided and bolstered up by a powerful society, which still expend huge sums for the support of the colony. The first have succeeded; the latter have virtually failed. Let the lesson be pondered by those who are considering what shall be done about the Negro. But second, there is positive and tangible proof of the will and the ability of the colored people to work and support themselves, and gather substance even in the hard climate of Canada.

Regarding education, he reported: "An unusually large proportion of the colored population of Canada is made up of adults. Those from the free States had very little schooling in youth; those from the Slave States, none at all. Considering these things, it is remarkable that so many can now read and write. Moreover, they show their esteem for instruction by their desire to obtain it for their children. They all wish to have their children go to school, and they send them all the time that they can be spared." Howe stated his opinion that separate schools and "colored" teachers were a mistake on the part of the Canadian fugitives and that they would have done better to stay in the public schools and integrate them as the law supported. While Howe's opinion was clearly his own, it is evident that he did not recognize the struggles Canadian blacks went through to go to school at all.

He summed up his findings by stating, "Finally, the lesson taught by this and other emigrations is, that the Negro does best when let alone, and that we must beware of all attempts to prolong his servitude, even under pretext of taking care of him. The white man has tried taking care of the Negro, by slavery, by apprenticeship, by colonization, and has failed disastrously in all; now let the Negro try to take care of himself."

"All the blood and tears of our people in this revolutionary struggle," Howe wrote, would be a small price to pay to "re-establish our Union in universal freedom." As for those enslaved, he concluded that "the misery which this people may suffer in their efforts for self-guidance and support," would be worth it, too, to "bring about emancipation from the control of the whites."

Attached to Howe's report were comments offered by the Reverend William King:

> The whole of my plan was this: to provide these people with a home and their children with an education, and, with these two things, I felt confident every blessing would come . . . I had an anti-alienation clause inserted in the deeds so that these people could not transfer their land to a white man until they had been here for ten years. That has kept them a compact body, so that the political power they have got will protect them. Prejudice has melted before that political power and now the people are respected and elected to office . . .

King summed up his assessment and gave his recommendations:

> I consider that this settlement has done as well as any white settlement would have done under the same circumstances; and I am prepared to prove that a coloured community can be made industrious and self-supporting, if they are properly treated. I have no doubt that the coloured people of your country, as soon as the war is over, if they are put on farms in the South, will become self-supporting. A finer class of laborers cannot be found in the world

for raising cotton. Only introduce Northern capital, or Southern capital, give them full remuneration, and in a short time you will find them an industrious, respectable, self-supporting community.

Howe's report was published in 1864. It would be used by Dr. Charles Sumner when he argued in Congress on behalf of the Fourteenth Amendment.

Along with the Emancipation Proclamation, Lincoln passed a law authorizing the recruitment of black troops, which offered Canadian blacks the opportunity they had been looking for to get directly involved. The fight against slavery they had conducted from Canadian land now would be fought on American soil.

Canadians, including Josiah Henson, Mary Ann Shadd Cary, Abraham Shadd, and Martin Delany, as well as American abolitionists closely aligned with Canada, such as such as Frederick Douglass, Harriet Tubman, Laura Haviland, and George DeBaptiste, now turned their attention to helping the Union win the war and free the slaves.

Frederick Douglass was one of the first to respond. On March 21, 1863, he published in *Douglass' Monthly*:

Men of Color, to Arms! Who would be free themselves must strike the blow." "Better even to die free, than to live slaves." This is the sentiment of every brave colored man among us. There are weak and cowardly men in all nations. We have them amongst us. They will tell you that this is the "white man's war"; and you will be "no better off after than before the war"; that the getting of you unto the army is to "sacrifice you on the first opportunity." Believe them not; cowards themselves, they do not wish to have their cowardice shamed by your brave example. Leave them to their timidity, or to whatever other motive may hold them back. I have not thought lightly of the words I am now addressing you. The counsel I give comes of close observation of the great struggle now in progress, and of the deep conviction that this is your hour and mine.

In good earnest, then, and after the best deliberation, I now for the first time during the war feel at liberty to call and counsel you to arms. By every consideration which binds you to your enslaved fellow-countrymen, and the peace and welfare of your country; by every aspiration which you cherish for the freedom and equality of yourselves and your children; by all the ties of blood and identity which makes us one with the brave black men now fighting our battles in Louisiana and in South Carolina, I beg you to fly to arms, and smite with death the power that would bury the government and your liberty in the same hopeless grave. . . . The day dawns—the morning star is bright upon the horizon! The iron gate of our prison stands half open. One gallant rush from the North will fling it wide open, while four millions of our brothers and sisters shall march out into liberty. The chance is now given you to end in a day the bondage of centuries, and to rise in one bound from social degradation to the place of common equality with other varieties of men. Remember Denmark Vesey of Charleston; remember Nathaniel Turner of Southampton; remember Shields Green and Copeland, who followed noble John Brown, and fell as glorious martyrs for the cause of the slave. Remember that in a contest with oppression, the Almighty has no attribute which can take sides with oppressors. The case is before you. This is our golden opportunity. Let us accept it and forever wipe out the dark reproaches unsparingly hurled against us by our enemies. Let us win for ourselves the gratitude of our country, and the best blessings of our posterity through all time. . . .

Canadian blacks had not been waiting for their "call." According to historian C. Peter Ripley, they had attempted to enlist in Northern armies immediately at the onset of the Civil War, but it was not until 1863 that they were actually allowed to do so. Many of Canada West's most prominent men and women then heeded the call by Lincoln and Douglass. According to Civil War historian William Gladstone, over a thousand Canadian blacks fought in the Civil War. The number is only an estimate, as identification of Civil War soldiers who were born in the United States but enlisted from Canada would be identified in any records as American recruits.

When the Emancipation Proclamation was passed, Josiah Henson was seventy-three, a man past his prime for actual fighting. But that did not stop him from doing what he could to aid the war effort. He not only encouraged all able-bodied men to join the army; he also advanced money to those who registered and personally escorted many of them to recruiting stations in Detroit to make sure they would get the bounty they were offered to join. Unfortunately, Henson's efforts caused him to be accused of "inducing enlistments" illegally. Queen Victoria had proclaimed British neutrality in May 1861. But this attempt to stay out of the war did not stop some from trying to make money by enlisting soldiers, using shady recruiting techniques called "crimping," which involved drugging or intoxicating men and taking them across the border and forcing them into service. Despite the fact that he was doing nothing wrong, Henson was accused of illegal recruiting, though charges against him were eventually dropped, based on the character of the informant.

Recruitment issues continued to plague the North. Enlistments were down and the war dragged on; two years into the fighting, it was clear that more troops would be needed. In order to solve the problem, Lincoln issued a draft, called the 1863 Enrollment Act of Conscription, which was not well received, especially in New York, where a very anti-Lincoln Democratic party ruled the city and an influx of Irish immigrants was already in economic competition with blacks. The first draftees were drawn on July 11, 1863. But news of Gettysburg and its horrific death toll had just reached the already-angry public, who were feeling duped into fighting a war over slavery rather than just for the preservation of the Union. And despite antislavery views, many whites in the North were not willing to lay their lives on the line for the freedom of blacks.

Lincoln put out the call for 300,000 new soldiers. Unfortunately, the Enrollment Act allowed wealthy persons to buy their way out of the draft, which left the poor, mostly the Irish immigrant population, hardest hit. They focused their anger on blacks. When the names of those selected were published, some fifty thousand mobbed New York City streets. The riots went on for three days. Federal troops were called. By the end, a black church and orphanage had been burned, several blacks had been lynched, and the death toll had reached between twenty-four and a hundred persons.

But blacks were willing to fight, and black recruiters proved invaluable to the cause. Recruitment posters aimed at blacks were placed around the North: "Colored men, rally 'round the flag of freedom. Pay, $13 a month! Good food and clothing! State aid to families!" By war's end, over 178,000 blacks had responded to the call and had served on behalf of the Union.

Henson was not the only Canadian recruiting for the Union army. When Governor John Andrew of Massachusetts was authorized to raise the first black regiment in the North, to be called the Fifty-fourth Massachusetts, he called on his network of abolitionist and black friends to aid him. Andrew had met many prominent blacks through Lewis Hayden, a member of the Boston Vigilance Committee, an Underground Railroad conductor, a personal friend, and the Grand Master of the Prince Hall Grand Lodge of Massachusetts. It was at Hayden's house that John Brown stayed on one of his last visits to Boston. According to Prince Hall historian Joseph Walkes, Jr., Governor Andrew often ate Thanksgiving dinner with Hayden and introduced him to many others in the Prince Hall Masonic brotherhood, men from New York, Pennsylvania, Ohio, and Rhode Island, as well as his own state of Massachusetts. As proof of their close relationship, Andrew presented Hayden with a gavel "made from a whipping post at Hampton, Va.," writing in a letter:

I know of no place more fitting for the preservation of these memorials of the barbarous institution that is now tottering with its rapidly approaching fall, than the association of free colored citizens of Massachusetts over which you preside. Some among you may be reminded by them of the suffering and bondage from which the hand of God has delivered you, while others, whose happier lot it has been to be born and reared as free men in a free state, as they look upon this thing, will thank Him that He has been graciously pleased that their lives should fall in more pleasant places; and to those who shall come after you let the sight of these things be a perpetual memorial of God's favor to their fathers, in delivering their oppressors.

That blacks would use fraternal ties to help them, as did whites, is not unusual. But the fraternal connection did not end there. Walkes has uncovered the fact that many of the black soldiers of the Fifty-fourth were bonded together fraternally and even held lodge meetings when stationed near Fort Wagner, South Carolina. It was Capt. Luis F. Emilio, a white officer who served with the Fifty-fourth Massachusetts, who initially noted the fraternal connections: "First Sergeant Gray of Company C had received a Masonic charter and organized a Lodge on Morris Island. The meeting place was a dry spot in the marsh near our camp, where boards were set up to shelter the members."

One of the Prince Hall Masons tapped to aid recruitment for the Fifty-fourth Massachusetts was Dr. Martin Delany, who had returned to the United States from Africa, putting aside his emigrationist dreams in order to fight for the cause he had been fighting for all his life—freedom for all those still enslaved.

Delany was mustered into service on February 27, 1865 as a major, United States Colored Troops. Upon his commission, Secretary of War Stanton said, "Major Delany, I take great pleasure in handing you this commission. . . . You are the first of your race who has been thus honored by the government; therefore much depends on and will be expected of you. But I feel assured it is safe in your hands." (It should be noted that Dr. Alexander Augusta, also a black man, was mustered into the Union army as a major in 1863.)

By the time Delany had formed the 104th Regiment of Colored Troops, the Confederates had already surrendered. He was then sent to Hilton Head, South Carolina, to work with the Bureau of Refugees, Freedmen and Abandoned Lands. Though the war was over, he did not temper the fiery rhetoric that had served him throughout his life, and while stationed in South Carolina, he was accused of "calculating to do harm, by inciting the colored people to deeds of violence" in a lecture he gave to the 104th Negro South Carolina troops. He said on this occasion:

I want you to understand that we would not have become free, had we not armed ourselves and fought out our independence. . . . If I had been a slave, I would have been most troublesome and not to be conquered by any threat or punishment. I would not have worked, and no one would have dared to come near me. I would have struggled for life or death, and would have thrown fire and sword between them.

Your masters who lived in opulence, kept you to hard work by some contemptible being called overseer—who chastised and beat you whenever he pleased—while your master lived in some Northern town or in Europe to squander away the wealth only you acquired for him. He never earned a single Dollar in his life. You men and women, every one of you around me, made thousands and thousands of dollars for your master. Only you were the means for your masters to lead the idle and inglorious life, and to give his children the education, which he denied to you, for fear you may awake to conscience. If I look around me, I tell you all the fine houses on this Island and in Beaufort, they are all familiar to my eye, they are the same structures, which I have met with in Africa.

Delany exhorted the assembled:

Now go to work, and in a short time I will see you again, and other friends will come to show you how to begin. Have your fields in good order and well tilled and planted, and when I pass the fields and see a land well planted and well cared for, then I may be sure from the look of it, that it belongs to a free Negro, and when I see a field thinly planted and little cared for, then I may think it belongs to some man who works it with slaves.

It was reported by a man sent to spy on Delany that the crowd erupted in cheers throughout the speech and that whites who were present "listened with horror depicted in their faces to the whole performance."

Martin Delany had also turned to his friends to help him recruit soldiers. Since he had been successful in raising troops for the Fifty-fourth Massachusetts, he was hired to recruit for the state of Connecticut. According to Jane Rhodes, Delany invited Mary Ann Shadd Cary to join him in the field in recruiting in December 1863. Delany offered her "$15 for every slave and $5 for every freeborn African American she could muster for the 29th Regiment Connecticut Volunteers."

Shadd's position in life had changed in the previous few years, due partly to the death of her husband, which left her to provide for herself and her two small children. Despite her differences with Delany regarding their views on emigration, she agreed to use her connections and talents on behalf of the Union effort. While other Canadians recruited in Canada, Shadd chose to tour throughout the United States and tap into sources she had cultivated on her many lecture tours. Her success brought her even more requests to recruit for other states, including Indiana.

Despite her efforts on behalf of the American Civil War, though, Shadd never gave up her attachment to her Canadian identity. Rhodes writes, "Two months before Lee's surrender at Appomattox, she was issued a Canadian passport with the following description; height—five feet, six inches; color of hair—black; complexion—mulatto; nose—pug; general appearance—slight figure; age—thirty-five years." (For whatever reason, Shadd did not give her real age, forty-one.)

Shadd solicited her old friend Osborne Perry Anderson, the only survivor of John Brown's original group from Harpers Ferry, to help her recruit for the United States Colored Troops of Indiana and Arkansas. Some historians suggest that Anderson served as a noncommissioned officer during the war, but no records have been found to document his service. Jean Libby notes that after the war, Anderson visited Harpers Ferry in 1871, accompanying Richard Hinton, a Brown supporter who had been stationed by Brown just outside the general

Harpers Ferry area during the raid. Anderson "pointed out the scenes of battle," enabling Hinton to write *John Brown and His Men* in 1894.

When news of the recruitment of black troops had reached Buxton on August 12, 1863, a town hall meeting was called and the Reverend William King addressed the crowd, saying: "Those who would be free must strike the blow." King, who had urged caution regarding John Brown's raid, now urged Buxton settlers to join the Union army. Forty men immediately volunteered; thirty more would join shortly after. Most served with the Massachusetts, Michigan, or Indiana black regiments. Included in this number was Abraham W. Shadd, Mary Ann's brother, who fought with the Fifty-fifth Massachusetts, reached the rank of captain, and became chief clerk to Maj. Martin Delany. Also enlisting from Buxton was Solomon, the young boy William King had purchased before leaving Louisiana. Solomon was now a young man twenty years of age. He became a recruiter in Canada as well as in Kentucky.

James Harlin Newby was another Buxton settler who joined the Northern forces. His parents, Solomon and Margaret, were both free when they moved from Indiana to become one of the founding families of the Buxton settlement. One year after arriving in Buxton, James Newby enlisted in the Union army. He was a sergeant in Company One, Third Regiment, serving for three years in the Charleston, South Carolina, area. Newby returned to Buxton after the war and married Eliza Rann. They had six children and lived in Buxton until their deaths, James in 1928, Eliza in 1932.

Buxton's schools produced many talented men and women ready to serve in other capacities as well. Anderson Ruffin Abbott was one of the first six graduates of the Buxton schools and the first Buxton student to go on to receive a higher education. He studied at the Toronto Academy in conjunction with Knox College, where he received honors for his class work, went on to Oberlin College, and then returned to Canada to study medicine at the University of Toronto. He received a license to practice medicine in 1861. With the outbreak of the Civil War, Abbott enlisted and became a surgeon in the Union army, serving under Dr. Alexander Augusta, another prominent black doctor who had received his medical training in Canada.

Dr. Augusta, commissioned as a major, was the first black surgeon in the Union army, serving with the Seventh U.S. Colored Troops until his assistant surgeons complained to President Lincoln about having to serve under a black man. Augusta was transferred to the Freedmen's Hospital in Washington, D.C., and later became the first black person to achieve the rank of lieutenant colonel.

Dr. Augusta can be credited with ending discrimination on Washington, D.C., streetcars. Decades before Rosa Parks refused to give up her seat on the bus in Alabama, Augusta was thrown off a streetcar while attempting to get to a court hearing and thus arrived at the hearing late. When the judge demanded an explanation, Augusta presented him with a written statement about the event on the streetcar. Augusta sent a copy of the report to Senator Charles Sumner, who read it in Congress and subsequently offered legislation to end discrimination on public transportation.

Dr. Abbott left several manuscripts that provide interesting insights into his life. In one, owned by Abbott's daughter, Mrs. F. L. Hubbard, he revealed many of his experiences during the war, some with Dr. Augusta. Regarding the history of the U.S. Colored Troops, he wrote:

> The year 1863 opened very auspiciously for the colored man. On the 1st of January 1863 the President issued that immortal document, the Emancipation Proclamation, by which 4,000,000 of the Afro-American race emerged from two centuries and a half of the most barbarous human bondage that ever cursed the earth. Contemporaneously with this departure, the government disburdened itself of the temporizing policy it had pursued in respect of the employment of colored men in the military service. Tentative legislation looking to the accomplishment of this end soon followed upon the utterances of the Proclamation of Freedom. The government began to realize the fact that the rebellion could not be suppressed without his aid; and hesitated no longer in adopting a most vigor-

ous policy in securing his incorporation into the ranks of the country's defenders.

Another tale involved his friend, Dr. Augusta:

An amusing story was told me in reference to the Drs. [Augusta] examination by one of the officers of the Army Medical Department. He says that Dr. Cronyn who was president of the examining board having occasion to go into Surgeon General Hammond's office a short time after Augusta had passed was asked by the General "I say Cronyn how did you come to let that nigger pass?" Dr. Cronyn replied, "The fact is, general, that the nigger knew more than I did and I could not help myself."

Abbott also described a scene that occurred in the White House when both he and Augusta were invited to a function with President Lincoln:

Mr. Lincoln on seeing August advanced eagerly a few paces forward, grasped his hand, and, as he held the doctor's hand Robert Lincoln, who had been standing beside his mother about six paces off, came up to the President and asked a question very hastily, the purport of which I took to be—"Are you going to allow this innovation?"—referring doubtless to our presence there. The President replied promptly "Why not?" Nothing more was said and Robert Lincoln returned to his mother's side, while the President turned again to the doctor who gave his hand a hearty shake, and then I was introduced and the President shook hands with me also . . .

They then proceeded to the East Room:

The moment we entered the room, which was crowded and brilliantly lit up, we became the cynosure of all eyes. I never experienced such a sensation before as I did when we entered the room. We could not have been more surprised ourselves or created more surprise if we had been dropped down through a sky-light. I suppose it was because it was a first time in the history of the U.S. when a coloured man had appeared at one of these Levees. What made us more conspicuous of course was our uniforms. Colored men in the uniforms of U.S. military officers of high rank had never been seen before. I felt as though I should have liked to crawl into a hold. But, as we had decided to break the record, we held our ground.

Dr. Abbott must have established a personal relationship with President and Mrs. Lincoln, since upon the president's death, Mrs. Lincoln presented him with a plaid shawl. According to an article by Henry S. Robinson in the *Journal of the National Medical Association*, "the plaid shawl [was the one] which Lincoln wore on his way to his first inauguration and which, it is alleged, formed a part of a disguise which he wore on that occasion." (The necessity for the disguise was warranted after Lincoln's contentious election to the presidency.)

Abbott also moved to Washington, D.C., to continue his army service at the Freedmen's Hospital. In 1866, he returned to Chatham, where he resumed his medical practice and became a leader in the community until his death in 1913.

Dr. Augusta, after his discharge, taught at the newly formed Howard University Medical Department. He remained in the United States until his death in 1890, and was buried with full honors at Arlington National Cemetery.

The Civil War had ended in 1865 with Lee's surrender to Grant at Appomattox. Reconstruction—the period of rebuilding the country and providing for the assimilation of over four million newly freed blacks— was to begin. But the assassination of Abraham Lincoln less than one week after the end of the war left blacks without their most powerful ally in the White House. In Canada as well as in the United States, they mourned the death of the man who had given them hope. Black armbands were worn throughout Canada West. When Lincoln's funeral train reached Buffalo, hundreds of Canadians crossed the suspension bridge to pay homage. When Martin Delany heard of Lincoln's assassination, he grieved publicly and challenged those faithful to the president:

> I suggest that, as a just and appropriate tribute of respect and lasting gratitude from the colored people of the United States to the memory of President Lincoln, the Father of American Liberty, every individual of our race contribute one cent, as this will enable each member of every family to contribute, parents paying for every child, allowing all who are able to subscribe any sum they please above this, to such national monument as may hereafter be decided upon by the American people. I hope it may be in Illinois, near his own family residence.

Delany published his plea in May 1865. It is acknowledged to be the first public statement on behalf of erecting a monument to honor President Lincoln.

Andrew Johnson became the new president of the United States. Reconstruction was now in his hands.

On January 16, 1865, General Sherman had issued Field Order No. 15, setting aside the Sea Islands and a large portion of the Low Country rice-growing coastal lands of Charleston, South Carolina, as well as thirty miles inland, for exclusive settlement by blacks. He authorized the loan of mules to each family, thus the phrase "forty acres and a mule."

Constitutional conventions were held in 1867 and 1868 to rewrite the southern state constitutions in order to bring them into compliance with Reconstruction policies. Many newly enfranchised blacks took an active role and often, because they outnumbered whites in the area, held the voting majority.

But new gains for the freedmen and women brought a dramatic backlash from white southerners, who felt they were being unfairly punished, facing not only the confiscation of their slave "property" but also the fact of Yankee control over their lives and the certainty of increasing black equality under the law. Many southern states responded with new black codes, some prohibiting land ownership by blacks outside city limits, some establishing curfews for blacks, some instituting poll taxes for blacks trying to vote. Others included the barring of interracial marriages. This period also gave rise to the establishment of a new terror organization, the Ku Klux Klan.

Just as many sons and daughters of Canada West extended their efforts during the war, others left their mark during Reconstruction. Particularly noteworthy was the Buxton community's response. King biographer Ullman states, "No single community in either the United States or Canada contributed so much to the emancipated Negroes as the sons and daughters of Buxton."

Many Buxton settlers still considered the South their homeland. After the war, they asked King to consider redirecting their mission work from Africa to the southern states, urging him to establish a "Buxton Settlement in the South." Each family would sell their farm in Canada and use the proceeds as a down payment toward the purchase of four or five hundred acres of land in the South. On these acres, side by side, they would re-create the Buxton community that had served them so well.

Being the cautious man that he was, and not trusting fully the news of Reconstruction coming out of the South, William King decided to go to Washington, D.C., to confer with General Howard, head of the Freedmen's Bureau. As he may have suspected, the support King had hoped to gain for the Buxton project was not forthcoming. Howard expressed his own frustrations with the new president, Johnson, and concerns regarding his ability to carry out Lincoln's original plans for Reconstruction. Howard indicated that a state of lawlessness existed in the South and that it was not safe for blacks to move there to initiate such a project.

When he returned to Buxton to give the community the news, King must have felt that he had succeeded with his mission of establishing a group of educated, self-sufficient people, for he did not try to convince the settlers to stay in Canada. He suggested that "those now educated in the settlement could go and give instruction to their brethren in ignorance . . . they could go as individuals and make themselves useful." Many began leaving their Buxton homeland immediately.

This exodus from Buxton was duplicated throughout Canada West. Census figures indicate that Canada West's black population went from approximately thirty-five thousand to forty thousand in 1861 to about thirteen thousand five hundred in 1871. Buxton's population had been reduced from its peak of two thousand to about thirteen hundred by 1871.

One of the South's most successful blacks during the Reconstruction years had come from Buxton. James Rapier was the youngest of four sons born free in Florence, Alabama. Despite all the laws against blacks receiving schooling, his extended family persevered in educating their children. John Rapier, Jr., one of his older brothers, a friend of Frederick Douglass as well as Dr. Anderson Abbott, had obtained a medical degree and later served as a surgeon with the Freedmen's Hospital in Washington, D.C. In 1856, though, eighteen-year-old James was still spending his time gambling and drinking on the steamboats of the Mississippi River. When he agreed to go back to school, he went to live with his uncle, Henry K. Thomas, in Buxton.

Thomas, born enslaved, owed his freedom to his mother, who had worked many jobs while she herself was still enslaved, in order to save money to purchase her children's freedom before the Civil War. Thomas had eventually settled in Buffalo, New York, where he owned a thriving barbershop in the prestigious Niagara Hotel. After the passage of the 1850 Fugitive Slave Act, he moved his family to the outskirts of Buxton, where he purchased over a hundred acres of farmland and became a successful businessman, serving on the board of the Canada Mill and Mercantile Association.

James Rapier began school in Buxton in October 1856, studying several languages as well as mathematics, grammar, writing, and geography, as did the other students. He seemed to get serious about his education after having a religious conversion the next year. In a letter to his brother, he wrote, "I am delivered." Continuing his studies, which now included Latin, Greek, and Spanish, James became one of King's best students.

In 1860, the Prince of Wales stopped in Buxton on his tour of Canada and the United States, and Rapier was selected to address him on behalf of the settlement. Expressing the satisfaction black settlers had found in Canada, specifically Buxton, Rapier said, "Here we enjoy true freedom, a blessing denied us in the land of our birth."

Rapier continued his higher education at a Toronto Normal School, and despite financial hardship received a teaching certificate in 1863. Returning to Buxton, he became the first teacher at the new school in what is now North Buxton. When the Civil War began, he too felt compelled to return south. In remarks made later at a celebration of the Fifteenth Amendment, he recalled, "You can imagine my feelings when I heard that Gen. Beauregard had ordered the firing on Fort Sumter. I listened to the sounds, and though many miles away, I fancied I heard the cannon, in thunder tones say, 'The year of jubilee has come, return you exiles, home.' "

In 1864, Rapier moved to Nashville, Tennessee, to begin the rest of his life's work. In 1865, he entered the national debate over black suffrage. With even staunch white abolitionists such as Charles Sumner and Thaddeus Stevens against granting blacks the right to vote, black leaders had to pick up the cause. Rapier suggested that a survey be conducted detailing the advances made by blacks since emancipation, thereby giving a foundational basis for arguing the black-suffrage cause. He told members at the state constitutional convention, "It is only a question of time." Rapier urged them to act as other states had already done, but he was not able to sway enough voters, and in Tennessee not only was black suffrage denied but antiblack legislation passed instead.

Despite this failure, Rapier began emerging as a leader and

spokesperson. He moved to his birth state of Alabama and became a successful farmer, watching political events unfold until the right environment would allow him to reenter politics. In 1867, when Congress finally took over Reconstruction efforts in Alabama as well as in some other southern states, Rapier and other sympathetic whites and blacks wasted no time. Voter registration among blacks became a priority; in October 1867, they voted for the first time in Alabama history. Seventy-two thousand blacks and eighteen thousand whites voted in favor of the constitutional convention to determine a new state constitution.

James Rapier was elected one of the delegates. In this role, he showed his ability to lead without exercising retribution against white citizens, suggesting that voting rights be given to black males, but also that amnesty be offered to those whites who had fought for the Confederacy. This was in contradiction to those who wished to punish the rebel states. Venturing into the area of civil rights, Rapier also argued for fair treatment on public transportation: "It is past my comprehension the manner in which colored gentlemen and colored ladies are treated on railroads and common carriers. I do not consider myself honored by sitting in a car beside a white man, simply because he is white." Other black delegates also took up the cause against separate accommodations based on race.

In a July 7, 1870, letter to the Reverend William King, Rapier thanked his teacher and mentor and brought him up-to-date on other Buxton men who had left Canada:

My dear friend: After a long silence on my part without any good cause, I take advantage of the present opportunity to address you this letter knowing full well, you have always taken a lively interest in me, and not only in myself, but all the boys who attended the old log schoolhouse and church. Whether I have profited by the education I received there or not, is not for me to practice. John Riley [another of Buxton's first graduates, who became a Presbyterian minister, in several southern cities, including Washington, D.C.] was preaching to a large congregation in Louisville, Kentucky; his brother Jerome [who went on to get a medical degree from Howard University and helped found the Freedmen's Hospital] was practicing medicine in the hospital in Washington. I hope to visit Canada this fall on private business, when I hope to see you. Remember me to the friends in Buxton.

Rapier went on to help establish a black labor union, from which platform he argued for homesteading lands to be opened up to black farmers who were struggling to purchase land. He even met with President Grant to pursue his case. Rapier also advocated a national education cabinet post: "We want a government schoolhouse, with the letters U.S. marked thereon in every township in the State. We want a national series of textbooks which will teach the child that to respect the government is the first duty of a citizen."

In 1872, Rapier began publication of the *Republican Sentinel*, which was, according to Loren Schweninger's biography of him, the "first black-owned, black-edited, and black-organized journal in Alabama." Rapier used the newspaper as a means to support Grant, the Republican party, and the needs of freedmen. He also had other goals in mind. He wrote to William King, "I have long wished to try for membership in Congress." Elected to that body in 1872, his first act was to submit legislation to improve the common school system and to fund it as necessary. His success in his first year in Congress, 1873, has been summed up by Schweninger: "During the first session of the Forty-third Congress Rapier not only voted on economic matters, wrote important legislation, and answered critics at home, he also listened to the first skirmishes of the House debate on civil rights."

The Freedmen's Bureau was abolished in 1872. Northern sympathizers of black causes had grown weary of efforts to bring black equality to the whole country. The economy was booming and legislators had other issues on their mind. Rapier tried for reelection in 1874 and 1876 but was defeated both times. He and other southern blacks began watching the erosion of the political and social gains they had made. By 1879, many of them began leaving the south for Kansas and Indiana.

Schweninger notes that "by May [1879] the total was estimated at fifty thousand, a figure that represented the greatest single migration of blacks in the nineteenth century."

Rapier had reluctantly come to a similar conclusion; emigration from the increasingly hostile South was "the only viable solution to the problems facing blacks." In this, he went against the beliefs of other prominent spokemen such as Frederick Douglass, who, in line with his previous views on emigration to Canada, urged southern blacks to stay put as "conditions in the Southern states were improving so steadily that ultimately blacks would realize 'the fullest measure of liberty.' "

Rapier was selected for one last governmental appointment but did not live to take the position. He died in 1883 in Montgomery, Alabama, at the age of forty-five of pulmonary tuberculosis.

Educational and leadership skills learned in Buxton were put to use in other southern states, as well. Thomas Stringer, originally a fugitive from Mississippi, lived for a while with his family in Ohio, where he became active in the African Methodist Episcopal Church. Stringer was an adult when he first moved to Buxton; he attended King's evening classes. One of the founders of the African Methodist Episcopal Church in Buxton, he is credited with organizing many churches throughout Canada West. In 1865, he moved back to Mississippi and established the first AME church in Vicksburg; eventually he established thirty-five churches.

In 1870, Stringer became the first black man elected to the Mississippi State Legislature. He was also active in developing Masonic lodges throughout Mississippi and was recognized for his efforts (in 1876, the Vicksburg Lodge was renamed the Most Worshipful Stringer Grand Lodge). Ullman notes that Stringer also organized the Fraternal Life Insurance Benefit Company, which became the "most successful cooperative Negro business venture in the Black Belt."

Isaac D. Shadd, brother to Mary Ann, partner in publishing the *Provincial Freeman,* and staunch supporter of John Brown, also moved to Mississippi during Reconstruction, along with his wife, Amelia Freeman. She taught school in Davis Bend and he worked as a book-keeper until he was elected Speaker of the Mississippi House of Representatives in 1874.

The young women of Buxton stand out as well. Although records are not as detailed for them, and gender constricted the roles available to them, King had encouraged many to become teachers. Their skills too would prove invaluable. There was a desperate need in the South for teachers at the newly established schools for former slaves. Once again, the fact that fugitives from Canada West were educated enabled them to also take leadership roles in this field. One woman mentioned specifically is Harriet Rhue Hatchett, who moved from Buxton to Licking River, Kentucky, and taught there for ten years. Hatchett returned to Buxton after this time period, when she found the southern black codes intolerable. As a young woman, she had taken piano lessons from King's second wife, Jemima, whom he had married in 1853. Hatchett's lessons ended suddenly, according to Ullman, when Mrs. King had a "spell." King seldom mentioned Jemima in any of his written records, but, again according to Ullman, it was well known throughout the Elgin settlement that Mrs. King had some form of "mental derangement." Hatchett must have been a good student. When she returned to Buxton, she continued to play and began writing hymns. "That Sacred Spot," her first to be published, became the official marching song of the Canadian army during World War I.

The Niagara Frontier also contributed its share of black men and women to the cause. The area's most famous resident, Harriet Tubman, had already moved back to New York by the time the Civil War broke out. It was Governor John Andrew of Massachusetts, again tapping into his network of prominent blacks, who suggested that Tubman be put to use with the Union army in South Carolina. She began her work in Beaufort with the "Port Royal Experiment," as it was dubbed, a government project to demonstrate how newly freed slaves could live given the right opportunities and conditions. Tubman distributed clothing and food and set up a washhouse to train the newly freed black women how to support themselves by washing and sewing for the Union soldiers.

After the war, Tubman continued her services, working as a nurse among wounded soldiers. Like Mary Ann Shadd, she became active in the women's suffrage movement, and, like her male peers, worked on behalf of black suffrage.

While many of the Detroit-area men had enlisted in the Michigan regiments, the Niagara blacks enlisted in East Coast regiments such as the Fifty-fourth Massachusetts. Writer Tom Derreck has been researching the Niagara region connection to the Civil War and has identified at least nine men from the St. Catharines area who fought, some with the Fifty-fourth Massachusetts. Pvt. William Henry of Fort Erie, who joined at the age of nineteen, was one. Henry was eventually wounded during the Battle of Olustee, in Florida, but his whereabouts after the war are unknown.

By the end of the war, the population of blacks in Canada West was less than one-third what it had been during its peak decade of 1850–1860. The British American Institute in Dawn, which had unofficially ceased operations, was finally sold in 1868. The Elgin settlement, or Buxton, whose population had gone from two thousand to less than thirteen hundred after the war, dissolved as a formal entity. Many of the settlers who remained moved to the northern edges of the settlement and established the community now known as North Buxton.

Chatham had lost many of its black leaders to the United States. Martin Delany, Mary Ann Shadd, Osborne Anderson, and Isaac Shadd all remained in the United States after the war. Henry Bibb had been dead for over a decade. The Refugee Home Society he had fostered officially ended with the end of the Civil War. Left behind were sixty families who had been settled under its auspices. The *Voice of the Fugitive* and the *Provincial Freeman* had ceased publication even before the war began. Canada West's black families had often separated, some remaining in Canada, others moving back to the United States.

Dr. Anderson Abbott expressed his views on the success of the Buxton settlement in a report written in 1894:

A large number of white settlers now occupy the land, but that makes no difference. The two classes work together on each other's farms, go to the same churches, their children attend the same schools, the teachers are white and coloured, and the pupils fraternize without any friction whatever. The teacher of the North Buxton School, Alfred Shadd, is an Afro-Canadian. He holds a second-class certificate from the normal school, Toronto, and has been a successful teacher for a number of years. One-third of his pupils are white. There are three hundred pupils in the schools. The various offices of the municipality, such as councilors, school trustees, path masters, constables and justices of the peace are fairly distributed among both classes. The coloured farmers who now occupy the land are of the best classes. Very few of them had any means at first; their only resources were their courage and determination to succeed . . . When they appear in the Chatham market side by side with their white neighbors, as vendors, there is nothing to distinguish but their colour.

While historians argue the successes and failures of Reconstruction, they cannot deny the accomplishments made under the auspices of the Freedmen's Bureau. This department succeeded in setting up over a hundred hospitals and establishing over four thousand schools, including institutes of higher learning such as Fisk University, the Hampton Institute, and Howard University. The Thirteenth, Fourteenth, and Fifteenth Amendments to the United States Constitution were all passed during the period of Reconstruction. Slavery was officially abolished; over four million formerly enslaved were freed. They became citizens of the United States and were granted the right to vote, a privilege protected by law. At least some of the accomplishments occurring during this time period can be credited to the educational and leadership abilities of those blacks who had lived in freedom under the protection of the British government and chose to risk that freedom to return to fight on behalf of those still enslaved.

Afterword

The antebellum history of Canada West has not been lost; it is kept alive today, in many instances, by descendants of the original settlers. From the eastern portal of Buffalo, Niagara, and St. Catharines, to the western portal of Detroit and Windsor, a shared black history is honored and celebrated.

On Labor Day weekend every year, the population of the small village of North Buxton, Ontario, swells to ten times its usual number. In North Buxton, it is Homecoming Weekend, when friends, families, and descendants of the original settlers return to celebrate their heritage.

The festivities begin on Friday with an international history and genealogy conference, in which Civil War scholars from across the United States and Canada meet and share their research. On Saturday, teams of families descended from the original Buxton settlers play Family Feud softball for the right to hold a traveling trophy for a year. Buxton's Next Generation of young adults sponsors an evening Party in the Park, with dancing until the early-morning hours. Sunday, the Liberty bell peals out its welcome from the Reverend William King's St. Andrew's Church, just as it did for all those early fugitives who reached freedom. In the evening, locals and friends reenact episodes from Buxton's early history.

Monday, Labor Day, begins with a parade, and continues with picnic lunches on the Buxton Historic Site and Museum grounds. The final championship softball game is played to determine the current year's winner. Civil War reenactors walk among the crowd and invite them into their camps. Cries of recognition can be heard throughout as families and friends, separated now by distance and time, reunite within sight of the old pear tree, which designates the site of the original Homecoming celebration over eighty years ago.

All weekend, the newly restored 1861 schoolhouse and the Buxton Museum welcome visitors to tour and view artifacts of the early Buxton settlers. The graveyard beside the church reveals familiar names, including that of Eliza Parker of Christiana resistance fame. Many of the gravestones are etched with the acronym USCT, indicating service in the United States Colored Troops. Evenings during Homecoming are spent around family campfires. As curator Shannon Prince says, "Homecoming is when visitors become family."

In Chatham, black history is honored by the Chatham-Kent Black Historical Society on King Street, where local artifacts are on display and genealogy materials are available. Every year in May, a John Brown Conference is held to bring Brown scholars together for a day of lectures and discussions. Just a few yards down the street is the First Baptist Church of Chatham, designated the John Brown Meeting House. Mary Ann Shadd's contributions to Chatham history are noted with a plaque, also on King Street.

A few miles away lies the town of Dresden, where a walking trail tells the history of the community, both black and white. At Dresden's edge is Uncle Tom's Cabin Historic Site, which invites visitors to tour Josiah Henson's cabin as well as other buildings representative of that period. As well as the Henson story, the museum exhibit features the history of the British American Institute and the story of slavery in the United States and Canada. Original artifacts from the Henson family and days of slavery and freedom are prominently displayed. In the adjacent cemetery is Josiah Henson's tombstone. Graves from other settlers of the British American Institute lie just opposite the museum property.

On the eastern border of Ontario is the town of St. Catharines, which celebrates its Harriet Tubman connections. Her commemorative plaque is outside Salem Chapel, the St. Catharines British Methodist Episcopal Church on Geneva Street. A few miles away, just off the street in Centennial Park, is the Richard Pierpoint plaque. Anthony Burns is buried in Victoria Lawn Cemetery, and farther along the same road the Welland Canal and the St. Catharines Museum offer visitors the opportunity to see a working canal and learn the black history of the Niagara region, including the legacy of the Colored Corps, the militia who were asked to keep the peace among workers building the canal.

In the Niagara River and Falls area, along the Niagara Parkway, visitors can find the "Crossing" stone, so designated to honor the area where a ferry brought many of the fugitives across the river.

At the western end of Ontario, in Amherstburg, the Nazrey African Methodist Episcopal Church National Historic Site stands next to the North American Black Historical Museum. The stone walls of the church and the pulpit inside were built by former slaves. The museum houses local artifacts and celebrates the black history of this western portal for many hundreds of fugitives. Sandwich, though now a part of Windsor, is still designated a historical black history area. The First Baptist Church dates its congregation's history back to 1840. The church itself was built in 1851.

John Hope Franklin, deemed by scholars to be the "dean of African American historians," in a 1979 presidential address to the American Historical Association, stated:

In recent years historians have focused much more on the period of slavery than on the period of freedom. Some historians have been most enthusiastic about the capacity of slaves to establish and maintain institutions while in bondage, to function effectively in an economic system as a kind of upwardly mobile group of junior partners, and to make the transition to freedom with a minimum of trauma. . . . Does this pattern suggest that historians have thought that the key to understanding the place of Afro-Americans in American life is to be found in the slave experience and not in the struggles for adjustment in the early years of freedom? Or does it merely mean that historians find the study of slavery more exotic or more tragic and therefore more attractive than the later period of freedom?

The story of the fugitives and free blacks who reached Canada and lived free in the decades before the Civil War is a different story from those usually told, one not limited by the experience of slavery, but defined by the experience of living in freedom. It is a story that celebrates a new beginning.

ACKNOWLEDGMENTS

It has been a humbling experience to attempt to cross the borders of race and country in order to tell a story that embraces each. But the task was made much easier with the help of all those I met along the way. To my friends in Chatham, Buxton, Dresden, and Amherstburg, my sincere thanks.

I did not have to create a new path when researching this area. As in most cases, no work of nonfiction can be written without the efforts of those who have gone before. In this case, there are several whose seminal works I relied on for guidance: Robin Winks, Daniel Hill, Donald Simpson, Arlie Robbins, and Victor Ullman. They each carved out the path and left footprints for the rest of us to follow. We are all indebted to them for their pioneering work.

In many places I resarched, I was guided by the descendants who are keeping their ancestors' stories alive and honoring them. I offer my thanks for your help and your support in letting me be a part of telling your story.

In Buxton, I spent many a long night sitting at Bryan and Shannon Prince's kitchen table, listening to stories, laughing, and exchanging thoughts until the wee hours of the morning. My thanks for letting me be a part of your family. Bryan, you are indeed the griot for your community and deserve the Queen's Golden Jubilee Medal you received in honor of your work preserving black history. I am not kidding when I say that I think your kitchen table should be on the list of historical sites. History is not just discussed there, it is made.

In addition, my appreciation and thanks:

To Elise Harding Davis, for giving me special access to the archives at the North American Black History Museum in Amherstburg, and to Charlotte Watkins, for sharing your family story with me and for touching me deeply with your piano renditions of the spirituals.

To Marie Carter, for a guided tour of Dresden and for helping me and others understand your area's rich black and white history. My thanks to Gwen Robinson, Daniel Milne, and Millie Jackson of the Chatham-Kent Black History Museum for opening up your archives to me and helping me understand that Chatham was indeed "a Black man's Paris."

To Barbara Carter and Steven Cook, my thanks for helping me get to know your ancestor, Josiah Henson, the real man and story behind the myth of "Uncle Tom."

To Toni Parker, for being wise beyond your years in understanding the importance of your William and Eliza Parker family history and sharing it with me. To Dr. Afua Cooper, for sharing your amazing seminal work on Henry Bibb that brought him and the issues surrounding him and his wife, Mary, to life for me. To Virginia Travis: You offered me your friendship, your home, and access to the John Brown Church. Your faith in me kept me going on many a dark, starless night.

My thanks also to William Gladstone, Tom Brooks, and Bennie McCrae, for sharing your knowledge of black Civil War soldiers; to Dr. Ronald Palmer, for your work on George DeBaptiste, and for the work of C. Peter Ripley and Roy E. Finkenbine, whose efforts led to the publication of the *Black Abolitionist Papers* that have allowed all of us to reach into the past and let the ancestors speak for themselves. To John Polacsek, for explaining to me in great detail early Great Lakes maritime history. And to Jean Libby for sharing your perspective and work on John Brown history and pictography.

My thanks to my agents, Madeleine Morel and Barbara Lowenstein, for helping me continue to tell the stories I want to tell. Writers cannot do what they do without your efforts. And to Hettie Jones, who believed in the story, signed on to help me tell it, and made me a better writer and the book a better story. I am honored to have shared this journey with you.

A special note of appreciation to my copyeditor, Carol Edwards, who went beyond her role and helped me with the facts. My thanks also to my editor, Clarence Haynes, for his support of this project from the beginning.

This book would not have been written had not my friend Joseph Walkes, Jr. asked me many years ago, "Have you been to Buxton yet?" I hope this book contains my response. Many thanks for your continued guidance and support.

As always, to my husband Stewart, who enabled me to make this all happen, my love and thanks. And to my children, Jasmine and Alex, and my new son-in-law, Patrick, I hope my work inspires you to value your own family stories. My thanks also to my friend Patty Stillwell, who walked the journey with me, and to those other friends who made me realize that sometimes you just have to stop, look up into the night sky, and dance to the moon.

And, finally, a special thank-you goes to Andrea Moore, whose support and respect stayed with me throughout the writing process. Although she did not live to see *From Midnight to Dawn* completed, her work lives on in so many ways, portions of this book included.

TIME LINE

1619	August 20, first African slaves arrive in Jamestown, Virginia, on a Dutch ship
1628	Olivier Lejeune, a young slave from Madagascar, becomes first recorded slave brought to Canada
1629	King Louis XIV allows slaves to enter New France (later called Canada)
1663	The first known slave revolt in the colonies occurs in Gloucester County, Virginia
1689	Louis XIV passes Code Noir, allowing slavery in all colonies
1708	First slave revolt on Long Island, New York
1712	April 6, New York slave rebellion occurs
1749	October 26, British Parliament formally legalizes slavery in colony known as Georgia
1770	March 5, Boston Massacre occurs
1775	May 10, black patriots help capture Fort Ticonderoga
1775	June 17, the Battle of Bunker Hill occurs; several blacks participate
1775	November 24, Continental Congress bars blacks from Continental army
1776	Free Black Loyalists who fought with the British are evacuated to Nova Scotia
1780	March 1, Pennsylvania becomes first state to abolish slavery

1783   American Revolution ends; those loyal to Britain, including blacks (not just free), move to Canada

1787   May 6, first black Masonic lodge organized by Prince Hall, a Revolutionary War veteran

1787   Northwest Ordinance declares that "there shall be neither slavery nor involuntary servitude in the said territory"

1787   U.S. Constitution provides that slaves are to be counted as three-fifths of a person for representation in Congress

1790   October 23, first slave revolt in Haiti takes place

1793   First Fugitive Slave Act passed in the United States

1793   Upper Canada under Simcoe passes bill for the gradual abolition of slavery

1793   Eli Whitney invents the cotton gin

1794   February 4, France abolishes slavery

1804   January 1, Haiti becomes the first independent black-led republic

1804   January 5, Ohio enacts Black Laws

1807   Britain abolishes slave trade

1808   United States passes law prohibiting importation of slaves

1811   January 8, slave rebellion in Louisiana

1812   War of 1812 commences; black soldiers in Canada fight for Canada

1822   June 16, Denmark Vesey leads slave revolt in South Carolina

1828   First African Methodist Episcopal Church in Upper Canada built in Amherstburg

1829   Wilberforce originates when Ohio fugitives flee enforcement of black codes

1829   David Walker, a free black, publishes *Walker's Appeal*

1829   Mexico abolishes slavery; some slaves escape south

1831   August 21, Nat Turner and seventy slaves revolt over two-day period in Virginia; November 11, he is hanged

1831   William Lloyd Garrison begins publication of the *Liberator,* an antislavery newspaper

1832   Laura Haviland and Elizabeth Chandler organize Logan Female Anti-Slavery Society in Michigan Territory

1833   December 4, William Lloyd Garrison and some sixty abolitionists meet in Philadelphia and found the American Anti-Slavery Society

1833   Blackburn Riots in Detroit

1833   August 28, Britain abolishes slavery in British Empire; Emancipation Act effective August 1, 1834

1839   June 28, Mende tribal member Cinque leads rebellion aboard the slave ship *Amistad*

1842   Dawn settlement founded near Dresden by Hiram Wilson and Josiah Henson

1844   Levi Coffin, Underground Railroad conductor, tours Canada West

1845   *Narrative of the Life of Frederick Douglass* published

1847   Frederick Douglass begins publication of the *North Star,* an antislavery paper

1847   William Wells Brown publishes autobiography

1849   The Elgin settlement and Buxton Mission for fugitives established by the Reverend William King

1850   September 18, second Fugitive Slave Act passed; both fugitive and free blacks move to Canada for safety

1850   Harriet Tubman begins her work on the Underground Railroad by helping her niece and her niece's two children to escape

1851   North American Convention of Colored People meets in Toronto

1851   Henry and Mary Bibb begin publication of *Voice of the Fugitive,* first black-owned antislavery newspaper in Canada

1851   Refugee Home Society established by Michigan and Canadian abolitionists to purchase land for fugitives settling near Windsor

1851   First Anti-Slavery Society of Canada founded in Toronto

1851   Harriet Tubman moves to St. Catharines; continues to live there until 1857

1852   September 11, Christiana resistance occurs in Pennsylvania

1852   Harriet Beecher Stowe publishes *Uncle Tom's Cabin;* it becomes an instant best-seller

1853   Mary Ann Shadd publishes *Provincial Freeman,* second black-owned antislavery newspaper in Canada; first published in Windsor, later in Toronto and Chatham

1854   May 24, fugitive slave Anthony Burns returned to the south from Boston

1856   British Methodist Episcopal Church of Canada separates from American Methodist Episcopal Church to show loyalty to Britain's abolition of slavery

1856   Benjamin Drew publishes *The Refugee: or the Narratives of Fugitive Slaves in Canada* after interviewing over one hundred fugitives throughout Canada West

1856   Michigan and Amherstburg Baptist churches unite

1857   Dred Scott decision passed down by U.S. Supreme Court

1858   John Brown holds his constitutional convention in Chatham

1858   George DeBaptiste and William Lambert organize the African-American Mysteries, a secret order, in Detroit

1859   October 16, John Brown raids Harpers Ferry; Osborne Anderson of Chatham fights with him

1859   December 16, Shields Green and John Anthony Copeland, two black
         Harpers Ferry conspirators, are hanged
1861   April 12, American Civil War begins
1861   September 25, first blacks admitted into Union navy
1862   April 16, slavery abolished in Washington, D.C.
1862   May 12, black slaves take Confederate ship *The Planter*
1863   January 1, Emancipation Proclamation passed
1863   Samuel Gridley Howe tours Canada West on behalf of President Lincoln
         and the Freedmen's Bureau to make recommendations for freeing slaves
         in the United States
1863   Congress authorizes recruitment of black soldiers in Union army; many
         blacks from Canada rush to enlist
1863   March 10, all-black Fifty-fourth Massachusetts Voluntary Infantry cre-
         ated; several blacks from Canada are in this regiment
1863   July 13, New York draft riots
1865   March 3, Freedmen's Bureau established
1865   April 9, Civil War ends when Lee surrenders to Grant
1865   April 15, President Abraham Lincoln dies; Andrew Johnson becomes
         president
1865   December 6, Thirteenth Amendment, abolishing slavery, ratified
1865   Mississippi begins enacting black codes
1865   Ku Klux Klan created in Tennessee
1866   Civil Rights Act passes over Johnson's veto
1866   Fourteenth Amendment to U.S. Constitution approved by Congress;
         sent to states for ratification
1866   May 1, Memphis race riot; July 30, New Orleans race riot
1867   Platform of Republican party convention in New Orleans includes equal-
         ity for blacks
1868   Fourteenth Amendment ratified; all persons born or naturalized in the
         United States entitled to citizenship and equal protection under U.S. laws
1868   British American Institute (Dawn) officially closes
1868   Thaddeus Stevens, Radical Republican in Congress, dies
1868   Ulysses S. Grant elected president
1870   March 30, Fifteenth Amendment ratified, giving voting rights to all male
         citizens regardless of race or former servitude
1870   Hiram Revels elected as first black to U.S. Senate
1872   Freedmen's Bureau abolished
1873   Elgin settlement officially closes

BIBLIOGRAPHY

Books

Adams, Ephraim Douglass. *Great Britain and the American Civil War*. Gloucester, Massachusetts: Peter Smith, 1925.

Adams, Nehemiah. *A South-Side View of Slavery; or, Three Months at the South in 1864*. 1864. Reprint. Port Washington, New York: Kennikat Press, 1969.

Anderson, Osborne P. *A Voice from Harper's Ferry*. 1861. Reprint. New York: World View Forum, 2000.

Andrews, William L., and Henry Louis Gates, Jr., comps. *Slave Narratives*. New York: Penguin Putnam, 2000.

Aptheker, Herbert, ed. *A Documentary History of the Negro People in the United States*. New York: Citadel Press, 1951.

Bald, F. Clever. *Detroit's First American Decade, 1796–1805*. Ann Arbor: University of Michigan Press, 1948.

Barry, Joseph. *The Strange Story of Harpers's Ferry: With Legends of the Surrounding Country*. 1903. Reprint. Shepherdstown, West Virginia: The Woman's Club of Harpers Ferry District, 1964.

Berlin, Ira, Marc Favreau, and Steven F. Miller, eds. *Remembering Slavery: African Americans Talk About Their Personal Experiences of Slavery and Emancipation*. New York: The New Press, 1998.

Blackett, R. J. M. *Running a Thousand Miles for Freedom: The Escape of William and Ellen Craft from Slavery*. 1860. Reprint. Baton Rouge: Louisiana State University Press, 1986.

Blight, David W., ed. *Passages to Freedom: The Underground Railroad in History and Memory*. Washington, D.C.: Smithsonian Books, 2004.

Blockson, Charles L. *The Underground Railroad: Dramatic Firsthand Accounts of Daring Escapes to Freedom*. New York: Berkeley, 1987.

———. *Hippocrene Guide to the Underground Railroad*. New York: Hippocrene Books, 1994.

Bolster, W. Jeffrey. *Black Jacks: African American Seamen in the Age of Sail*. Cambridge: Harvard University Press, 1997.

Bordewich, Fergus. M. *Bound for Canaan: The Underground Railroad and the War for the Soul of America*. New York: Amistad/HarperCollins, 2005.

Bradford, Sarah. *Scenes in the Life of Harriet Tubman*. Auburn, New York: W. J. Moses, 1869.

Bridges, Flora Wilson. *Resurrection Song: African-American Spirituality*. Maryknoll, New York: Orbis, 2001.

Bristow, Peggy, coordinator, and Dionne Brand, et al., eds. *"We're Rooted Here and They Can't Pull Us Up": Essays in African Canadian Women's History*. Toronto: University of Toronto Press, 1994.

Brown, William Wells. *The Rising Son; or, the Antecedents and Advancement of the Colored Race*. 1874. Reprint. New York: Negro Universities Press, 1970.

Brown-Kubisch, Linda. *The Queen's Bush Settlement: Black Pioneers 1839–1865*. Toronto: Natural Heritage Books, 2004.

Browne, Ray B., and Lawrence A. Kreiser, Jr. *The Civil War and Reconstruction*. Westport, Connecticut: Greenwood Press, 2003.

Buckmaster, Henrietta. *Let My People Go: The Story of the Underground Railroad and the Growth of the Abolition Movement*. Columbia: University of South Carolina Press, 1992.

Carter, Marie, and Jeffrey Carter. *Stepping Back in Time: Along the Trillium Trail in Dresden*. Dresden, Ontario: Catherine McVean Chapter IODE, 2003.

Catton, Bruce. *The American Heritage Picture History of the Civil War*. New York: American Heritage, 1960.

Charlebois, Peter. *Sternwheelers and Sidewheelers: The Romance of Steamdriven Paddleboats in Canada*. Toronto: N. C. Press, 1978.

Coffin, Levi. *Reminiscences of Levi Coffin*. Cincinnati: Robert Clark, 1880.

Conrad, Earl. *General Harriet Tubman*. Washington, D.C.: Associated Publishers, 1990.

Cooper, Afua. "Doing Battle in Freedom's Cause: Henry Bibb, Abolitionism, Race uplift, and Black Manhood. 1842–1854." Ph.D. diss., University of Toronto, 2000.

Creel, Margaret Washington. *"A Peculiar People": Slave Religion and Community-Culture Among the Gullahs.* New York: New York University Press, 1988.

Cruden, Robert. *The Negro in Reconstruction.* Englewood Cliffs, New Jersey: Prentice-Hall, 1969.

Danforth, Mildred E. *A Quaker Pioneer: Laura Haviland, Superintendent of the Underground Railroad.* New York: Exposition Press, 1961.

Davis, David Brion, and Steven Mintz. *The Boisterous Sea of Liberty: A Documentary History of America from the Discovery Through the Civil War.* Oxford: Oxford University Press, 1998.

Davis, Harry E. *A History of Freemasonry Among Negroes in America.* Chicago: R.R. Donnelley and Sons, 1946.

DeCaro, Louis, Jr. *"Fire from the Midst of You": A Religious Life of John Brown.* New York and London: New York University Press, 2002.

Diamond, Arthur. *Prince Hall: Social Reformer.* New York: Chelsea House, 1992.

Dillon, Merton L. *Benjamin Lundy and the Struggle for Negro Freedom.* Urbana and London: University of Illinois Press, 1966.

Douglas, R. Alan. *Uppermost Canada: The Western District and the Detroit Frontier, 1800–1850.* Detroit: Wayne State University Press, 2001.

Douglass, Frederick. *My Bondage and My Freedom.* 1855. Reprint. Urbana and Chicago: University of Illinois Press, 1987.

Drew, Benjamin. *The Refugee: A North-Side View of Slavery.* 1855. Reprint. Reading, Massachusetts: Addison-Wesley, 1969.

Du Bois, W. E. B. *Black Reconstruction in America, 1860–1880.* 1935. Reprint. New York: Atheneum, 1992.

————. *John Brown.* 1909. Reprint. New York: International Publishers, 1996.

Dunbar, Willis Frederick, and George S. May. *Michigan: A History of the Wolverine State.* Grand Rapids, Michigan: William B. Eerdmans, 1965.

Escott, Paul D. *Slavery Remembered: A Record of Twentieth-Century Slave Narratives.* Chapel Hill: University of North Carolina Press, 1979.

Ferrell, Claudine L. *Reconstruction.* Westport, Connecticut: Greenwood Press, 2003.

Fitzgerald, Michael W. *The Union League Movement in the Deep South: Politics and Agricultural Change During Reconstruction.* Baton Rouge: Louisiana State University Press, 1989.

Fitzgerald, Ruth Coder. *A Different Story: A Black History of Fredericksburg, Stafford and Spotsylvania, Virginia.* Fredericksburg, Virginia: Unicorn, 1979.

Foner, Philip S., and Robert James Branham, eds. *Lift Every Voice: African American Oratory, 1787–1900.* Tuscaloosa: University of Alabama Press, 1998.

Forbes, Ella. *But We Have No Country: The 1851 Christiana, Pennsylvania Resistance.* Cherry Hill, New Jersey: Africana Homestead Legacy, 1998.

Franklin, John Hope. *From Slavery to Freedom: A History of Negro Americans.* 3d ed. New York: Alfred A. Knopf, 1967.

———. *Reconstruction After the Civil War.* Chicago: University of Chicago Press, 1994.

———, and Loren Schweninger. *Runaway Slaves: Rebels on the Plantation.* Oxford and New York: Oxford University Press, 1999.

Gara, Larry. *The Liberty Line: The Legend of the Underground Railroad.* Lexington: University of Kentucky Press, 1961.

Genovese, Eugene D. *Roll, Jordan, Roll: The World the Slaves Made.* New York: Pantheon, 1974.

Gladstone, William A. *Men of Color.* Gettysburg, Pennsylvania: Thomas Publications, 1993.

Hagedorn, Ann. *Beyond the River: The Untold Story of the Heroes of the Underground Railroad.* New York: Simon and Schuster, 2002.

Harding, Vincent. *There Is a River: The Black Struggle for Freedom in America.* Orlando, Florida: Harcourt Brace Jovanovich, 1981.

Haviland, Laura S. *A Woman's Life-Work: Labors and Experiences of Laura S. Haviland.* 1881. Reprint. Salem, New Hampshire: Ayer, 1984.

Heglar, Charles J. *Rethinking the Slave Narrative: Slave Marriage and the Narratives of Henry Bibb and William and Ellen Craft.* Westport, Connecticut: Greenwood Press, 2001.

Henson, Josiah. *The Life of Josiah Henson, Formerly a Slave.* 1849. Reprint. Dresden, Ontario: Uncle Tom's Cabin Historic Site, 1969.

Hill, Daniel G. *The Freedom Seekers: Blacks in Early Canada.* Toronto: Stoddart, 1981.

Hochschild, Adam. *Bury the Chains: Prophets and Rebels in the Fight to Free an Empire's Slaves.* Boston: Houghton Mifflin, 2005.

Horton, James Oliver. *Free People of Color: Inside the African American Community.* Washington, D.C.: Smithsonian Institution Press, 1993.

Horton, James Oliver, and Lois E. Horton. *In Hope of Liberty: Culture, Community and Protest Among Northern Free Blacks, 1700–1860.* New York: Oxford University Press, 1997.

———. *Slavery and the Making of America.* New York: Oxford University Press, 2005.

Howe, Samuel Gridley, *Report to the Freedmen's Inquiry Commission 1864: The Refugees from Slavery in Canada West.* Reprint. New York: Arno Press and the New York Times, 1969.

Jenkins, Wilbert L. *Seizing the New Day: African Americans in Post-Civil War Charleston*. Bloomington: Indiana University Press, 1998.

Johnson, Charles, and Patricia Smith. *Africans in America: America's Journey Through Slavery*. New York: Harcourt Brace, 1998.

Johnson, Michael P., and James L. Roark. *No Chariot Let Down: Charleston's Free People of Color on the Eve of the Civil War*. Chapel Hill: University of North Carolina Press, 1984.

Katz, Jonathan. *Resistance at Christiana: The Fugitive Slave Rebellion, Christiana, Pennsylvania, September 11, 1851*. New York: Thomas Y. Crowell, 1974.

Katz, William Loren. *Eyewitness: A Living Documentary of the African American Contribution to American History*. New York: Simon and Schuster, 1995.

Katzman, David M. *Before the Ghetto: Black Detroit in the Nineteenth Century*. Urbana: University of Illinois Press, 1973.

Kuyk, Betty M. *African Voices in the African American Heritage*. Bloomington: Indiana University Press, 2003.

Larson, Kate Clifford. *Bound for the Promised Land: Harriet Tubman, Portrait of an American Hero*. New York: Ballantine, 2004.

Levine, Robert S. *Martin Delany, Frederick Douglass, and the Politics of Representative Identity*. Chapel Hill: University of North Carolina Press, 1997.

Libby, Jean, ed. *John Brown Mysteries*. Missoula, Montana: Pictorial Histories Publishing Co., 1999.

Litwack, Leon, and August Meier, eds. *Black Leaders of the Nineteenth Century*. Urbana: University of Illinois Press, 1988.

Lundy, Benjamin. *The Life, Travels and Opinions of Benjamin Lundy, Including His Journeys to Texas and Mexico*. 1847. Reprint. New York: Negro Universities Press, 1969.

McKivigan, John R. *The War Against Proslavery Religion: Abolitionism and the Northern Churches, 1830–1865*. Ithaca, New York: Cornell University Press, 1984.

McPherson, James M. *The Negro's Civil War: How American Blacks Felt and Acted During the War for the Union*. New York: Vintage, 1993.

Mellon, James, ed. *Bullwhip Days: The Slaves Remember*. New York: Avon, 1988.

Meyler, Peter, and David Meyler. *A Stolen Life: Searching for Richard Pierpoint*. Toronto: Natural Heritage Books, 1999.

Middleton, Joyce Shadd, Bryan Prince, and Karen Shadd Evelyn. *Something to Hope For: The Story of the Fugitive Slave Settlement, Buxton, Canada West*. North Buxton, Ontario: Buxton National Historic Site and Museum, 1999.

Middleton, Stephen. *Black Congressmen During Reconstruction*. Westport, Connecticut: Praeger, 2002.

Mitchell, Rev. W. M. *The Underground Railroad*. 1860. Reprint. New York: Negro Universities Press, 1970.

Morgan, Carl. *Birth of a City: Commemorating Windsor's Centennial, 1992*. Tecumseh, Ontario: TraveLife, 1991.

Newman, Richard, Patrick Rael, and Phillip Lapsansky, *Pamphlets of Protest: An Anthology of Early African American Protest Literature, 1790–1860*. New York: Routledge, 2001.

Osofsky, Gilbert. *Puttin' on Ole Massa: The Slave Narratives of Henry Bibb, William Wells Brown, and Solomon Northup*. New York: Harper & Row, 1969.

Pease, William H., and Jane Pease. *Black Utopia: Negro Communal Experiments in America*. Madison: State Historical Society of Wisconsin, 1963.

Penn, Garland I. *The Afro-American Press and Its Editors*. Salem, New Hampshire: Ayer, 1988.

Pirtle, Carol. *Escape Betwixt Two Suns: A True Tale of the Underground Railroad in Illinois*. Carbondale: Southern Illinois University Press, 2000.

Polacsek, John F. "The Extension of the Tracks of the Underground Railroad." Manuscript, 2003.

Power, Michael, and Nancy Butler, *Slavery and Freedom in Niagara*. Niagara on the Lake, Ontario: Niagara Historical Society, 2000.

Prince, Bryan. *I Came as a Stranger: The Underground Railroad*. Toronto: Tundra, 2004.

Proctor, Samuel DeWitt. *The Substance of Things Hoped For: A Memoir of African-American Faith*. New York: G. P. Putnam's Sons, 1995.

Putney, Martha S. *Black Sailors: Afro-American Merchant Seamen and Whalemen Prior to the Civil War*. New York: Glenwood Press, 1987.

Quarles, Benjamin, ed. *Narrative of the Life of Frederick Douglass: An American Slave Written by Himself*. Cambridge: Harvard University Press, 1960.

———. *Allies for Freedom and Blacks on John Brown*. New York: Oxford University Press, 1974.

———. *Black Abolitionists*. New York: Oxford University Press, 1969.

———. *The Negro in the Making of America*. 1964. Reprint. New York: Touchstone, 1996.

Raboteau, Albert J. *Canaan Land: A Religious History of African Americans*. Oxford and New York: Oxford University Press, 2001.

Rael, Patrick. *Black Identity and Black Protest in the Antebellum North*. Chapel Hill: University of North Carolina Press, 2002.

Redpath, James. *The Roving Editor, or, Talks With Slaves in the Southern States*. 1859. Edited by John R. McKivigan. University Park: Pennsylvania State University Press, 1996.

Rhodes, Jane. *Mary Ann Shadd Cary: The Black Press and Protest in the Nineteenth Century.* Bloomington: Indiana University Press, 1998.

Richmond, Ben, ed. *Reminiscences of Levi Coffin.* 1876. Richmond, Indiana: Friends United Press, 1991.

Ripley, C. Peter., ed. *The Black Abolitionist Papers.* Vol. 2, *Canada, 1850–1865.* Chapel Hill: University of North Carolina Press, 1985.

———. *Witness for Freedom: African American Voices on Race, Slavery, and Emancipation.* Chapel Hill: University of North Carolina Press, 1993.

Robbins, Arlie C. *Prince Hall Masonry in Ontario: 1852–1933.* Authorized by Most Worshipful Prince Hall Grand Lodge Free and Accepted Masons of the Province of Ontario and Jurisdiction, 1980.

———. *Legacy to Buxton.* Chatham, Ontario: Ideal Printing, 1983.

Robinson, Gwendolyn, and John W. Robinson. *Seek the Truth: A Story of Chatham's Black Community.* Chatham, Ontario: privately published, 1989.

Rollin, Frank A. *Life and Public Service of Martin R. Delany.* New York: Arno Press and the New York Times, 1969.

Russell, William Howard. *My Diary North and South.* New York: Harper Colophon, 1954.

Sadlier, Rosemary. *Mary Ann Shadd: Publisher, Editor, Teacher, Lawyer, Suffragette.* Toronto: Umbrella Press, 1995.

———. *Tubman, Harriet Tubman and the Underground Railroad: Her Life in the United States and Canada.* Toronto: Umbrella Press, 1997.

Schneider, Dorothy, and Carl J. Schneider. *An Eyewitness History of Slavery in America.* New York: Checkmark 2000.

Schweninger, Loren. *James T. Rapier and Reconstruction.* Chicago and London: University of Chicago Press, 1978.

Sernett, Milton C. *North Star Country: Upstate New York and the Crusade for African American Freedom.* Syracuse: Syracuse University Press, 2002.

Shreve, Dorothy Shadd. *The AfriCanadian Church: A Stabilizer.* Jordan Station, Ontario: Paideia Press, 1983.

Siebert, Wilbur H. *The Underground Railroad: From Slavery to Freedom.* 1898. Reprint. Gloucester, Massachusetts: Peter Smith, 1968.

Silverman, Jason H. *Unwelcome Guests: Canada West's Response to American Fugitive Slaves, 1800–1865.* Millwood, New York: Associated Faculty Press, 1985.

Simpson, Donald. *Under the North Star.* Toronto: Harriet Tubman Resource Centre on the African Diaspora, York University, 2003.

Slaughter, Thomas P. *Bloody Dawn: The Christiana Riot and Racial Violence in the Antebellum North.* New York and Oxford: Oxford University Press, 1991.

Still, William. *The Underground Railroad*. 1871. Reprint. Chicago: Johnson Publishing, 1970.

Stouffer, Allen P. *The Light of Nature and the Law of God. Anti-Slavery in Ontario 1833–1877*. Baton Rouge: Louisiana State University Press, 1992.

Stowe, Harriet Beecher. *Uncle Tom's Cabin*. Boston: John P. Jewett, 1852.

―――. *A Key to Uncle Tom's Cabin: Presenting the Original Facts and Documents Upon Which the Story Is Founded, Together with Corroborative Statements Verifying the Truth of the Work*. 1853. Reprint. Bedford, Massachusetts: Applewood Books, 1998.

Strangis, Joel. *Lewis Hayden and the War Against Slavery*. North Haven, Connecticut: Linnet Books, 1999.

Switala, William J. *Underground Railroad in Pennsylvania*. Mechanicsburg, Pennsylvania: Stackpole, 2001.

Taylor, Nikki M. *Frontiers of Freedom: Cincinnati's Black Community, 1802–1868*. Athens: Ohio University Press, 2005.

Thomas, Owen. *Niagara's Freedom Trail: A Guide to African-Canadian History on the Niagara Peninsula*. Thorold, Ontario: Niagara Economic and Tourism Corp., 1999.

Trefousse, Hans L. *Thaddeus Stevens: Nineteenth-Century Egalitarian*. Mechanicsburg, Pennsylvania: Stackpole, 2001.

Trudeau, Noah Andre. *Like Men of War: Black Troops in the Civil War 1862–1865*. Boston: Little, Brown, 1998.

Ullman, Victor. *Look to the North Star: A Life of William King*. Toronto: Umbrella Press, 1969.

Vinet, Mark. *Canada and the American Civil War: Prelude to War*. Quebec: Waden, 2001.

Walker, James W. St. G. *The Black Loyalist: The Search for a Promised Land in Nova Scotia and Sierra Leone 1783–1870*. Toronto: University of Toronto Press, 1992.

Walkes, Joseph A., Jr. *Black Square and Compass: 200 Years of Prince Hall Freemasonry*. Richmond, Virginia: Macoy, 1979.

Ward, Samuel Ringgold. *Autobiography of a Fugitive Negro*. 1855. Reprint. Chicago: Johnson Publishing, 1970.

Warren, Robert Penn. *John Brown: The Making of a Martyr*. Nashville: J. S. Sanders, 1993.

Winch, Julie. *A Gentleman of Color: The Life of James Forten*. New York: Oxford University Press, 2002.

Winks, Robin W. *The Blacks in Canada: A History*. New Haven and London: Yale University Press, 1971.

————. *The Civil War Years: Canada and the United States.* Montreal: McGill–Queen's University Press, 1998.

Woodford, Frank B. *Father Abraham's Children: Michigan Episodes in the Civil War.* Detroit: Wayne State University Press, 1999.

Woodson, Carter G. *A Century of Negro Migration.* New York: Dover, 2002.

Wright, Roberta Hughes, and Wilbur B. Hughes III. *Lay Down Body: Living History in African American Cemeteries.* Detroit: Visible Ink Press, 1996.

Yacovone, Donald, ed. *Freedom's Journey: African American Voices of the Civil War.* Chicago: Lawrence Hill, 2004.

Newspapers
Detroit Advertiser and Tribune

Detroit Daily Post

Emancipator

Frederick Douglass' Paper

Liberator

Liberty Standard

New National Era

North Star

Provincial Freeman

Signal of Liberty

Voice of the Fugitive

Articles
Landon, Fred. "The Anti-Slavery Society of Canada." *Ontario History* 48, no. 3 (1956): 125–131.

————. "The Negro Migration to Canada After the Passing of the Fugitive Slave Act," *Journal of Negro History* 5, no. 1 (1920): 22–36.

Lumpkin, Katherine Dupre. "The General Plan Was Freedom: A Negro Secret Order on the Underground Railroad." *Phylon* 28 (1967): 63–77.

Manuscript and Special Collections
Black Abolitionist Papers Collection. Seventeen reels of microfilm. New York: Microfilming Corporation of America, 1981–1983; Ann Arbor, Michigan: University Microfilms International, 1984–.

The Burton Historical Collection. Detroit Public Library, Detroit, Michigan.

Buxton Historical Site and Museum, Buxton, Ontario

Detroit Historical Museum (Detroit), and the Dossin Great Lakes Museum (Belle Isle).

Talman Collections. Fred Landon Papers and Donald Simpson Papers. University of Western Ontario, London, Ontario.

Videos

Celebrating the Legacy: The History of Chatham's Black Community. Heritage Room, Chatham-Kent Black Historical Society, Chatham, Ontario. Video released 2001.

Father Henson: His Spirit Lives On. An Uncle Tom's Cabin Historic Site Video. Uncle Tom's Cabin Historic Site, Dresden, Ontario. Video released 2002.

Mother Tongue: The Other Side of History. Episode 1, "Buxton," tells the story of Eliza Parker. Video released 2004.

Tales of the Underground Railroad: On the Erie Canal. Gribbins Films. Video released 2004.

INDEX

The Old Pear Tree, North Buxton, site of original homecoming festivities
that now sits across the road from where homecoming celebrations are
currently held. "A living symbol of our survival."—Arlie Robbins
(Photograph by Jacqueline Tobin)

ABOUT THE AUTHORS

Jacqueline L. Tobin is the author of *Hidden in Plain View: A Secret Story of Quilts and the Underground Railroad* and *The Tao of Women*. She is on the adjunct faculty at the University of Denver, where she teaches courses in writing and research. She has spent the last fifteen years researching and writing on African American Civil War history and uncovering untold stories. Jacqueline lives in Denver with her husband, Stewart, and her dog, Sheba. She has two grown children, Alex and Jasmine, and a son-in-law, Patrick.

Hettie Jones has written seventeen books, including *How I Became Hettie Jones*, a memoir of the "Beat Scene"; the poetry collection *Drive*, which won the Poetry Society of America's 1999 Norma Farber Award; *Big Star Fallin' Mama (Five Women in Black Music)*; and *No Woman No Cry*, a memoir with Bob Marley's widow, Rita. Jones's poetry and short prose have appeared in the *Village Voice*, the *Washington Post*, and elsewhere. She lives in New York City, where she teaches writing at the New School and at the Ninety-Second Street Y Poetry Center.

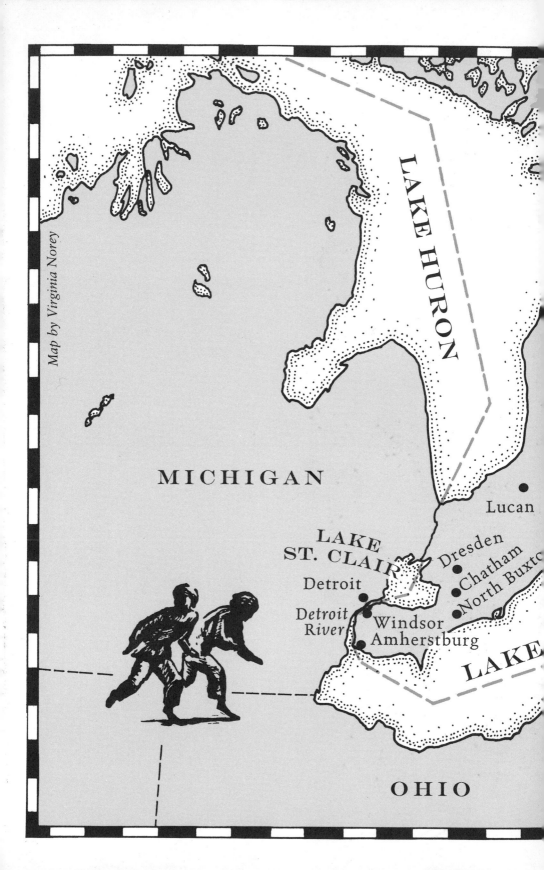

Map by Virginia Norey

LAKE HURON

MICHIGAN

Lucan

LAKE
ST. CLAIR

Dresden

Chatham

North Buxto

Detroit

Detroit
River

Windsor
Amherstburg

LAKE

OHIO